Peter Jones

History of the Ojebway Indians : with especial reference to their conversion to Christianity ; with a brief memoir of the writer

Peter Jones

History of the Ojebway Indians : with especial reference to their conversion to Christianity ; with a brief memoir of the writer

ISBN/EAN: 9783337305888

Printed in Europe, USA, Canada, Australia, Japan

Cover: Foto ©ninafisch / pixelio.de

More available books at **www.hansebooks.com**

HISTORY

OF THE

OJEBWAY INDIANS;

WITH ESPECIAL REFERENCE TO THEIR

CONVERSION TO CHRISTIANITY.

BY

REV. PETER JONES,

(KAHKEWAQUONABY,)

INDIAN MISSIONARY.

WITH A BRIEF

MEMOIR OF THE WRITER;

AND

INTRODUCTORY NOTICE BY THE REV. G. OSBORN, D.D.,

SECRETARY OF THE WESLEYAN METHODIST
MISSIONARY SOCIETY.

LONDON:

A. W. BENNETT, 5, BISHOPSGATE STREET WITHOUT.
HOULSTON AND WRIGHT, PATERNOSTER ROW.

———

1861.

PREFACE.

THE name of the Rev. Peter Jones will still be familiar to many who recollect his visit to this country in 1831, for the purpose of urging upon the Government the territorial rights of his fellow-countrymen. There is probably no one who can speak with more authority than he, on the past state of the North American Indians, probably of the Ojebway nation, to which he himself belonged ; and of the amelioration of their condition consequent on their conversion to Christianity. It must ever be a matter of regret that his graphic and interesting narrative was never completed by his own hand. To the lovers of philology, and to all who take an interest in these remarkable people, his brief account of the different languages in use among the various tribes will possess great interest. The sketch of his life is drawn up by his widow, with whom he left his many interesting MSS.

The publisher has the pleasure of appending the following letter from the Rev. G. Osborn, D.D., Secretary of the Wesleyan Methodist Missionary Society :—

" Sir,—I have read with much interest the proof-sheets you were kind enough to send me, of a posthumous work by the late Rev. Peter Jones, formerly a missionary in connexion with this Society, among the Chippeway—or, as it is now written, Ojebway Indians, in Upper Canada.

Mr. Jones was a man of sterling piety, with much natural good sense and shrewdness; and had evidently taken great pains in the cultivation and improvement of his mind. His appearances in this country, on two successive visits, afforded high and just gratification to immense numbers of persons, who saw in him an undeniable proof, both of the capacities of his countrymen, and of the power of Christianity to reclaim and elevate those who were at the utmost distance from European civilization.

"Mr. Jones's researches into the antiquities, customs, and language of his nation, will doubtless be duly appreciated by students in philology and ethnology, &c.; while the philanthropist will have his sympathies excited on behalf of an aboriginal people struggling to maintain themselves against those destructive forces which the neighbourhood of the 'white man' appears to generate wherever he goes. But for the influence of 'the glorious Gospel of the blessed God,' the progress of their decay would have been more rapid, if indeed they would not ere now have become extinct; but we may hope that under its influence they may yet be preserved, and prosper. The fatal 'fire-water'—supplied, alas! by those who bear the Christian name,—appears to have been regarded by Mr. Jones as their worst foe, and his estimate is probably correct.

"The book would doubtless have been more complete, had Mr. Jones lived to publish it himself; but as it is, it well deserves a wide circulation, and a careful reading; and wishing it may obtain both, I remain, sir,

"Yours truly,

"G. OSBORN."

INDEX.

LIST OF ILLUSTRATIONS.

A BRIEF SKETCH

OF

THE LIFE OF THE AUTHOR.

In the annals of the Wesleyan Methodist Church in Canada, as in those of the church of God in general, we constantly find noble examples of the power of the Gospel to rescue our fellow men from the dominion of error and sin, and to make them wise unto salvation through faith in Jesus Christ. We record the holy lives and the happy deaths of such men; not for the purpose of eulogising them— they are now alike unaffected by our praise or our censure —but for the purpose of magnifying the name and the work of our blessed Lord and Master, from whom all wise counsels, all holy desires, all moral excellences proceed. In those beloved disciples of Christ, those witnesses of truth, we see the grace of God and are glad. In their happy experience we find delightful proof that wisdom's ways are ways of pleasantness, and all her paths are peace : in their upright and useful deportment we see that good men are not only blessed, but are made a blessing—that as trees planted by rivers of water, they bring forth their fruit in season ; and assured that God is no respecter of persons, that what His grace does for one it can do for all, we are en-

B

couraged to seek that grace, and thus participate in the present and eternal advantages of common salvation. We greatly need such encouragement. The inroads of death upon the ranks of our church have, during the past few years, been painfully frequent and sudden; our fathers in the ministry, our companions and fellow-labourers in the Lord's vineyard, have been cut down by our side, have been swept away from the midst of us; we look for them, but they are not—their bodies sleep in the dust, their spirits have returned to God. We mourn over their departure; but "we sorrow not as those who have no hope; for if we believe that *Jesus* died and rose again, even so them also which *sleep in Jesus* will God bring with Him." . . . . "For the Lord Himself shall descend from heaven with a shout, with the voice of the archangel, and with the trump of God; and the dead in Christ shall rise first; then we which are alive, and remain, shall be caught up together with them in the clouds, to meet the Lord in the air; so shall we ever be with the Lord." Most thankful ought we to be, that by the grace of God we may so live in this world, as to be prepared for, and secure, unending happiness in the world to come. The *possibility* of our realising this blessedness is assured to us not only by Divine teaching, but by human example—by a great cloud of witnesses who have run the race, reached the goal, won the prize, and received the crown of life which fadeth not away. To find such examples of victorious piety, we have not to go back to the remote ages of antiquity, they are to be found amongst those who were once our own cotemporaries—brethren beloved, with whom we have taken sweet counsel, who have walked with us to the house of God, whose faith we are to follow, considering the end of their conversation, Jesus Christ, the same yesterday, to-day, and for ever. The moral government which the Divine Ruler of the universe exercises over the world, and over the church, is one of the most interesting, instructive, and cheering subjects of human investigation. So far as we can understand that government, we feel assured that the Lord reigneth, and though clouds and darkness are about Him, justice and judgment are the habitation of His throne, mercy and truth go before His face. The care which God takes of His church is strikingly exhibited in the agents, which, from time to time, he raises up and sends forth to vindicate His sacred cause, and to extend the triumphs of His blessed truth in our benighted and ruined world. All those agents were vessels of honour, sanctified and meet for the Master's use ; many of them were stars of the first magnitude ; Christ held them in His own right hand ; Christ gave them all their lustre—He appointed their orbit—He upheld them in their course ;—

> " As giants they ran their race,
> Exulting in their might ;
> As burning luminaries chased
> The gloom of hellish night."

In the simplicity and depth of their piety, in the vigour of their faith and the ardour of their zeal, in their diligence in acquiring knowledge, and in their aptitude to communicate it, in their courage and self-denial, in their deadness to the world and their entire devotion to God, we see that He laid His hand upon them, He endowed them with their varied gifts and graces. . . . . He made them able ministers of the New Testament. Such an example of the power and the goodness of God was *Kahkewaquonaby*— Peter Jones. About thirty-six years ago he and his tribe in Canada were nearly all pagans. They knew not the true and living God. They worshipped the sun, the moon, and the stars, thunder, serpents, beasts, and birds, with a great many other imaginary gods. Their physical, intellectual, and moral condition at that time was extremely low and miserable ; darkness covered their minds ; hunger and whisky destroyed their health ; wicked and designing men took advantage of their ignorance and their weaknesses, and they were fast dying off from the face of that magnificent country which their forefathers once proudly called their own. In the year 1823, the Lord, in His tender compassion, visited them ; He enabled some of them to see the vanity of idol worship, and the sinfulness and wretchedness of their own moral condition. They listened with deep interest and solemn attention to the preaching of the gospel—the word came to them in demonstration of the Spirit, and with power; they were pricked in their heart; they cried aloud for mercy and salvation ; and He who made of one blood all the nations that dwell upon the face of the earth ; who sent His Son to seek and save the lost ; who commanded His ministers to beseech a rebel world to be reconciled to Him—heard the poor Indians' penitential cries, and appointed unto them beauty for ashes, the oil of joy for mourning, and the garments of praise for the spirit of heaviness.

The word of the Lord spread very rapidly from one tribe to another; so much so, that within a very few years fifteen Christian settlements were formed among those very people who used to worship stocks and stones ; some hundreds of whom were turned from idols to serve the living and true God. The real test of all religious profession is—"by their fruits ye shall know them :" apply this test to those Indian converts, and it will be found that in works of faith, in labours of love, and in the patience of hope, they were examples to many of their more highly favoured white brethren. Peter Jones was one of the first-fruits of this good work among the red men of the wilderness. He was born in the woods, on a prominent tract of land called Burlington heights, in the year 1831. He spent ten years in wandering about with his own tribe, and grew up under the influence of the heathen notions and habits of his own nation. At the age of sixteen, his father, of Welsh descent, and a government surveyor, got him baptized by the Rev. Ralph Leeming, English Episcopal minister, at the Mohawk Church, on the Grand River near Brantford. This outward profession of Christianity imposed some restraint upon his conduct, but left him still under the powerful influence of his pagan prejudices and practices. About three years after his baptism, he was truly converted to God. A camp meeting was being held near Ancaster, to which he and one of his sisters resorted. His own account of this important crisis in his life is deeply interesting. He says that he was tempted by curiosity to go and see how the Methodists worshipped the Great Spirit in the wilderness. "On arriving at the encampment," he says, " I was immediately struck with the solemnity of the people, several of whom were engaged in singing and prayer. Some strange feeling came over my mind, and I was led to believe that the Supreme Being was in the midst of the people who were engaged in worshipping him. The encampment contained about two acres, enclosed by a bush fence. The tents were pitched within this circle ; all the under-brush was taken away, while the large trees were left standing, and formed a most beautiful shade. There were three gates leading into the encampment. During the night the whole place was illumined with fire stands, which had a very imposing appearance among the branches and leaves of the various trees. The people came in their

waggons from various parts of the country, bringing their
sons and daughters with them for the purpose of presenting them to the Lord. I should judge that there were
about a thousand persons present. The Rev. William Case,
the presiding elder, had the general oversight of the encampment and the religious services. There were a number
of ministers present, who alternately delivered powerful
discourses to the listening multitude. After each sermon
a prayer meeting was held, in which any one was at liberty
to exhort the penitents and unite in prayer for the divine
blessing. On the Sabbath, the 3rd of June, there was a
vast concourse of people, several sermons were preached,
and prayer meetings were held during the intervals. By
this time I began to feel very sick in my heart, but I did
not make my feelings known. Some of the sermons deeply
impressed my mind; I understood a good deal of what was
said; I thought the *black coats* understood all that was in
my heart, and that I was the person to whom they were
speaking. The burden on my soul began to increase, and
my heart said—what must I do to be saved? I saw myself
in the gall of bitterness, and in the bond of iniquity. The
more I understood the plan of salvation, the more I was
convinced of the truth of the Christian religion, and felt
my need of its blessings. In spite of my old Indian heart,
tears flowed down my cheeks at the remembrance of my
sins. I saw many of the white people powerfully awakened,
and heard them cry aloud for mercy; while others stood
and gazed, and some even laughed. My elder brother
John was at that time studying the art of surveying at
Hamilton. He came to the meeting on the Sabbath, but
appeared quite indifferent about religion; so much so, that
I reproved him for speaking lightly of these people, and
told him I believed they were sincere—that they were the

true worshippers of the Great Spirit. "Oh," said he, "I see you will yet become a Methodist!" The meeting continued all Monday, and several discourses were delivered from the stand. My convictions became more deep and powerful during the preaching : I wept much ; this, however, I endeavoured to conceal by holding down my head behind the shoulders of the people. I felt anxious that no one might see me weeping like an old woman, as all my countrymen say that weeping is a sign of weakness, which is beneath the dignity of an Indian brave. In the afternoon of this day my sorrow and anguish of soul greatly increased, and I felt as if I should sink down into hell for my sins ; which I now saw to be very many, and exceedingly offensive to the Great Spirit. I was fully convinced that if I did not find mercy from the Lord Jesus, of whom I heard so much, I certainly would be lost for ever. I thought if I could only get the good people to pray for me at their prayer meeting, I should soon find relief to my mind, but I had not sufficient courage to make my desires known. Oh ! what a mercy it was, that Christ did not forsake me when my heart was so slow to acknowledge him as my Lord and Saviour. Towards evening, I retired into the solitary wilderness to try to pray to the Great Spirit. I knelt down by the side of a fallen tree—the rushing of the leaves over my head made me uneasy. I retired further back into the woods, and there wrestled with God in prayer. I resolved to go back to the camp and get the people of God to pray with me ; but when I got to the meeting my fearful heart again began to hesitate. I stood by the side of a tree, considering what I must do—whether I should give up seeking the Lord or not. It was now about dusk, and while I was thus halting between two opinions, a good old man named Reynolds came up to me and said

—" Do you wish to obtain religion and serve the Lord ?" I
replied, " Yes." He then said—" Do you desire the people
of God to pray for you?" I told him that was what I
desired. He then led me into the prayer meeting. I fell
upon my knees, and began as well as I could to call upon
the name of the Lord Jesus Christ. The old man prayed
for me, and exhorted me to believe in the name of the
Lord, to trust in the atonement of Him who gave himself
a ransom for all—for Indians as well as white people.
Several of the ministers prayed for me. When I first began
to pray my heart was soft and tender, and I shed many
tears ; but, strange to say, some time after, my heart got
as hard as a stone. I tried to look up, but the heavens
seemed like brass. I then began to say to myself, there is
no mercy for poor Indians : I felt myself an outcast, a sinner
bound for hell. About midnight I got so fatigued and discouraged that I retired from the prayer meeting, and went
to our tent, where I immediately fell asleep. I know not
how long I had slept, when I was awakened by the Rev.
Edmund Stoney and the Rev. George Furguson, who,
having missed me at the prayer meeting, came with a light
to search for me. Mr. Stoney said to me, " Arise, Peter, and
go with us to the prayer meeting and get your soul converted ; your sister Mary has already obtained the spirit of
adoption, and you must also seek the same blessing." When
I heard that my sister was converted and had found peace,
not knowing before that she was seeking the Lord, I
sprung up and went with the good men, determined that if
there was still mercy left for me, I would seek until I found
it. On arriving at the prayer meeting, I saw my sister
apparently as happy as she could be. She came to me, and
began to weep over me, and exhorted me to give my heart
to God, and told me how she had found the Lord. Her

words came with power to my sinking heart, and I fell upon my knees, and called upon God for mercy. My sister and others prayed for me, especially Mr. Stoney, whose zeal for my salvation I shall never forget. At the dawning of the day I was enabled to cast myself wholly on the Lord, and to claim an interest in the atoning blood of my Saviour Jesus Christ, who bore my sins in his own body on the tree ; and when I received Him unspeakable joy filled my heart, and I could say, "Abba Father." The love of God being now shed abroad in my heart, I loved him intensely, and praised Him in the midst of the people. Every thing now appeared to me in a new light, and all the works of God seemed to unite with me in uttering the praises of the Lord. There was a time when I thought that the white man's God was never intended to be our God ; that the white man's religion was never intended to be the red man's religion ; that the Great Spirit gave us our way of worship, and that it would be wrong to put away that mode of worship and take to the white man's mode of worship. But I and my people now found that there is but one true religion, and that the true religion is the religion of the Bible. Christianity has found us, and has lifted us up out of a horrible pit, and out of the miry clay; it has placed our feet upon a rock ; it has established our goings, and has put a new song into our mouths, even praise unto our God."

It belongs to a more extended history of his life to narrate his now commenced public career—his prayers and exhortations—his travels, labours, success—the conversion of his own and kindred tribes—his transatlantic voyages and ministrations—his appointments to Indian missions, missionary tours, and usefulness in regard to both the temporal and spiritual interests of his countrymen, during more than a quarter of a century.

Having furnished satisfactory evidence to the fathers and brethren of the Wesleyan church that he was called by the Lord of the harvest to the office of a Christian minister, he was solemnly set apart to that work as deacon, by the imposition of hands, at the Kingston Conference, by the Rev. Bishop Hedding, in 1830; and as priest, at the Toronto Conference, in 1833, by the Rev. George Marsden.

During the following twenty-three years of his valuable life he continued to labour among his Indian brethren, in word and doctrine, with encouraging success. He often went forth bearing precious seed, and sowed that seed in tears; but in due season he reaped in joy. He was instrumental in turning hundreds of Pagan idolaters from the error of their ways, and of bringing the poor lost wanderers into the fold of the good Shepherd. Whenever sinners were converted under his ministry he evinced the deepest emotion, and rejoiced over them as one who had found great spoil. He was not satisfied by merely holding so many religious services; he longed to see the end of all preaching answered in the salvation of those who heard him, and in the building up of believers on their most holy faith. He not only brought considerable numbers of his own people to the knowledge of the truth and into fellowship with the church of Christ, but he watched over them with unceasing vigilance and tender solicitude. Upon him, in a special degree, rested the care of the *Indian churches.* His position as a Christian pastor and a ruling chief of his tribe, gave him great influence, not only among his own people, but among all the tribes of the Ojebway nation, with whom he had an opportunity of holding personal intercourse. That influence for the good of the red men generally would have been greatly increased, had the oft-

expressed wishes of the Indians, that he should be made a
general Indian agent, been granted. For that responsible
and somewhat delicate office he was, by his education, his
prudence, and his piety, well qualified; and not a few of
the best friends of the Indian were deeply grieved because
his claims to that distinction were, as they thought, unjustly
ignored. Disappointments of this kind, however, neither
altered his character, nor turned his attention from the
grand and main object of his life;—he ever sought to promote the glory of God and the well-being of his fellow
men; generally and especially the improvement of the
intellectual, the moral, and the physical condition of his
own people. He evinced his great zeal in the promotion
of these objects, by his abundant labours in Canada, in the
United States of America, and in the British Islands. In
public meetings and in private intercourse with the people
of these countries, he made many effective appeals to their
Christian sympathy and charity, and obtained the means of
originating and sustaining some of the best schools and
churches, which are, even now, exercising a beneficial influence over the destiny of the red men of the wilderness.
All his public appeals, both in the pulpit and on the platform, were marked by great clearness, simplicity, and
pathos; and no one could listen to him without feeling
that he was speaking the truth in love and with earnestness
of purpose.

The following sketch of his character, drawn by a master
hand—a hand, alas! which has long lost its cunning—
evinces a just appreciation of the distinguishing excellences
of the beloved and lamented Peter Jones:—"Previously
to that important epoch which was connected with the
conversion of his soul, he was brought up in all the ways
and customs of his own pagan and nomade tribe; inured

to the same forest life, and covered with the same thick darkness of superstition and idolatry. But his spirit was now emancipated from that debasing enthralment. He was roused from the apathy which would otherwise have stolen over him, and paralyzed his naturally good abilities. He began to thirst for knowledge, and, happily for him, he found the means of satisfying that thirst. He obtained a very fair English education, and made considerable progress in the cultivation of his intellectual faculties; while by habitual study of the word of God, and attention to the ordinances of religion, he sought to abound in divine knowledge yet more and more, to approve things which are excellent, to be sincere and without offence until the day of Christ, and to be filled with the fruits of righteousness which are by Jesus Christ to the glory and the praise of God. His whole intellect and demeanour, though somewhat marked by his English education and intercourse with different classes of society, were essentially of the Indian caste, and it was his being so striking a representative of the Indian race, elevated and beautified by the influence of Christianity, that caused him to be regarded with such lively interest by wise and good men in his own and other lands. His still and sombre countenance, when in a state of repose; or, if kindled by any incident or feeling, the flashes of his dark and lustrous eye; brought vividly before the imagination what tale or history has told of the solemn and stately manners, the freedom and unshackled fortitude, and the once tameless spirit, of the man of the wilderness." What a striking and lovely example was he of the saving power and the transforming and elevating influence of the Gospel! He, who in his infancy had been dedicated by his pagan mother to the eagle,—*i. e.*, the thunder god,—now dedicated himself, unreservedly, to the

living and true God, and recognizing the claims of his redeeming Lord, glorified him in his body and spirit, which
were his. He, who on the day of his heathen baptism was
presented with a war-club and a bunch of eagle feathers, as
the insignia of his future office as an Indian chief and warrior,
on the day of his spiritual baptism took unto himself the
whole armour of God, determined to fight the good fight of
faith, and to win the crown of life, which fadeth not away.

From the day of his conversion to Christianity until the
day of his death, he maintained his religious integrity, and
adorned the doctrine of God his Saviour in all things.
He was humble, calm, and earnest in the discharge of his
duty; and in works of faith, in labours of love, and in the
patience of hope, he was a living epistle, known and read
of all men.

At length, his never very vigorous constitution began to
yield to excessive exposures, colds, and fevers. In the
spring of 1850 he had so severe a fit of sickness that few
who saw him had any expectation of his recovery. But
many prayers continued to be offered up by both Indians
and whites for the blessing of God upon the means employed for his recovery, and his valuable life was prolonged
a few years.

On his recovery, he said, "The prayers of the good
people have kept me out of heaven." In the autumn of
the same year he experienced a very severe trial, in the
death of a beloved and promising boy; but his sweet resignation under so heavy a blow exemplified the supporting
grace of God to the heart of a true Christian. At length,
from his failing and precarious health, and by the advice
of his physician, it was not deemed advisable for him to
attempt to continue any longer in charge of a mission
station; he was therefore superannuated.

At the same time, whenever health permitted, he was
ready to go forth and preach the Gospel, or attend missionary meetings. He often journeyed to the New Credit
settlement, where he attended both to the spiritual and
temporal concerns of his tribe—settling their accounts,
attending frequent councils, communicating with the Indian
department, &c., &c.

During the summer of 1853, while on a visit to New
York, he experienced a great deepening of the work of
grace in his heart—a fresh baptism of the Holy Spirit—
even that "perfect love that casteth out all fear." His
own account of this experience is as follows, in a letter to
his wife : " On Tuesday afternoon I attended one of Mrs.
Palmer's meetings in her house. Dr. Bangs, and about
forty others, were present. These meetings are held for
the special purpose of promoting holiness of heart. Several
rose and declared that the blood of Christ had cleansed
them from all sin. Among those who spoke was a sailor,
who said that the Lord had enabled him to enjoy this
blessing on board his ship. My own soul was greatly
blessed. Glory be to God for what I enjoy! My soul is
happy. Of a truth God *is* love. I know that the precious
blood of my dear Saviour cleanseth my poor heart from all
sin. Join with me in praising God for what he hath done
for my soul. My heart is full of Jesus. Little did I think
when I came to this bustling city that I was going to obtain such a baptism from above. Continue to pray for me,
that I may retain this simple power to believe what God
has promised in his holy word." This deeper work of
grace continued to strengthen and mature ; and the effect
of it was manifest in his increasing deadness to the world,
his simple faith in the promises of Christ, and his fervent
appeals to the consciences of his hearers.

In December, 1855, he rode in a lumber-waggon over bad roads to the New Credit Settlement of his tribe, a distance of about twenty miles; sat in council all the next day, feeling very unwell; and then returned home through a drizzling rain. No sooner did he reach his own house, than he was obliged to lie down. The next day medical aid was called in. Until the 2nd of January, 1856, he was able to sit up part of the time. The following month he was entirely confined to his bed—at times sickness at the stomach, attended with extreme general prostration, reducing him so low that the effort to move him often produced faintness. About the beginning of March he appeared to rally a little. On the 24th of April, accompanied by his wife, he went to St. Catharine's, to try the effect of the celebrated waters, but was disappointed; the medical advice sought there communicating the sad tidings that his case was beyond all human power—that to alleviate his sufferings was all that could be done. He took leave of his kind and sympathising friends at St. Catharine's, amidst their tears and prayers that the Lord would still spare his valuable life. Medical gentlemen at St. Catharine's having recommended him to consult Dr. Bovel of Toronto, he left home for that purpose on the 20th of May, hoping at the same time that he might be able to attend to some business with the Indian department in behalf of his people; but the disinterested and kind medical aid received here could only mitigate suffering; and medical consultation only confirmed previous apprehensions.

"During his stay of seven weeks in Toronto," said his kind host, Dr. Ryerson, "I had the melancholy pleasure of entertaining him, and the opportunity of witnessing his calm resignation, his simple faith, his devout gratitude, his ardent solicitude for the welfare of his people, his enlightened

and exalted views of Christian truth and privilege, and his
tender affection for his family.   After two days he was
entirely confined to his bed.   Among other ministers who
visited him was the Rev. Dr. Hannah (Representative of
the British Conference), who, at his request, administered
to him and others present the memorials of the broken
body and shed blood of our blessed Saviour.   It was a
deeply affecting solemnity.   Seeing he grew rapidly worse,
medical advice was taken as to the practicability of removing him home, where he so much desired to be.   He
was conveyed on a litter to the railroad, where a room
was kindly allotted to him and his friends.   He reached
home the same evening, being carried by kind friends from
the rail-car to his own house, a distance of about half a
mile.   Many tears were shed when those who awaited his
arrival witnessed the sad change that so short a time had
made; but a song of thankfulness was in his heart, that
he was permitted to see his dear children, and enter once
more his much-loved home.   This was on the 18th of June,
from which time he became rapidly worse, being unable
to retain any nourishment on his stomach, and discharging
little else than blood the last week.   But he uttered not a
murmuring word.

The Rev. John Ryerson (happening to be in Brantford
a day or two) visited him, and was much affected at his
emaciated appearance; but he said, " Not a wave of trouble
has crossed my breast; I feel resting on the Rock of Ages."
When the Indians of the New Credit came, much sorrow
filled their hearts to see their best earthly friend so low,
that they proposed, at their own expense, to despatch a
messenger to Rice Lake for a noted Indian doctor, and
they assembled several times a day in an adjoining room,
when they prayed, and sang, and wept aloud !

The following particulars of his last hours are given by an eye-witness :—

"Many friends came from day to day to see him; to each of whom, as long as he was able, he addressed a few appropriate words. To one, pressing both his hands in his, he said: 'I am going home—going to my Father's house above; all is well; meet me there.' To the doctor (Griffin) he said : 'I thank you for all your kind attentions. You have done all you could ; but it is the will of God to take me home. I hope you will give God all your heart, and meet me in a better world.' To others he said : . 'God bless you; be faithful unto death, and you shall receive a crown of glory.' Hearing him say, 'Blessed Redeemer!' it was remarked, 'You can say, I know that my Redeemer liveth.' 'O yes,' he replied, 'I could say that all the time.' On Friday he took leave of his dear children, presenting the three elder ones with the bibles he had long used, and the youngest with his Wesleyan hymn book, with other appropriate tokens of remembrance. He put his dying hands upon each of their heads, saying : 'God bless you, my dear boys. Be good children. Be affectionate and obedient to your dear mother. Be kind and loving to each other. Give God your hearts, and meet me in a better world.' He then took the hand of his dear wife, saying: 'I leave these dear boys to the care of their heavenly Father, and yours, for you to train them and teach them the good way. God bless you all!' On Saturday he continued to sink, and knowing that his death was fast approaching, and being in the full possession of his mental faculties, he gave, with the greatest composure, several instructions as to what he wished done. His voice soon became inaudible. The last intelligible words were (addressing his sorrowing partner): 'God bless you, dear.

C

About nine o'clock in the evening, the weary wheels of life seemed about standing still, and the happy spirit waiting for the welcome message—'Come up hither.' Surrounded by his weeping wife and children, friends and Indians, his sister and aged mother, who had been converted by his instrumentality, the solemnity and affecting character of the scene can be better conceived than described. The contest between spirit and flesh seemed long. At length, a little after two o'clock on sabbath morning, June 29th, 1856, the deep breathing gave way, and becoming fainter and yet lower still, the last quiver of the lips told that all was over. 'Victory! victory! O death, where is thy sting? O grave, where is thy victory?'

"On Tuesday, July 1st, his precious remains were conveyed from their late happy home to an adjoining grave, where the Rev. Dr. Ryerson, from Toronto, delivered an address founded on Acts xi. 24; and from thence to the cemetery at Brantford, followed by upwards of eighty carriages, and great numbers of white people and Indians on foot. At the grave, into which many flowers were thrown, the beautiful burial service was read by the Rev. T. B. Howard."

Dr. Ryerson adds: "Mr. Jones was a man of athletic frame as well as of masculine intellect; a man of clear perception, good judgment, great decision of character; a sound preacher, fervent and powerful in his appeals; very well informed on general subjects, extensively acquainted with men and things, serious without gloom, cheerful without levity, dignified and agreeable in his manners; a faithful friend, a true patriot, a persevering philanthropist; a noble specimen of what Christianity can do for the Indian Gentiles of Canada, and therefore for the Gentiles of the whole world. Mr. Jones died at the age of fifty-four years, leaving a widow and four sons to mourn their loss, but ‘ not as those who have no hope.’ ”

On the 1st of July, 1857,—a year from the day on which the remains of this exemplary Christian and zealous minister were committed to their final resting-place,—a handsome marble monument was raised to his memory in the cemetery at Brantford. There were present at this inauguration several ministers of the town, a large number of the inhabitants, D. Thorburne, Esq., Indian Commissioner, and Indians from the Credit and Mohawk.

Mr. Thorburne remarked that he was present at the inauguration of a monument raised to the memory of *Brant*, and he felt extremely happy now in being present to do honour to the memory of one of the most illustrious soldiers in the service of Christ ; one who had been a burning and a shining light, working good wherever his duties called him, and who was esteemed by all who had ever been acquainted with him.

The Rev. T. B. Howard (Wesleyan minister) said, he felt this to be a solemn occasion. He deemed it a privilege to be present to give his testimony to the great worth of him who now sleeps beneath the sod. He had been acquainted with Peter Jones for many years, had journeyed with him in the prosecution of his great work of missionary labours, and had always esteemed him most highly as a Christian and a gentleman. “ It was,” he said, “ a strong proof of magnanimity and affection on the part of the red men, who, out of their poverty, have raised this monument to the memory of their beloved chief. The stone on which we now see his name engraved will in the course of time perish, and be lost to view ; but in the Lamb’s book of Life it is written in characters that will never be effaced. He prayed that God would perpetuate the

c 2

good work commenced by our departed friend among the
natives of the country, and bless his widow and family."

The Rev. J. C. Usher (Church of England minister)
expressed himself as having felt a deep interest in the welfare of the Indians for the last twenty years. With the
Rev. Mr. Jones he had not had much personal acquaintance; but, from what he had heard from those intimately
acquainted with him, he had come to the conclusion that he
was really a good and a great man; and from personal
observation he always saw something which stamped him
to be first-class. He was happy at being unexpectedly
present on this occasion, and concluded by wishing prosperity, temporal and spiritual, to the widow and children
of the late Mr. Jones.

Mr. G. H. M. Johnson (Indian chief of Six Nations) said
he had known Mr. Jones for thirty years, had greatly pro-
fited by his example and advice, and his loss was deeply
felt by the Indian tribes. He died in his arms. Almost
the last words he said were—That God would bless his
people. He had done much to convert the Indian, and
was ever a regular visitor to all the Indian stations in the
country.

A venerable chief (Sawyer) of the Mississauga tribe,
returned his sincere thanks to all for their attendance on
that solemn occasion.

Lewis Bunnell, Esq., said he had been acquainted with
Peter Jones since he was sixteen years of age. He was in
youth an exemplary person; and a great portion of the
good he had accomplished will never be known till the con-
summation of all things. He prayed that God would bless
all his people, and bring them to His eternal kingdom.

Dr. Digby said there was no stain on the life of the good
Peter Jones, whose piety, he blessed God that he (Dr. D.)

Mr. Matthews being called on, said he had long known and respected Peter Jones. He was present when he was ordained in Kingston by Bishop Hedding, from which time a great work had been carried on by him. His after-life had borne out all the expectations raised at his conversion. He concluded by expressing himself happy at having had an opportunity of giving testimony to the worth of the late Rev. Peter Jones.

Mr. Thorburne then called on the Rev. James Usher to pronounce the benediction, when the assembly dispersed.

The following inscription, from the pen of the Rev. Dr. Ryerson, is a beautiful epitome of his excellent character:

Erected by the

OJIBEWAY AND OTHER INDIAN TRIBES,

TO THEIR REVERED AND BELOVED CHIEF,

KAHKEWAQUONABY,

(THE REV. PETER JONES),

Died June the 29th, 1856. Aged 54 years.

He was a man of deep piety and catholic spirit ; an able Minister, and powerful advocate of Christian missions.

A true Patriot, an affectionate Husband, Father, and Friend. He was the means of promoting, in the highest degree, the spiritual and temporal good of his race.

Sinking under excessive attacks of disease, caused by exposures and labours in the Missionary work, he died, triumphing in the faith which he preached during his memorable ministry of thirty-one years in the Wesleyan Methodist Church.

A Tablet is also raised to his memory by his bereaved

family, in the Indian Church, at the New Credit Settlement; on which is the following fitting inscription: —

In Memory of

KAHKEWAQUONABY,

(PETER JONES),

THE FAITHFUL AND HEROIC OJIBEWAY MISSIONARY AND CHIEF;

THE GUIDE, ADVISER, AND BENEFACTOR OF HIS PEOPLE.

Born January 1st, 1802.

Died June 29th, 1856.

HIS GOOD WORKS LIVE AFTER HIM,

AND HIS MEMORY IS EMBALMED IN MANY GRATEFUL HEARTS.

The editor cannot withhold the observations of the late Mrs. James Wood, of Bristol, England, respecting her late excellent husband, during his visit at her house, in the summer of 1831. . . . . "My weakness prevents my giving a particular account of Mr. Jones, further than that he is a converted North American Indian Chief, come over to England on business concerning his nation. What I wish to record of him is, that he is an exemplary Christian, a man of deep piety, great humility and simplicity, walking closely with God—in short, he is a Bible Christian. The above traits of character have also been eminently exhibited under our roof during a season of affliction which put to the test all his graces.

"On his arrival in England, he took cold through exposure to a severe frosty night on the top of a stage-coach from Liverpool, where he landed April 30th, on his way to London.

"Pleasing accounts being received of him here, Mr. Wood

wrote, requesting him to come to our Bristol missionary meeting, and to make our house his home. He did so; arriving on Saturday, May 14th. He preached twice on Sunday, and gave his experience in the evening in King Street Chapel. He attended the missionary meeting at Downend, where he increased his cold, so that he was entirely laid up. His presence on the platform had been published so extensively, that it was thought absolutely needful that he should appear there. He was conveyed to the meeting in a car just before it was time for him to speak. He delivered a short and suitable address with great simplicity. The audience were much delighted, but expressed great concern to see his debilitated appearance. He remained on the platform about twenty minutes, returned to our house, and the next day took to his bed. The physician and surgeon who attended him had considerable doubt of his recovery. After being confined to his bed for three weeks he is now slowly convalescent. Through the whole of this severe affliction, endured in a foreign land, among strangers, whose customs and habits differ so materially from his own—with a probability of never again visiting his native country, or seeing his dearest relatives or connexions—he manifested the utmost submission to the will of his heavenly Father, and with great meekness of spirit passed through the fiery trial unhurt. He has so won the hearts of all our family by his temper and affability of manners, together with his gratitude for all that has been done for him, that the name of Kahkewaquonaby will always be remembered by us with respect and Christian affection."

CHAPTER I.

The former and present condition of the North American Indians.

As the continent of America is now so well known, I need not attempt to give a general description of it. I shall, therefore, confine my remarks principally to that part of the new world occupied by my countrymen.

At the same time it may not be uninteresting to glance over what I suppose to have been the condition of our forefathers long before the European planted his footsteps on our shores, when the red man could cast his eye from the Atlantic on the east to the Pacific ocean on the west, from the frozen regions of the north to Cape Horn in the south, and, viewing the immense continent in its length and breadth, exclaim,

> " I am monarch of all I survey,
>   My right there is none to dispute ;
> From the centre all round to the sea,
>   I am lord of the fowl and the brute."

Before the treacherous Spaniard made his appearance in our country the Indian could sleep peacefully in his wigwam without fear of being hunted by bloodhounds ;* as if the owners of the soil were beasts of prey rather than men of like passions with themselves ; or as if the rich mines of Mexico were of greater value than the lives and souls of the poor aborigines, whom the Good Spirit had made lords of the land where His providence had seen fit to place them.

* *Vide* Appendix A.

And long before the adventurer from Europe, eager to get
gain, ever thought of such a country as America, the red
man roamed undisturbed through the mighty forest;
killing the buffalo, the deer, and the bear; or, when traversing the lakes and the rivers, partaking the pleasure of the
fish that swam in their waters.

But oh, how has the scene changed since the white man
discovered our country! Where are the aborigines who
once thronged the shores of the lakes and rivers on which
the white man has now reared his dwelling and amassed
his wealth? What doleful tales do those bleaching bones
tell which the husbandman has ploughed up, that he may
sow his seed and reap an abundant harvest! Where is the
pensive mourner who was once seen approaching the
graves and bones of his departed fathers to weep there?
He is gone the way of all flesh, and his bones lie by the
side of his ancestors. But where are his widow, and the
fatherless children? —are none left to weep over his grave?
The red man is gone, and a strange people occupy his
place.

This solemn fact leads me to inquire, What have been the
causes of the rapid decrease in numbers of my countrymen? I have put the question to the Indian whose head
was white with the frost of many winters, and who has
heard the expiring wail of once numerous and powerful
tribes of my people. In reply, he has given me the following melancholy picture:—

"Ah! my son, my heart sickens when I look at that
which has happened to our forefathers since the pale face
came amongst us.

"My son, before the white man landed on our shores the
red men of the forest were numerous, powerful, wise, and
happy. In those days nothing but the weight of many

winters bore them down to the grave. The Indian mother could then rear a large family of healthy and happy children. The game in the forest, the fish in the waters, abundantly supplied their wants. The Indian corn grew rank and tall, and brought forth much, and plenty smiled upon the land. The old men made their feasts, smoked their pipes, and thought upon their *munedoos* (gods), they sang and beat upon the *tawaegun* (drum). The young men and women danced. The *pow-wows* (medicine men) visited the sick, sang and invoked their gods, applied their medicines gathered from nature's stores, and thus drove away the grim monster Death. These were happy days of sunshine and calm to our forefathers.

" My son, while our fathers were in this happy state they cast their eyes towards the sun-setting, and beheld a big canoe with white wings approaching nearer and nearer to the shore, and outbraving the waves of the mighty waters. A strange people landed, wise as the gods, powerful as the thunder, with faces white as the snow. Our fathers held out to them the hand of friendship. The strangers then asked for a small piece of land on which they might pitch their tents; the request was cheerfully granted. By and by they begged for more, and more was given them. In this way they have continued to ask, or have obtained by force or fraud, the fairest portions of our territory. As the white man advanced in his encroachments, the Indian retired farther back to make room for him. In this way the red men have gradually been stripped of their hunting-grounds and corn-fields, and been driven far from the land of comfort and plenty. Their children began to cry for food, their souls fainted for want, their clothes dropped from their shivering backs, the fatal small-pox and measles visited them for the first time, and swept away the poor

Indians by thousands. Goaded to despair, they clutched the deadly tomahawk, and sought to wield it against the encroaching whites; but, instead of conquering, the act only afforded to the calculating, remorseless foe, a pretext for a more general slaughter of the defenceless natives. Then, as if disease and the musket—both imported by the whites—could not mow down the Indian fast enough, the *fire-waters* crept in and began to gnaw their very vitals, debasing their morals, lowering their dignity, spreading contentions, confusion and death!

"My son, these are the causes which have melted away our forefathers like snow before a warm sun. The Great Spirit has hidden his face from his red children, on account of their drunkenness and their many crooked ways."

I have often heard my brethren, both in public and in private, give utterance to the sentiments just expressed; and it must be acknowledged that they were much better off in their former comparatively happy state, when they could feast unmolested on the abundance which nature had provided for them. It should also be remembered that the pagan ideas of bliss are almost entirely sensual, and relate to the unrestrained indulgence of the animal appetites. Alas! they know nothing of that real peace which the world can neither give nor take away. From experience of my early life, I can truly say, that their imaginary bliss is so mixed up with everything that is abominable and cruel, that it would be vain to look for real happiness among savage tribes. "The dark places of the earth are full of the habitations of cruelty."

When I consider the prevalence of intemperance among my people,—an evil formerly not confined to the men, for even women and youth were addicted to it,—and the long catalogue of vices and diseases which follow in the train of the monster, I am not surprised at the appalling decline in number of my countrymen.

If the enlightened and polished European settlers and their descendants had no means of staying the progress of this devastating curse among themselves, what shield or protection had the rude and simple natives against the same insidious foe ?

I cannot suppose for a moment that the Supreme Disposer has decreed that the doom of the red man is to fall and gradually disappear, like the mighty wilderness, before the axe of the European settler.

Some persons may affect to ascribe this waste of life to a divine decree, in order to screen themselves from the terrible responsibility which rests upon their own souls. But that the Great Spirit never determined this is plainly declared; for He hath said, " I have no pleasure in the death of the wicked, but that the wicked turn from his way and live." " God so loved the world that he gave his only begotten Son, that whosoever believeth in Him should not perish, but have everlasting life." " The Son of man came not to destroy men's lives, but to save them." May we not well reply to such infidelity, " Woe unto them that call evil good, and good evil ; that put darkness for light, and light for darkness."

Oh, what an awful account at the day of judgment must the unprincipled white man give, who has been an agent of Satan in the extermination of the original proprietors of the American soil ! Will not the blood of the red man be required at *his* hands, who, for paltry gain, has impaired the minds, corrupted the morals, and ruined the constitutions of a once hardy and numerous race ?

When I think of the long catalogue of evils thus entailed on my poor unhappy countrymen, my heart bleeds, not only

on their account, but also for their destroyers, who, coming
from a land of light and knowledge, are without excuse.
Poor deluded beings! whatever their pretensions to Christianity may have been, it is evident the love of God was
not in their hearts; for that love extends to all mankind,
and constrains to acts of mercy, but never impels to deeds
of death.

Of all the causes which have contributed to the rapid
decrease of the Indian tribes, the abuse of ardent spirits,
while following their native mode of life, is, in my opinion,
the primary and most important. For when an Indian is
intoxicated, all the savage passions of his nature assume
the entire control, often leading him to commit the most
barbarous acts of cruelty and even murder. This is the
way in which the natives have been continually falling one
after another, like the tall trees before the rushing blast;
and thus will they continue to fall until the gospel of our
Lord Jesus Christ shines into their hearts. Then the lion
will be changed into a lamb, and every fierce passion be
hushed into peace. "O Lord, hasten the time! Come
from the four winds, O breath, and breathe upon these
slain, that they may live."

CHAPTER II.

Tradition of Nanahbozhoo—My own opinion as to their origin—Reasons for not supposing them descended from the ten lost tribes of Israel—Desire that this subject should be inquired into.

For several years past I have made it a subject of inquiry among the aged sachems of the Ojebway* nation of Indians,—What are the opinions entertained by them, and transmitted from our forefathers, regarding the origin of our race? All the information I have been able to gain in relation to this question amounts to the following:—That many, many winters ago, the Great Spirit, whom we call in Ojebway *Keehe-munedoo*, or *Kezha-munedoo*, the Benevolent Spirit, created the Indians, and placed them on the continent of America,—that every nation speaking a different language is a separate creation; but that all were made by the same Supreme Being. How they were created is not known.

They say that when the Great Spirit made the different nations of the earth, He gave them various languages, complexions, and religion, as well as divers customs, manners, and modes of living. When He gave the Ojebways their religion, He told them how they were to act; and with this knowledge they think it would be wrong, and give great offence to their Creator, to forsake the old ways of their forefathers.

* Of which Chippeway is a corruption,

The different tribes of the Ojebway nation who now inhabit the shores of Lakes Ontario, Erie, Simcoe, &c., have a tradition current amongst them, that they originally came from the great western lakes, Huron and Superior. The former tribes who resided on the shores of these lakes were called *Nahdooways** or *Hurons*, whom the Ojebways dispossessed of their country by conquest, and the mounds that cover their bones are still pointed out by the Ojebways in different locations. After this the Nahdooways, acknowledging they were conquered, freely gave up their country; at the same time entering into a treaty of friendship with the Ojebways, both agreeing ever after to call each other " *Brother;*" which treaty is still observed between the two nations.†

One of the main difficulties which the Christian missionary has to encounter in planting the gospel amongst the aborigines of North America, arises from their unwillingness to believe what is taught in the unerring Word of God, that the whole human race originally sprang from one pair. But even this difficulty, with many other obstacles to the truth, gives way when the light of the gospel shines into the heart. Of late years a host of living witnesses from among their own people have risen up, declaring that " God hath made of one blood all nations of men, to dwell on all the face of the earth;" thus proving, in their own experience, that " of a truth, God is no respecter of persons: but in every nation he that feareth Him, and worketh righteousness, is accepted with Him."

Some tribes believe that a great man, endued with the spirit of the gods, by the name of *Nanahbozhoo* (the meaning of which is now lost) made the world and the Indians

---

* This word is also applied to the Six Nations Indians.

† The renewal of this treaty will be given in the chapter on wars.

in America. This tradition, as preserved by the Ojebways, is the following :—

Before the general deluge, there lived two enormous creatures, each possessed of vast power. One was an animal, with a great horn on his head; the other was a huge *toad*. The latter had the whole management of the waters, keeping them secure in its own body, and emitting only a certain quantity for the watering of the earth. Between these two creatures there arose a quarrel, which terminated in a fight. The toad in vain tried to *swallow* its antagonist, but the latter rushed upon it, and with his horn pierced a hole in its side, out of which the water gushed in floods, and soon overflowed the face of the earth. At this time Nanahbozhoo was living on the earth, and observing the water rising higher and higher, he fled to the loftiest mountain for refuge. Perceiving that even this retreat would soon be inundated, he selected a large cedar tree which he purposed to ascend should the waters come up to him. Before they reached him he caught a number of animals and fowls, and put them into his bosom. At length the water covered the mountain. Nanahbozhoo then ascended the cedar tree, and as he went up, he plucked its branches and stuck them in the belt which girdled his waist. When he reached the top of the tree he sang, and beat the tune with his arrow upon his bow, and as he sang the tree grew and kept pace with the water for a long time. At length he abandoned the idea of remaining any longer on the tree, and took the branches he had plucked, and with them constructed a raft, on which he placed himself with the animals and fowls. On this raft he floated about for a long time, till all the mountains were covered, and all the beasts of the earth and fowls of the air, except those he had with him, perished.

D

At length Nanahbozhoo thought of forming a new world, but how to accomplish it without any materials he knew not, till the idea occurred to him that if he could only obtain a little of the earth which was then under the water he might succeed in making a new world out of the old one. He accordingly employed the different animals he had with him that were accustomed to diving.—First he sent the loon* down into the water in order to bring up some of the old earth; but it was not able to reach the bottom, and after remaining in the water some time, came up dead. Nanahbozhoo then took it, blew upon it, and it came to life again. He next sent the otter, which also failing to reach the bottom came up dead, and was restored to life in the same manner as the loon. He then tried the skill of the beaver, but without success. Having failed with all these diving animals, he last of all took the *musk rat*;† on account of the distance it had to go to reach the bottom, it was gone a long time, and came up dead. On taking it up, Nanahbozhoo found, to his great joy, that it had reached the earth, and had retained some of the soil in each of its paws and mouth. He then blew upon it, and brought it to life again, at the same time pronouncing many blessings on it, saying, that as long as the world he was about to make should endure, the musk-rat should never become extinct. This prediction of Nanahbozhoo is still spoken of by the Indians when referring to the rapid

* The *loon* is a water fowl of the penguin species, about the size of a goose, with a large pointed bill; the feathers cast a variety of colours; there is a white ring round the neck, the back and neck are also spotted with white. Their skins are used by the natives as pouches; they also make pretty bags. The loon lives on small fish. When it is pursued it will dive under the water for a long time, and some of the Indians have informed me that they have known it to disappear for a day.

† A well known animal of the beaver species, whose fur is made into hats, which are passed off as *beaver hats!*

increase of the musk-rat. Nanahbozhoo then took the earth which he found in the musk-rat's paws and mouth, and having rubbed it with his hands to fine dust, he placed it on the waters, and blew upon it; then it began to grow larger and larger, until it was beyond the reach of his eye. In order to ascertain the size of the world, and the progress of its growth and expansion, he sent a wolf to run to the end of it, measuring its extent by the time consumed in the journey. The first journey he performed in one day, the second took him five days, the third ten, the fourth a month, then a year, five years, and so on, until the world was so large that Nanahbozhoo sent a young wolf that could just run, which died of old age before he could accomplish his journey. Nanahbozhoo then said the world was large enough, and commanded it to cease from growing. After this Nanahbozhoo took a journey to view the new world he had made, and as he travelled he created various tribes of Indians, and placed them in different parts of the earth ; he then gave them various religions, customs, and manners.

This Nanahbozhoo now sits at the North Pole, overlooking all the transactions and affairs of the people he has placed on the earth. The Northern tribes say that Nanahbozhoo always sleeps during the winter ; but, previous to his falling asleep, fills his great pipe, and smokes for several days, and that it is the smoke arising from the mouth and pipe of Nanahbozhoo which produces what is called " Indian summer."

The reader will observe many resemblances in this tradition of Nanahbozhoo to that beautiful account of Noah's flood handed down to us in sacred history, which leads me to conclude it is a corruption of the same,—Nanahbozhoo being substituted for Noah, the raft for the ark, the sending of the animals to search and fetch the earth for the raven and the dove, and Nanahbozhoo making Indians to people the earth for the rapid increase of mankind after the flood. As the Indians had no means of preserving records, the true history of any event would in the course of time be lost, and I have noticed that even this tradition is related quite differently by various tribes of Indians, either by adding to or omitting some parts of the story. From all that can be gathered from the wise old Sachems and their traditions on this subject, it appears that their notions as to their origin are little better than a mass of confusion. Many of their traditions are founded on dreams, which will account for the numerous absurd stories current amongst them.

I am inclined to the opinion that the aborigines of America came originally from the northern parts of Asia, and that they crossed over at Behring's Straits. I think this supposition may account for the prevailing opinion among almost all the tribes, that their forefathers were first placed somewhere in the west, whence they took their journey towards the sun-rising. The notion they entertain of the souls of the dead returning to a good country towards the sun-setting, may be derived from a faint remembrance of their having come from that direction, and the love they still feel for the better land they have left behind.

The love of country is a feeling implanted in the breast of every man, however poor and obscure he may have been in the land of his birth and among his own people. When he emigrates to foreign parts nothing is more common than to hear such an one extol his native land, and speak with rapture of the many happy days he has spent in it. His temporal condition and prospects may be far better in his adopted country, yet he will still remember the " leeks and onions in Egypt." Thus it is with the American Indian. He looks forward to a happy return to a land of plenty

and great joy, not literally, but in spirit; and this desire
and hope fill his soul with exultation when he sees the
glorious orb of day sinking near the abodes of departed
spirits.

Much has of late years been said and written on the
theory of the North American Indians having descended
from the ten lost tribes of Israel. There are many things
to favour this opinion, and many against it. When I read
the book called "The Star in the West," and "Smith's
View of the Hebrews," I was strongly inclined to favour
the theory. Certainly many of the customs and sacrifices
of the Indians resemble very much those of the children of
Israel, such as observing days of purification, offering the
first-fruits of the earth, burnt offerings, and reckoning
time by moons. But, on the other hand, they have no
Sabbaths, no circumcision, no altars erected, and no distinction between clean and unclean animals. It would seem
almost impossible for the descendants of the Israelites ever
to have lost the recollection of their Sabbath days, and the
rite of circumcision, both of which were so solemnly
enjoined upon them. One of the above-mentioned works
gives an account of circumcision existing among some
tribes in the west; but I have inquired of several old
Indian men whether they ever heard of such a practice
being observed by our forefathers previous to the landing
of Europeans on the shores of America, and they have
always expressed themselves quite ignorant on the subject.*

From all I have heard and read on the subject, I am
inclined to favour the opinion that the Indians are
descendants of the Asiatic Tartars, as there appears to me
a more striking similarity in features, customs and manners,
between them and my countrymen than any other nation.†

* *Vide* Notes B and C, Appendix.   † Appendix D.

If it were possible for a few of the most enlightened Indians in each nation to visit that part of Asia which lies nearest to Behring's Straits, for the purpose of examining minutely into the language, customs, and manners of the Tartars, they would, in my opinion, discover such a similarity between the people of the two countries, as to lead to the satisfactory conclusion that the aborigines of America are descended from the Asiatics.* It would be exceedingly gratifying to me were the fact ascertained, and I hope I may yet see the day when the attention of some of the learned and scientific men in Europe and America shall be turned to this subject. I think the plan is quite feasible, and might be accomplished without very great expense. It would not only be satisfactory to know the origin of my countrymen, but might be the means of introducing pure Christianity among the Tartars, by sending native missionaries from America to the other side of the great waters. I leave the subject for the consideration of all who feel any interest in this puzzling question.

* In a letter from the author, dated April 4th, 1853, he states : "The other day I had an interview with a young Chinese who is studying for the Church. In appearance he resembles H. P. Chase, and when he read the Lord's Prayer in his language I fancied I was listening to Echo, the fire-keeper of the Six Nations. I am more and more convinced that our Indians are a branch of the Tartar or Chinese family, there are so many striking resemblances between the two races."

CHAPTER III.

INDIAN LOCALITIES.

Country of the Ojebways—Lake Superior—Surrounding country—Its Mission stations—Lake Huron—Residence of the Thunder Gods—Manitaulin Island—Attempts to settle Indians there—Lake Michigan—Island of Mackinaw—St. Clair River and Lake—Detroit River—Lake Erie—Grand River—Niagara River and Falls—Grand and Navy Islands—Lake Ontario—St. Lawrence and Ottawa Rivers—Mountains—Queenston Heights—Climate and soil—Mode of clearing a farm—Natural productions.

THE Ojebway nation is found scattered in small bodies in the country extending from the River St. Lawrence, thence along the northern shores of lakes Ontario, Erie, St. Clair, Huron, both sides of Lake Superior, and on to Hudson's Bay territory, and the head waters of the Mississippi. A few of the same people are also found intermingled with the Ottawas and others on the south shore of Lake Huron, and in the vicinity of Lake Michigan. Within the range of the same tract of country are to be found several other nations of Indians, as the Six Nations, of whom are the following: Mohawks, Onondagas, Senecas, Oneidas, Cayugas, Tuscaroras; and also Delawares, Munceys, Minominees, Wayandots, Ottawas, and Pottawatamees, &c. Each band or community has its own chiefs, and manages its own affairs, within the limits of its territory, quite independently of other tribes of the same nation; but in matters which affect the whole nation, a general council is called, composed of all or a majority of the chiefs of the different tribes.

THE OJEBWAY COUNTRY.

The country originally occupied by the Ojebway nation, and in which scattering tribes are still found, is situated between the latitudes of 42° and 50° north, and longitudes 75° and 100° west of Greenwich.

Within this range lie the immense fresh-water lakes or inland seas so noted for their size and grandeur; a short description of which I shall here insert, commencing at the fountain head with

LAKE SUPERIOR.

This lake is so called from its being the largest of all the lakes in North America.* It is reckoned to be about 420 miles from east to west, and its greatest breadth about 135 miles. Its circumference is about 1,000 miles. The waters of this lake are as pure as the clearest spring. Its northern shore is studded with numerous islands of various forms and sizes; on the south they are but few, and these rather small.

There are several large bays on both sides of the lake; the most noted is *Kahkewaoonnahning*, commonly called *Kawawenah Bay*, situated on the south shore. At this bay the Rev. John Sunday, a native missionary, *planted the gospel in the year* 1832, and laboured with great success for seven months. Here the Methodist Episcopal Church of the United States has a mission, and I have been informed that the American Board of Missions conducted by the Presbyterians have also missions near this bay and at Fond du Lac.

The principal rivers which flow into Lake Superior are *St. Louis* at its western extremity, *Nipiyon, Black river, Wahbeshkah, Michipicoton, Montreal, Carp, Garlick, Ontonagon, Monraise, Bois Brule.* This great lake has its outlet in

* The Ojebway name is Ojebway Kechegahme.

Lake Huron by the river or straits of St. Marie, called by the Ojebways *Bahwetig,* or *the Falls,* because near the commencement of this river is the *Sault* or *Falls of St. Marie.* These falls are not perpendicular, but form a rapid of about a mile in length, in which distance there is a descent of about twenty feet.

The Sault St. Marie is a famous place for *white fish,* which are caught in great abundance by the Indians, and are most delicate and delicious food. Opposite the Sault, on the north side, is a mission station, under the care of the Church of England. The Rev. W. M'Murray,* the missionary stationed there, is an excellent and pious man, whose labours have been much blessed among the poor Indians. His wife is an Indian lady, daughter of the late Mr. Johnson, who married a Chippeway woman, and resided at Sault St. Marie. Here is also an establishment of the Hudson's Bay Company. On the American side is Fort Brady, where a few troops are stationed. The American Baptist Board of Missions have for a long time had a station at this place, and have been instrumental in making some converts and educating several of the Indian children. A short distance below Fort Brady, the Methodist Episcopal Church of the W. S. have also a mission, where a number of the Ojebways are settled in log-houses, and are faithful members of the society. These converts were first visited and taught in the Christian religion by John Sunday and other native teachers.

Soon after leaving the Sault, islands of various sizes begin to multiply, which increase in number as you travel towards the waters of Lake Huron. At the outlet of this strait is the island of St. Joseph, of considerable magnitude, and capable, I am informed, of producing wheat,

* Now (1860) Rector of Niagara.

potatoes, and other vegetables. Near this island is that of
St. Drummond's, where the British formerly had a fort;
but it is now entirely forsaken, and the buildings are gone
to ruin. So long as a military establishment was kept
up there, it was a place of general resort for the various
tribes of Indians from *Superior*, *Huron*, *Michigan*, and *Green
Bay*, who went there to receive the Government presents.

LAKE HURON.

This lake, next in size to Superior, is about 270 miles
from the River St. Clair to the Island of Mackinaw, and
about 150 at its greatest breadth; it is nearly 1,100 miles
in circumference. The principal bays in this noble sheet of
water are the Georgian, Gloster, Nahdoowasahge, and
Sangenah. It is said that there are 3,000 islands on the
north shore of this lake, of different shapes and sizes; most
of them are composed of granite, with trees of evergreen
growing from the interstices of the rocks, while others are
entirely barren.

Next to the stupendous Falls of Niagara, I think these
islands present to the eye of the traveller one of the most
wild and romantic scenes imaginable. Some of them,
towering far above the rest, are barren and rugged; others
beautifully wooded, with the diversified foliage of the cedar,
pine, and spruce. When on the lake, you see them stretch-
ing in the distance as far as the eye can reach, with swarms
of gulls and ducks flying about. The channels and bays are
so numerous that it is impossible for a person unaccustomed
to their windings to find his way; even those who are in
the habit of traversing them often go astray. I have never
taken this route without a guide well acquainted with the
coast; but with this precaution we have sometimes found
ourselves penned up in a bay, and been obliged to make
our way back again.

The La Croche mountains, on the main shore, which almost form islands, project over the waters of the lake in awful grandeur; being principally composed of white flint rock, when viewed from a distance they have all the appearance of snow-capped mountains. It is on these mountains the poor superstitious Indians say the thunder-gods, or eagles, have their abode, and hatch their young. The great and little Manitoulin Islands lie stretched along the lake, as if the father and mother of the thousands of small ones, whom they seemed formed to protect from the boisterous waves of the Huron. These two islands are in general barren, and destitute of game. The Colonial Government have made an attempt to locate the scattering tribes of Indians in Upper Canada on the great Manitoulin Island;* but, on account of many disadvantages, the Indians in general have refused to settle on it. Some of the Ottawa Indians have made attempts at improvements on this island, and have grown a few potatoes and some Indian corn. The government have also commenced an establishment, where the annual presents are issued to such Indians as may come for them.

The wonderful works of nature displayed in these islands show forth the power and greatness of their Creator, and lead us to exclaim, " O Lord, how manifold are thy works; in wisdom hast thou made them all !"

Scarcely one in a hundred of these islands is capable of cultivation, therefore in their present rude and wild magnificence they must remain, till all nature be put to confusion, and the elements melt away with fervent heat. The rivers which empty themselves into Lake Huron are French River, Moon, Severn, Coldwater, Nahdoowasahgee, Sahgeeng, Maitland, Auxsable, Bayfield, Sagana, Thunder, Messissauge,

* Properly, Manedoomini—the Spirit Island.

Spanish, and several others of less note. There are several excellent fisheries on this lake ; the most noted is that near Sahgeeng river, along the east shore. The principal fish caught are the salmon trout, of enormous size, white fish, herring, bass, sturgeon, pickerell, pike, mullet, sheephead, which form the chief food of the Indians along the coast of these lakes. The soil on the north shore is very rocky, and therefore unfit for cultivation, and I have been informed by Indian hunters that this rocky country extends a long distance into the interior. On the eastern shore the land is in general good and capable of producing excellent crops of wheat, oats, potatoes, turnips, &c., especially from the Sahgeeng to the outlet of the lake. The south-west shore is also rather stony and swampy, which will retard the settlement in that quarter. About Sagana Bay I have been informed there is some good land, which will no doubt speedily be settled by Americans, in whose dominions it is situated.

LAKE MICHIGAN.

This lake is an arm of Lake Huron, joined by the Straits of Mackinaw. Its course from Mackinaw is south-west ; it is about 300 miles in length, and eighty-five at its greatest breadth ; circumference about 1000. The principal bay in this lake is situated on the west side, and is called Green Bay, ninety miles long and about thirty-five broad. At the head of this bay the Oneida Indians from the State of New York have formed a settlement, and there is a mission station among them. On the east is Grand Traverse Bay.

The rivers which flow into this lake are Grand Traverse, Belisis, Sandy, Kallemazo, Grand, Calumot, Milwarkie, Menoominee, and Fox.

The islands in this lake are few in number ; the most

celebrated is that of *Meshenemahkenoong* (the Great Turtle,) commonly called Michilimackinack, or Mackinaw. This island is well situated for a fort, and is noted on account of there being a military establishment on it; and also as being the great depôt of the American Fur Company. There are many romantic spots on this island; one curious natural wonder is the stone *arch* and *cap*.

The following interesting description of a visit to this island in July, 1851, is given by the author in a private letter:—" We landed this morning at Mackinaw, which place has greatly improved since I was here twenty-five years ago. The village contains about 8,000 inhabitants. I am luxuriating on delicious white fish every day. After dinner a party of us sallied forth to see the wonders of the Island. We first went through a forest to see the *Arch Rock*, which hangs over a precipice of 100 feet or more, forming a natural bridge. Some daring ones walk over the arch, but to look at it was enough for me. It spans about forty feet, and is second only to the natural bridge in Virginia. We then wandered through the thicket to the *Harne's Foot*, which stands on the highest part of the island, from whence is presented a splendid view of the lakes and islands far and near. From thence we proceeded to see the *Sugar Loaf Rock* which rises out of the earth some thirty feet from its base, like a large turtle lifting its head; from which I have no doubt the Indians gave the name of the island *Meshenemahkenoong*, or the Great Turtle. From thence we went to see the *Skull Cave*, where a trader was concealed by an Indian when the British troops were massacred by the Indians. The account is in one of our Indian narratives. The cave is now nearly filled up with fallen stones. There is another object of curiosity, called the *Lover's Rock*, but we were too fatigued to go and see it. . . . . Towards evening I met a few Indians in a tent by the beach, to whom I conversed on religion, gave some advice, &c. One of them said he was converted to Christianity at the camp meeting dear Charles and I attended at Lake Superior, and that he was still holding on in the good way. The rest were pagans. They stated they resided on the shores of Lake Michigan, and that there were a number of Indians in that vicinity, most of whom were anxious to receive religious instruction, and had been waiting a long time for a missionary to come among them. I pitied them from the bottom of my heart. O, ye Christians of Britain, Canada, and the United States, will ye suffer these immortal souls to perish for the lack of knowledge! If it be true that one soul is of more value than ten thousand worlds like this, why then not care for these poor perishing souls, though they may be few in number? O Lord, raise up more labourers, for the harvest is truly great, and souls are perishing!"

The American Board of Missions have for a long time had a station on this island, and have educated several of the Indian youths, especially the half-breeds. Many of the traders under the employ of the American Fur Company have taken wives from this school, and it is to be hoped that the religious instructions there received will not be lost, but that they will infuse the savour of the Gospel among their Indian brethren wherever their lot may be cast.

The land around this lake is in general of a good quality, especially about the south shore, near which stands the city of Chicago, the landing-place of the thousands of emigrants who are bending their way to the far west.

Lakes Huron and Michigan forming the same sheet of water, empty themselves into Lake St. Clair, flowing about thirty miles down the beautiful river St. Clair. The channel at the outlet of Huron is rather narrow, not more than a musket-shot from one side to the other; near this is Fort Gratiot on the American coast, and on the Canadian shore is the St. Clair Mission. Approaching nearer the lake it forms itself into various channels, which cause a number of islands; on some of these the Indians plant, and find pasture for their cattle.

ST. CLAIR.

This is a small lake, called by the Ojebways *Wahweyah-tahnoong, (the Round Lake,)* so named from its shape. It is about thirty miles in diameter.

The rivers which flow into this lake are the Thames, called by the Indians *Ashkahnesebe, (the Horn River,)* from its resemblance in shape to the deer's horns. Bear Creek also empties into this lake.

The country around is in many parts very low and marshy, yet the soil is good and productive.

At the south extremity of this lake commences the noble river Detroit, reaching about thirty miles, when its waters empty themselves into Lake Erie. The banks of this river are well settled by French and other inhabitants, who possess extensive farms and have planted large orchards. On its west side stands the city of Detroit, and opposite the little village of Sandwich. Near the outlet of this river is the town of Amherstburg, a short distance north of which is an Indian settlement of the Huron or Wyandot tribe. Some of these people adhere to the Roman Catholic religion, and others to the Methodist doctrines.

Amherstburg is the most southern point of Canada. The climate is favourable for the growth of almost all kinds of grain and vegetables. Tobacco flourishes well here, and the farmers raise large quantities of it for market.

LAKE ERIE.

The Indians call this lake *Wahbeshkegoo-Kechegahme, (the White Water Lake).* It is so named from its colour, in contra-distinction to the beautiful green and blue waters of the upper lakes. It is about 250 miles in length, and 60 in breadth. Its course is east and west.

The rivers which flow into this lake are the Grand River, or Ouse, on the banks of which are settled the Six Nations of Indians, the Moumee, and Raisen. On either side it is well settled by white people, and the soil, on the whole, is very good for agricultural pursuits.

There are several villages scattered along the vicinity of this lake. The city of Buffalo stands on the east side, and Cleveland on the south shore. The enormous western and northern supplies of Lake Erie flow down the celebrated River Niagara, and, as they approach the stupendous cataract, come dashing and foaming against immoveable rocks for several miles before they reach the awful precipice over which they fall thundering into the chasm beneath : thence they flow into Lake Ontario. On the west side of the lake there are several islands. Above the Falls is the largest one, called Grand Island ; and another called Navy Island, which has lately become notorious on account of the rebels from Canada and the vagabonds of the United States making it their head-quarters. It is only a small swampy spot, and would not, in all probability, have come into notice but for the above-mentioned circumstance.

The Chippeway River empties itself into the Niagara, a few miles above the Falls, on the site of which is the village of Chippeway. The word *Niagara* is Mohawk, but is pronounced by the natives *Oo-noo-nah-gah-rah.*

The Ojebways call the falls *Kahkejewung, the Water*

Falls. At the mouth of the Niagara river is the town of Niagara, containing a large population. It is quite evident that the falls had their existence in the first place at Queenston Heights, about seven miles below their present situation ; and that they have been receding imperceptibly in that direction ever since the flood, and will continue so to do, there is no doubt, as the weight of water and the immense masses of ice which tumble over the rock are constantly wearing it away.

LAKE ONTARIO.

This is a fine sheet of water, about 200 miles long and 50 broad. Its course is nearly east and west. Circumference about 500 miles. The principal rivers besides the mighty Niagara which run into Ontario are the Credit, Nappane, Black, Oswego, and Genesee. In several of these most excellent salmon are caught.

The bays are Burlington at the head of the lake, separated from the main lake by a narrow sandy beach, on which grow scattering oak trees and wild grape vines. The Bay of Quinty is on the north side of the east end of the lake. Grape Island Mission was on this bay, but the Indians are now removed to the township of Alnwick.

At the east end of Ontario commences the well-known river St. Lawrence, which flows into the Atlantic Ocean, where the waters of these immense lakes and their numerous supplies are lost in the briny deep of the Gulf of St. Lawrence. The river Ottawa runs into it near Montreal, also St. Maurice, Chaudiere, St. Francis, Richelieu, St. Regis, and Oswegatche.

All these lakes, and their connecting rivers, are navigable for the largest ships and steamboats. During the summer seasons Ontario and Erie present very busy scenes of com-

E

merce, with first-rate steamboats and schooners constantly
plying up and down their noble waters.   Besides the great
lakes already mentioned, there are a number of less note,
such as Rice Lake, Simcoe, about thirty miles in diameter,
Nippissing, Nipigon, Rainy Lake, Winnipeg, Manitoba,
Mud Lake, Sturgeon, Pigeon, and Balsom.

MOUNTAINS.

There are but few mountains in the range of the Ojebway
country.   The principal one is that which stretches round
the head waters of Lake Ontario, and over which the
waters of the upper lakes precipitate with awful grandeur
into the bosom of Ontario, forming Niagara Falls.   The
scenery from this mountain at Queenston Heights is exceedingly grand, presenting to the eye in panoramic beauty
the extensive waters of Lake Ontario, the noble Niagara
river, winding its way through high banks, clothed in the
richest foliage, the wild forest and the cultivated farm, with
here and there a town or village, showing that prosperity
and comfort are rewarding the industry of the old settler
and the emigrant.

At the head waters of Lake Ontario this mountain takes
a majestic curve, presenting a landscape somewhat different,
but not less grand.   Immediately beneath, inclosed as it were
in a crescent, is the city of Hamilton; beyond stretches
the lovely Burlington Bay, separated from the lake by a
narrow sandy beach of six miles long.   When the late
Captain Joseph Brant, and my father, Augustus Jones, had
the whole country to choose from, Captain B. selected a
tract of land at the north-west end of the beach, built a
large frame-house, where he lived with his family; and my
father, choosing the other extremity, settled his family
on the opposite side.   The two families were constantly

crossing this sandy beach, living on friendly terms with each other. I think, without exception, this part of Canada outvies all others I have visited, as regards the beauty of its scenery, the quality of its land, the high state of cultivation, and the local advantages it has for carrying on trade. Perhaps I may be partial in my judgment, as it was on the romantic Burlington Heights I first drew my breath, and, in my youthful days, was accustomed to traverse the shores of its clear waters in the light birch-bark canoe; here I ranged the forest, and shot many a partridge, squirrel, and pigeon, where now may be seen the fine brick or stone house, and the productive farm of the white man. Here also I used to climb the mountain, and, after reaching the summit, indulge myself in viewing the country and waters below, till I would feel reluctant to quit a spot so charming and attractive.

CLIMATE AND SOIL.

The Canadian climate in general is clear, pure, and dry; the extremes of heat and cold are great; the thermometer, in summer, often rising to 120 degrees, and, in winter, falling to 20 degrees and sometimes 30 degrees below zero. Snow often falls in November, and continues on the ground till April; the depth of snow varies in different parts; along the shores of Lakes Ontario, Erie, and St. Clair, it seldom falls over two feet, whereas further north it is often three or four feet; persons much exposed during the extreme cold weather are often frost-bitten. Spring sets in suddenly, and the extreme heat of summer causes vegetation to spring up rapidly; the autumns are lovely, and the foliage splendid; I have often thought a correct representation of one tree would, by persons who had never seen such foliage, be considered unnatural and exaggerated.

E 2

The winters are far more healthy than the summers, when fevers are prevalent in many parts.

Along the chain of the great lakes the soil and climate is in general well adapted for the growth of winter and spring wheat, rye, oats, peas, barley, Indian corn, potatoes, turnips, melons, &c. The country on the north shore of Lakes Huron and Superior is unfit for cultivation, excepting now and then small spots, as these parts abound with rocks and cold cedar swamps. All vegetables that grow in the open fields in England thrive in Western Canada, especially in the southern parts; apple, pear, and plum trees are cultivated to great advantage. Peaches are grown on the south shore of Lake Ontario, and as far as to the head waters of Erie. The tobacco plant grows in the vicinity of Lakes St. Clair and Erie, and Detroit river; currants and gooseberries do well in most places; grapes may be raised in the open air in southern parts, but require care to preserve them from the severe frosts of winter. I sowed in my garden a number of flower-seeds sent me by a kind friend from England, nearly all of which flowered beautifully; they were much admired by the Indians, who said they far surpassed theirs on account of their scent. Many American wild flowers have to be raised in hot-houses in England.

Western Canada, as regards agriculture, is decidedly the garden of Her Majesty's possessions in North America; the rivers and lakes affording great facilities for carrying on extensive trade and commerce. Most of the settlers in this part of the country have risen to affluence and respectability by the industrious cultivation of their farms, and it is truly pleasing to observe their gradual ascent from the shanty to the brick or stone house. On many farms you may still see the humble log house, their first dwelling-place in the wilderness, where they have spent many a long and dreary

day in subduing the forest ; and after the hard toils of six
days' work were over, and the axe no longer heard to echo
through the dreary woods, no cheerful sound of the church-
going bell would salute their ear, to remind them that the
sacred Sabbath had returned, and summon them away from
earthly toil and care to spend its hallowed hours in the courts
of the Lord's house. They could not say with the poet—

> "Dear is the hallow'd morn to me
> When village bells awake the day,
> And by their sacred minstrelsy
> Call me from earthly cares away.
>
> "And dear to me the wingèd hour
> Spent in Thy hallow'd courts, O Lord,
> To feel devotion's soothing power,
> And catch the manna of Thy word."

Yet, no doubt, many pious souls who had not forgotten
the Sabbath privileges of their native land would unite their
voices even in the solemn stillness of a Canadian forest—

> "And there, like incense, softly rose
> The strains of prayer and praise,
> And broke the Sabbath-like repose
> With soft harmonious lays.
>
> "And oft as evening's purple shade
> Was lost in twilight dim,
> Together in the forest glade
> They sang their evening hymn."

The method pursued by a new settler to clear his farm
is, first to cut down all the under-brush, which he piles
into heaps ; he then begins to fell the trees, and to cut them
into such lengths as may be drawn by one or two yoke of
oxen. The limbs are next cut off, and carefully thrown
into heaps. After he has gone through as much land as
he wishes to clear, which is called a *fallow*, he leaves it
lying during the summer for the purpose of drying, and
then about the month of August sets it on fire, which runs

through the whole ground, burning up all the leaves, rubbish, and limbs. After the fire has done its first execution, the settler makes a *bee*, inviting a number of his neighbours to come and help him log and pile the large timber which the fire did not consume. The party commences by several yoke of oxen drawing the logs together to various parts of the ground, which are then piled up by means of handspikes; a dozen men will in this way log several acres a day. After these logs are nicely heaped they are set on fire, and by a little attention in rolling the brands together the whole of the timber is soon burnt up. On these occasions all work without wages; a dinner is provided, and the owner of the land too often provides plenty of *fire-water* with which to treat his friends. The next thing done is to save the ashes, which are drawn off the ground and put into a dry place till winter, when he takes them to the manufacturers of pot or pearl ashes. He next drags or harrows the ground two or three times before he sows it with wheat; which done, it is harrowed two or three times more; this completes the sowing. He next sets to work to make rails from such timber as is easily split, which he hauls round his field and then lays up in a zigzag manner so as to form a fence five or six feet high; such a fence will keep out all cattle and pigs. The stumps of the trees cut down in the fallow are left standing about three feet above-ground, where they remain till they rot out, which generally takes ten or more years. Wheat sown in September or October remains all the winter under the snow.

NATURAL PRODUCTIONS.

The Canadian forests consist in certain parts of immense tall groves of pine, with other trees intermingled. In some districts the forests abound with oak, elm bass-wood, white-wood, walnut, hickory, butter-nut, slippery elm, poplar, sassafras, and dogwood. In other parts, especially in the north, the land is covered with sugar maple, beech, birch, ash, hemlock, and ironwood. In low swampy ground grow spruce firs of various species, willow, alder, water ash, bird's-eye maple, cedar, larch, and sycamore, commonly called button-wood. The wild fruit trees are several kinds of wild plums, crab apple, thorn, cherry, elder, and bush cranberry. Many of the small lakes yield plentiful supplies of wild rice, which the Indians gather in great abundance, in the autumn, and make into soup. The woods and prairies abound with blackberries, huckleberries, strawberries, raspberries, gooseberries, black currants, wild grapes, and marsh cranberries. There is a root resembling in shape and taste the West India sweet potato. This serves for food, and grows in rich black soil. It is commonly called ground nut. There is another plant called *wahbezeepin*, or the swan potato, found in bogs or marshy soil. The Indians boil and eat it in cases of extreme hunger. Another root sometimes eaten by them is called *oduhpin*. It is long, white, and tender, and has a warm, pungent taste. But of all the natural productions *mundahmin* (the Indian corn or maize) is the most valued by the Indians; of which the following tradition, related to me by Chief Netahgawinene, of Cold Water, will show. Many winters ago the Great Spirit appeared to one of our wise forefathers, and showed him a plant of the mundahmin, or Indian corn, on which grew two ears. The Great Spirit then told him to preserve the two ears until the next spring, when he was to plant them. He was further commanded to preserve the whole crop, and send two ears to each of the surrounding nations, with the injunction that they were not to eat of it until the third crop. The wise

Indian did as he was commanded. His corn grew strong and brought forth much. The next summer he enlarged his ground, and planted all his seed, which yielded plentifully. He then sent two ears to each of the surrounding tribes, with proper directions, which they observed, and by this means the corn was distributed among all the American Indians. It is considered by them the best grain in the world, because the Great Spirit gave it to them for their bread. Pounded parched corn and pemegun is the celebrated food for warriors and travellers in the western and northern countries. The Great Spirit about this time is also said to have given the Indian the tobacco plant, that he might smoke the pipe of peace with his fellows, and cause the smoke of the calumet to ascend to the Great Spirit as sweet incense. The prairies and woodlands present a splendid appearance during the summer months, from the endless variety of beautiful wild flowers which, bursting forth in succession, display the most brilliant colours, although they have little or no fragrance. I have often been led into delightful contemplation of the goodness and power of the Supreme, when traversing the mighty forests, contrasting the sombre foliage of the trees with the delicate yet brilliant hues of the wild flowers which deck, like so many gems, the green verdure beneath, and I have been led in admiration and gratitude to exclaim, "My Father made them all!"

CHAPTER IV.

Treatment of the women by the men—Character of women—General description—Education of children—Family government—Treatment of the aged
—Cannibalism.

CONSIDERING the manners of life, dress, and habits of
the North American Indians, it may be said that they are
a moral people. This was strikingly characteristic of them
before they were contaminated by unprincipled European
adventurers, who introduced the *fire-waters* and many vices
amongst them. In their original state they were generally
true to each other, and as moral as a people unrenewed
by Divine grace could be expected to be. It is true the
depraved nature in them is as strong as it is in other
nations ; but the good counsel of the wise sachems, and the
mark of disgrace put upon unruly persons, had a very
desirable influence.

They are naturally suspicious, revengeful, stoical,* and
indolent. In time of peace they are kind and hospitable
to each other, particularly to strangers, with whom they
will divide the last morsel of food. " Hospitality," says
Morse, " is a prominent trait in the Indian character. To
the stranger, whether white or red, they are hospitable and
generous, furnishing the best food and accommodation
their dwellings afford, often relinquishing their own

* Appendix E.

for the refreshment and comfort of the stranger.* When aroused, however, to take up the tomahawk, vengeance sparkles in their eyes. They have a high sense of honour, and like to be thought good, kind, and brave. Carver says, " In danger they readily give assistance to those of their band who stand in need of it, without any expectation of return, except of those just rewards that are always conferred by the Indians on merit."

Their indolence leads them to be very improvident; the thought of laying up a store of provisions beforehand seems never to enter their minds; but so long as they have anything to eat, they will lounge about and sleep, and never think of hunting till hunger presses them to go in search of game. They spend their time when in their villages or wigwams, in smoking, making their implements

---

* Mr. Harmon, a clerk of the North-West Company, who resided in the Indian country for many years, remarks on Indian hospitality :—"February 11th, 1801. On the 1st instant, accompanied by eight of our people, and one of the natives as a guide, I set off, with a small assortment of goods, to go and trade with about fifty families of Crees and Assiniboins. When we had approached within about a mile of the camp of the natives, ten or twelve of their chiefs, or most respectable men, came on horseback, to meet and conduct us to their dwellings. We reached them through a crowd of people, who hailed us with a shout of joy. Immediately after our arrival, the principal chief of the village sent his son to invite me and my interpreter to his tent. As soon as we had entered it, and were seated, the respectable old chief caused meat and berries, and the best of every thing which he had, to be set before us. Before we had eaten much, we were sent for to another tent, where we received similar treatment; and from this we were invited to another; and so on till we had been to more than half-a-dozen tents. At all these we ate a little, and smoked our pipes ; for my interpreter informed me they would be greatly affronted, and think that we despised them, if we refused to taste of what was set before us. Hospitality to strangers is among the Indian virtues. During several days that we remained with these people, we were treated with more *real* politeness than is commonly shown to strangers in the civilized parts of the world."

for war and hunting, and talking over their various exploits in the chase and in the fight. To strangers they are reserved, but among themselves they are notorious talkers and newsmongers; no event occurs in any village but it is soon published abroad. In the presence of others they are seldom known to hold any conversation with their wives. Morse testifies, "Except when intoxicated they are not vociferous, noisy or quarrelsome in their common intercourse, but mild and obliging. Backbiting, whispering, cursing and swearing,—to our shame it must be said,—are vices not of *savage*, but of civilized man ! The Indians who have been *conversant with white men,* like the ancient Cretans, are liars. Many among them are full of subtilty, deceit, and artifice, implacable, unmerciful, without pity.* When enmity towards an individual family, or tribe, from whatever cause, is imbibed, it remains till death, unless previously gratified or removed by taking revenge on his enemy. The most horrid scenes of torture and cruelty are witnessed by whole tribes of both sexes, old and young, without any show of pity. But these dispositions, and the indulgence of them, unhappily are not confined to Indians. I would to God for the honour of our country they were. Were we to charge the Indians with the indulgence of these ferocious dispositions, we should expose ourselves to the just retort, ' Physician, heal thyself.' Thou that reproachest us as implacable, unmerciful, unpitying to white people, dost thou suffer thy warriors to indulge these same dispositions toward defenceless Indians, desolating and burning our pleasant villages, and slaughtering our shrieking wives and children ?"

* A Pawnee brave, the subject of a very interesting anecdote, may be considered as one among many other honourable exceptions to these general remarks.—P. J.

TREATMENT OF THE WOMEN BY THE MEN.

In accordance with the custom of all pagan nations, the Indian men look upon their women as an inferior race of beings, created for their use and convenience. They therefore treat them as menials, and impose on them all the drudgeries of a savage life, such as making the wigwam, providing fuel, planting and hoeing the Indian corn or maize, fetching the venison and bear's meat from the woods where the man shot it: in short, all the hard work falls upon the women ; so that it may truly be said of them, that they are the slaves of their husbands.

In the wigwam the men occupy the best places, leaving such parts as are most exposed to the inclemency of the weather to the poor women. In regard to their food, the women eat the coarsest parts of the meat, or what the men leave. When travelling the men always walk on before. It would be considered great presumption for the wife to walk by the side of her husband ; she therefore keeps at a respectful distance. I have often seen the husband start with nothing but his gun or bow and arrows, while the poor wife, at some distance behind, would be seen bending under the weight of all their goods, often with a child packed in the midst of materials for building the wigwam. These burdens they carry about with them in all their journeying, which soon makes them decrepid. The men have an idea that it is unmanly and disgraceful for them to be seen doing anything which they imagine belongs to the women's department. I have scarcely ever seen anything like social intercourse between husband and wife, and it is remarkable that the women say very little in the presence of the men.

Since the introduction of the *fire-waters* the miseries of the Indian women have been increased tenfold. Several instances have occurred within my own recollection of their dying from the injuries they had received.* Paganism and intemperance are the sad degradation and ruin of Indian females! If any class of persons have special cause to thank God for the blessings of the Gospel, surely it is the women of pagan countries. Christianity alone can deliver them from the wretched slavery produced by heathenism and drunkenness. Would to God its beneficial effects were felt ·by all now labouring under the iron sway of ignorance, superstition, and savage cruelty!

CHARACTER OF WOMEN.

Indian women, notwithstanding all the heavy burdens imposed on them, are generally true and constant in their affection to their husbands. No mothers can be fonder of their children, though some may think they are destitute of natural love. This mistake has arisen from the fact that some of the *drunken* Indian women have been known to sell their children for a bottle of whisky, or suffered them to perish for want of proper attention and care. Such instances, however, are few and far between, and confined to those abandoned wretches who have been ruined by the *fire-waters.*†‡ They are much more industrious than the men,

* The Rev. E. Adams stated at a missionary meeting, that when he was missionary at Muncey Town, an old pagan Indian got drunk, and drove his wife and family out of the wigwam, which soon after took fire and roasted the drunken man to death. At another time, an Indian quarrelled with his wife ; his mother reproved him for it ; upon which he threw her into the fire ; she managed to crawl out, but the drunken savage took up a tomahawk and killed her on the spot.

† Appendix F.

‡ An instance of an Indian mother's love is related of Osheowhmai, the wife of Little Wolf, one of the Iowa Indians, who died while at Paris, from an

and are generally employed in fetching meat from the woods, dressing skins, planting Indian corn, making clothing, belts, mocassins, mats, canoes, maple sugar, &c., &c. The Indians who are settled near to white people also make baskets and brooms, for which they find a ready sale. The women are naturally shy and distant to strangers. They are inordinately fond of trinkets and gaudy apparel. Many of the young are in the habit of painting their faces. Like the Jews, too, the women observe certain days of purification, during which they separate themselves as much as possible from the rest, having their own wigwam, fires, provisions, cooking utensils, all of which are considered as unclean, and are never used by any but themselves. They are very careful to remove the fire and ashes from the wigwam in which the family reside, and then strike fresh fire, believing that if this be not done sickness would immediately follow.

GENERAL DESCRIPTION.

The stature of the men averages five feet ten inches, that of the women five feet. Both males and females are well formed; the muscles and bones of the former are smaller in proportion than those of the latter; a fact which, no doubt, arises from the women having to perform the heavy drudgeries of an Indian life. The men are built more for fleetness than for strength; they are great walkers and runners, and think nothing of walking forty or fifty miles a day.

The women have larger heads than the men, round and

affection of the lungs, brought on by grief for the death of her young child in London. Her husband was unremitting in his endeavours to console and restore her to the love of life ; but she constantly replied, "No, no ; my four children recall me ; I see them by the side of the Great ! They stretch out their arms to me, and are astonished that I do not join them."

rather broad at the top, high cheek bones and black eyes, while many have large Roman noses; their mouths and lips in general are large, their teeth good and white, their hair jet black and straight.

The men have little or no beard, as they take pains to pluck out what scattering sprouts they may have had; in the course of generations no doubt their posterity have been affected by this custom. Their complexion is a reddish-brown; apart from want of cleanliness, there is no peculiar smell about their bodies.

I have often reflected on the causes of the different complexions of the human race,—whence this variety of colour in persons descended from one common stock, as revelation informs us that God made of *one blood* all the nations of the earth? It is my opinion that the complexion is greatly affected by the habits, modes of life, and food. For instance, a nation attentive to cleanliness, and dwelling in comfortable houses, will become fairer and fairer; on the contrary, a wandering people, like the American Indians, living in smoky bark wigwams, anointing their bodies with oil and paint, and neglecting the customs and comforts of civilized society, may be expected to become darker and darker. The following fact known to myself will illustrate what I have stated. James Johnson—or as he is commonly called, Yankee Jim—went among the Indians when very young, a fair-skinned boy, but adopting in every particular their mode of life, is now, in his seventieth year, almost as swarthy as any pure Indian.

EDUCATION OF CHILDREN.

The education and general knowledge of a people unacquainted with letters and with the arts and sciences must necessarily be very limited. Such was the condition of

the North American Indians before the missionaries brought
to them the words of eternal life, with the blessings of
civilization. The highest ambition of pagan Indian parents,
in regard to the education of their children, is, to make
them *good hunters.* At an early age they are first taught
to handle the bow and arrow, with which they wander
along the banks of the lakes and rivers, shooting at marks,
small birds, and squirrels. Constant practice soon makes
them expert marksmen. They are also taught how to handle
a spear and manage a canoe, so that they may become good
fishermen. When a little older they are allowed to shoot and
hunt with a gun and rifle; and as soon as the boys are able
to kill large game, they accompany their fathers in their
hunting excursions, when they are taught the art of
taking the game, by being made acquainted with the
nature of the various animals, the kind of ground they
occupy, when they are found eating, and when asleep.
They also teach them the virtue of the hunting medicines,
by which they charm the game.

When they are young a spirit of war is instilled into
their bosoms; and in order to excite them to courage and
ambition, their parents and the old wise men recount to
them the wonderful exploits of the braves in former days,
such as a single warrior stealing secretly up to a village,
killing a number of the enemy, taking off their scalps, and
making his escape before the remainder were apprised of
the slaughter. The brave warrior then carries the scalps
to his own village, where the men, women, and children
meet and bless him. He thus becomes a noted personage in
his tribe. Great care is taken to teach them the war
medicine song and dance, in which they often join.

Another part of their education consists in their being
taught the mysteries of their religion, such as fasting,

feasts, offerings, religious songs and dances, the initiation into the orders of the *Wahbahnoowin* and *Media*.

As an inducement to excel in the number and length of their fasts, the old men promise to relate to them in the evening, after lying down to rest, various traditions, which are always of the marvellous kind, illustrative of the blessings received and the power obtained by fasting and prayer. They tell them how some have become invincible in war, successful in the chase, or profound *pow-wow* or medicine men. They even speak of some young Indians becoming immortal through perseverance in fasting. The following is a specimen of their wonderful tales :—

Many winters ago several young people commenced fasting, which they continued day after day until they were reduced to mere skeletons ; and having now fully secured the blessings and aid of the munedoos, they were told that they had earned for themselves by their untiring faithfulness immortal lives. No sooner was this blessing pronounced, than they rose from the earth, and were wafted by some magical power wherever they willed to go, and are supposed by the Indians to be still in existence. They call them *pahgak*, or the *flying skeletons*. They say they have repeatedly heard them shout in the air, and those that hear them generally faint.

Another story they relate is about the robin, which they call *obeche*. They say that this robin was once an Indian female, who fasted a long time, and just before she was turned into a bird she painted her breast, and as she flew away she laughed for joy, saying that she would ever afterwards return to her friends early in the spring, and bring them the news of what was to happen during the year : if peace and plenty, then she would come to them laughing, making the following noise, " *Che—che—che ;*" that is—

F

Ha—ha—ha : but if war or trouble then she would say, " *Uh-nwoh-che-ga*," or I prophesy evil tidings.

The old sages also repeatedly give the young people gathered around the cheerful blaze of the hearth lectures on the duties of hospitality to strangers, teaching them to revere the aged, and to treasure up in their minds the counsels they hear from them, and to endeavour to maintain dignity of character. They are also taught that in the presence of their parents and the aged they should be reserved, especially at their meals; and that when engaged in common conversation they must not be boisterous, but speak in a low tone of voice, and never interrupt another when talking.

The Indians exhibit much natural politeness; they are, generally, very gentle and obliging in their manners; the women in particular show great bashfulness when spoken to. Carver, in his travels, tells of a young Indian with whom he fell in company when on a journey to the Falls of Niagara. He says, " When the young chief first came in sight of the cataract he addressed the Great Spirit, whose residence he supposed this to be; he then threw into the stream his pipe, tobacco, and various ornaments, as offerings; and continued fervently to petition the Great Spirit to afford them protection and a bright sun; and would not leave the place till they had together smoked his pipe in honour of the Great Spirit." He then goes on to state:—
" I was greatly surprised at beholding an instance of such elevated devotion in so young an Indian, and looked on him with greater respect for these sincere proofs he gave of his piety. Indeed the whole conduct of this young chief at once amazed and charmed me. During the few days we were together his attention seemed to be wholly employed in yielding me every assistance in his power; and even in so short a time he gave me innumerable proofs of the

most generous and disinterested friendship; so that on our return I parted from him with great reluctance. Whilst I beheld the artless yet engaging manners of this unpolished savage, I could not help drawing a comparison between him and some of the more refined inhabitants of civilized countries, not much I own in favour of the latter."

FAMILY GOVERNMENT.

In family government, I regret to say, my countrymen are very deficient; no discipline is enforced upon their children, consequently they grow up without restraint, and become self-willed and disobedient to their parents and guardians. As before stated they are not allowed to grow up without receiving the wise counsels of the sachems; but the evil lies in not insisting on the due observance of what they are taught. They scarcely ever inflict any punishment upon them beyond that of angry looks, and a little angry talk. Like Eli, when their children make themselves vile they restrain them not. Most of the Christian Indians now see and lament the want of family government; but not having been themselves instructed in the right way, they are quite ignorant how to exact implicit obedience from their children, and to " train them in the way they should go."

I fear it will be long before the Indians will learn the blessed art of family government, especially if no greater exertions are made to teach the rising generation the value and importance of governing themselves. Nothing appears more lovely to me than to see a well-ordered family where the law of kindness rules, and the parents are obeyed, feared, and loved. In such a family peace and harmony reign. There the blessing of God, which maketh rich, and addeth no sorrow, is enjoyed.

F 2

TREATMENT OF THE AGED.

Some have supposed that age is not respected by the Ojebways, but this is a great mistake. No people reverence old age more than the Indians. The advice of the *uhkewaihzee*, or long dweller upon the earth, is generally listened to with great attention, as it is from them that the youth receive their instructions respecting pow-wowism, medicines, and the traditions of their forefathers.

Where there is no literature it cannot be otherwise than that they should think much of those who impart to them all the knowledge they most prize, and who are supposed, from the length of time they have lived, to have gained great experience. These remarks refer particularly to the males, as the aged females are not in general looked up to with the same degree of reverence, although they are treated kindly by their relatives and friends. I knew an old crippled woman who, for many years before her death, was supported by her children and friends, and in their wanderings they often carried her on their backs, and never forsook her although a great burden to them. It has been reported that some Indians have put their aged to death when no longer able to hunt, or to render them any assistance. Cases of such brutal conduct may have occurred, but I never knew an instance of the kind, neither have I heard of any on which I could fully depend. Instances have been known of very aged and infirm Indians abandoning themselves to death. A case of this kind occurred at Grape Island. An old woman, by the name of Beaver, fancied that she had lived long enough, and as life was now burdensome, she left her son's house, and went out into the woods to die. The missionary hearing of it immediately got the Indians to search for her. They found her lying on the ground, and brought her back to her son, where she lived a few years longer. If she had been left to herself she never would have returned alive.

CANNIBALISM.

It has been ignorantly stated by some persons, that cannibalism prevails among the North American Indians. In confirmation of this report, they adduce the fabulous sayings of Indians about *weendeyoos*, or *giant men-eaters*, and also the sad fact that some northern Indians have been known through famine to eat one another. My firm conviction is, that North American Indians are not cannibals; and Mr. J. Carver, who travelled extensively through the interior parts of North America, among the Ojebways, Sioux, Sanks, &c., makes no mention of cannibalism.

Having heard such assertions some years since, I took particular pains to ascertain whether or no this was a fact, and the result of my enquiries amounted to this:—First, that cannibalism does not exist among them as it does among the New Zealanders. Second, that such is their abhorrence of cannibalism, that they have a common law among them that when an Indian is known to have eaten human flesh through starvation, it is right to put such an one to death as soon as possible. A few years ago I met with a wretched Indian woman at the narrows of Lake Simcoe, who had fled for her life from the north-west country, in consequence of having eaten her husband through extreme hunger. She was a most pitiable object, and appeared as though an evil spirit haunted her, as she wandered about in the woods, hiding herself behind the trees and logs. She was the terror of all the people, as they supposed that Indians who have once tasted human flesh became deranged, possessing the nature of a racoon, porcupine, or some other animal. They fall on such a person, and beat out his brains with a club. No doubt, if the Lake Simcoe Indians had not been Christians, this poor woman would have been put to death. Christianity saves in all ways.

That the poor Indians in the barren regions of the North should occasionally, through starvation, be driven to eat one another, is nothing more than might be expected. Has not the same thing often occurred among the white people when shipwrecked or cast upon some desolate island? Thirdly, the whole amount of cannibalism, if such it may be called, of some of the western war tribes, is this,—that they have been known to take the heart of their enemy, cut it into small pieces, and boil it in a large kettle of corn soup for a heathen feast or offering. Each warrior then takes a ladleful, as a bravado or triumph over his enemy. This, in Indian mode of speech, is called "*drinking the heart's blood of the enemy.*"

In Alexander Henry's travels among the Indians in Canada, between the years 1760 and 1776, he mentions an Indian family who had been so reduced by famine as to be compelled to eat each other. One young man arrived at the author's wintering place. The Indian was suspected of what he had done, and search being made, it was found he had lately eaten his surviving companion. He confessed the crime, and was forthwith put to death by tomahawk. He also mentions that some French Canadians, in a time of extreme hunger, proposed to kill and eat an Indian woman who was in their company.

. In no book of travels among North American Indians have I seen cannibalism mentioned as prevalent amongst them. Goldsmith, in his geography, says—"Murder is seldom heard of among them. A murderer is detested by all the tribe, and obliged, like another Cain, to wander up and down forlorn and forsaken even by his own relations and former friends."

CHAPTER V.

Wigwams—Ancient Domestic Implements—Mode of travelling—Dress.

IN their natural state, the Indians have no settled home, but wander about from place to place in pursuit of game or fish, on which they subsist. No sooner do these grow scarce in one part of the country than they remove to another. Each tribe or body of Indians has its own range of country, and sometimes each family has its own hunting grounds, marked out by certain natural divisions, such as rivers, lakes, mountains, or ridges; and all the game within these bounds is considered their property as much as the cattle and fowl owned by a farmer on his own land. It is at the peril of an intruder to trespass on the hunting grounds of another.

The game they hunt consists of deer, elk, bear, moose, beaver, otter, musk rat, hare, martin, mink, and a great variety of fish and fowl. The buffalo is taken in abundance towards the Rocky Mountains, and on the prairies of the great Mississippi. Before the introduction of guns they took their game by means of bows and arrows, spears and snares. The old Indians say that previous to the use of fire-arms the game was much tamer and in greater abundance. In time of peace, hunting and fishing constitute the chief employment of the men. It requires great judgment and perseverance to be a good hunter. The Indians who inhabit the prairie countries towards the

Rocky Mountains hunt on horseback; but the northern tribes, who live in the forest parts of America, hunt on foot, either following the tracks of the deer or bear, or accidentally coming upon them. A good hunter has such a thorough knowledge of the peculiar habits of the animals he wishes to take, that he knows exactly what section of country they frequent, the time of day they feed, and when and where they sleep. He will therefore act accordingly.

Many hunters use charms, made of roots and herbs, in which they place great confidence. There is one kind of medicine to give them good luck, another to make them invisible to the animal, and another which they put on guns or arrows to make them sure of killing. I have known some good hunters in one day kill ten or fifteen deer, and have heard of others killing as many as twenty. When they slaughter as many as these, they do not stop to skin or dress them, but leave them where they fall until the next day, when the women and children assist in taking the carcases to the wigwams.

The wild pagan Indians have no houses, but live in wigwams. The wigwams are made by placing poles, twelve or fourteen feet long, in the ground. These meet at the top, and are left open for the smoke to escape. Over them they spread nets, made of flags or birch bark, and sometimes the skins of animals. The fire is in the centre, around which the families take their seats on the ground, having skins or bark for their carpeting. A wigwam about twelve feet in diameter will contain about three families. Here they cook, eat, smoke, and sleep. When they make their wigwams long enough to have two fires, they will contain six or eight families. One family at each fire will cook at a time, and then divide the food with all belonging to the same fire. After the morning meal is over they

1 Pieces of Ancient Pottery 2 Ancient Bowl 3 Antique Pipe Heads.

have no set time for eating, but leave it to the direction of their craving appetites, or the good luck of having a supply of provisions. During the absence of a hunter, the portion of meat which he would have eaten is carefully saved for his return, on which he makes a hearty repast. When he is successful he will make a feast and sing his hunting chaunts to his munedoo for a whole night, and by the dawn of day he will be off again. If on this day, by uncommon perseverance, he has the good luck to kill a deer or bear, it is attributed to the virtue of the songs or medicine employed for the occasion. The Indians who live within the bounds of the English settlements depend, in a great measure, for their livelihood on making baskets, brooms, wooden bowls, ladles, and scoop shovels, which they sell to the white people in exchange for provisions.

ANCIENT DOMESTIC IMPLEMENTS.

Their mode of procuring fire, before the introduction of the steel and flint, was by friction. Three pieces of dry cedar or pine wood and a small bow were provided. One flat piece was put on the ground, with a small incision in it; then a round straight stick was placed perpendicularly into the incision of the bottom piece, round which the bow-string was twisted once; a flat piece was placed on the top round stick, to press it down. This done, the bow was pulled quickly backward and forward, and spun round till the wood ignited. Sometimes pieces of spunk wood were placed round the pivot, which greatly facilitated the ignition.

Their axes were made of hard stone sharpened at one end. The handle was split so as to receive the stone, which was fastened in with strings and glue made from the sturgeon's head. These rude axes, being very blunt, could only cut through soft or rotten wood and the bark of trees.

Thus they were able to peel off bark, which serves as a covering for wigwams and canoes. These axes have long since been superseded by hatchets or axes of European manufacture, which the Indians now obtain from the traders. The farmer frequently ploughs up these ancient edge tools, and also their flint arrow-points and earthenware.

Their *pipes* were made of soft stone, cut and carved into all sorts of shapes and figures. Some were also made from baked clay or granite. Their pots were made of the same materials, and baked thoroughly hard so as to stand the action of fire. The Indians are well pleased to discard these for English pots and kettles, which they find much more convenient. Their knives and awls were made of flint or sharp stones. They had no forks, but used their fingers in eating. Instead of dishes, they had wooden bowls and ladles. Their hunting implements consisted of bows and arrows. The arrows used in war were pointed with sharp flints or bones, and those for killing small game were blunt at one end. In their primitive state they roasted much of their meat, which was suspended on sticks, one end stuck in the ground, and the other turned towards the fire.

MODE OF TRAVELLING.

The Indians residing in the northern and woody parts of the country travel during the summer months either on foot or by water; but during the long winter months, having no horses, they employ the reindeer or dogs to draw them in sledges, which are made of a broad thin board turned up at one end for a runner. The dogs used are a species of bull-dog or Newfoundland. Two will draw a man and his provisions at the rate of thirty or forty miles a day. The harness is made of dressed deer-skin. These dogs are kept upon short allowance, being fed only when their day's journey is finished. It is said that when well fed they can only perform half the service. As the country becomes settled both Indians and whites travel in sleighs drawn by horses. To those well wrapped in furs this manner of travelling is very pleasant and easy. The horses wear strings of bells round their necks. When the snow is deep, the Indians use snow-shoes. When they travel by water, they use the well-known birch bark canoe, which is made as light as possible. They first sew the bark together with the roots of the spruce fir tree, and then line it with thin pieces of cedar. The ribs and supporters are made of the same wood. A canoe that will carry four or five persons can be borne on the shoulder of one man. Some of the canoes used by the Hudson's Bay Company are large enough to carry twenty or thirty persons. These are employed in transporting goods and furs. The smaller ones are used for fishing, trapping, hunting, and gathering the wild rice. The Indians who reside in southern and prairie countries, where horses abound, generally make their journeys on these animals. It is said by travellers that the natives are very expert riders. They both hunt the buffalo and go to war on horseback. The Indian men are swift travellers on foot. I have known them to walk with ease fifty and sixty miles a day, and some have accomplished the journey from Niagara to Toronto, a distance of eighty miles, in one day, and that too when there was only a narrow Indian footpath. Whenever they go on a journey they carry with them their blankets, guns, pipes, tomahawks, and provisions.

DRESS.

The clothing of the men consists of a loose coat coming down below the knees. This is made of dressed deer or moose skin fantastically decorated with tassels of the same material, or with porcupine quills, beads and silver brooches. Their leggings are made of the same skins. Round their waists they tie belts worked with worsted and beads. Their head-dresses are made from the skins and feathers of birds, such as the eagle, crow, hawk, owl, and duck; and sometimes from fur skins, such as the beaver, mink, musk rat, and the tails of the deer, wolf, and fox. The men generally wear their hair long, hanging down to their shoulders. This serves as a covering for their heads, and, being well greased, no rain can penetrate it. Some of the old men have the hair of their heads cut very close, and others have it plucked up by the roots, except a small tuft on the crown which is left as a bravado, so that in case they should fall into the hands of their enemies they may be scalped with ease. To this tuft they sometimes fasten a silver or leaden cube, three or four inches long. Many of them also have their ears cut from one end to the other, leaving the end fast to the ear, to which they fasten weights of lead, wampum, and other trinkets, so as to hang down in a loop. In a few years these strings of the ear stretch long enough to reach the shoulders, and they think this makes them look venerable. They seldom, however, keep them entire for any length of time; for in the first drunken brawl, ten chances to one they have the mortification of having them pulled off or broken. They have their noses pierced also, and in them they wear nose-jewels. Their pouches, containing their pipes and tobacco, are fastened to their belts, and a sheath for the scalping-knife hangs round the neck. Their mocassins are made of dressed deer skins worked with quills or beads. The women wear short gowns and petticoats made of deer skin, and a mantle thrown over the shoulders: they also wear leggings and mocassins neatly worked. The hair is tied up in a bunch behind. In winter both men and women clothe themselves with furs, such as the buffalo, bear, and hare. At present, those Indians who have the means of obtaining clothing of European manufacture have adopted the same, but the style of wearing it is somewhat after the fashion of their ancient dress. The Christian Indians have their hair tied behind and hanging down their backs. Many of them wear round beaver or straw hats, and neat shawls or cloaks.

CHAPTER VI.

COURTSHIP AND MARRIAGE.

Forming the Marriage Contract—No Ceremony or Vows—Wedding Dress—
Divorce—Polygamy.

In forming marriage contracts the most common practice observed by the Ojebways is for the parents of both
parties to make up the match; very often without the
consent, or even knowledge, of the young people. Sometimes this agreement is entered into when the children are
very young, and it generally happens that they yield to
the arrangements made by their parents, not only without any courtship, but even before they have spoken to
each other. When the contract is not made by the
parents, the Indian youth, having fixed his affections on
some young woman, will make his wish known to his
mother or some particular friend; to whose care he
commits the presents he has prepared for the occasion.
These usually consist of a fine blanket, gown, and
leggings for the object of his love; and a kettle, a sack of
corn, or some other article, for the parents. If these
presents are received it is at once understood that the offer
is accepted. Since the introduction of the *fire-waters* they
have formed a sad substitute for the kettle and other useful
articles as presents to the parents of the bride. There is
great reserve manifested by the young females, and not to
maintain it would be to lose the spotlessness of their
character, and bring on themselves the reproach of the old

people. The period of their courtship is not generally protracted beyond a few months, when it is terminated by the young man's taking his chosen companion on a wedding trip for several days.

Wherever night overtakes them there they pitch the wigwam, and spend the days in shooting or fishing, *the bride steering the canoe.* When this excursion is ended, they return with the product of the chase, which they present to the parents of the bride, laying it at the mother's feet; and with them they continue to reside, as the parents consider they have a claim on their industry and support till they have a family of their own to maintain. On this account the parents are always anxious that their daughters should marry good hunters. Although no public vows are made, nor any particular ceremonies are performed, at the marriages of the Indians, it is surprising how seldom their mutual engagements are violated.

There is a good understanding between them as to their individual duties and employments: the husband takes pains to please his wife by showing his skill as a hunter; thus practically proving that he is able and willing to supply her wants by his abilities in fishing and the chase. The wife, again, although her fatigues and drudgery are often great, performs her part cheerfully. Neither men nor women in general trouble themselves with each other's business, but there are many instances on record, and others known to myself, which prove how strong and sincere their love is for each other. A man has been known to go forty or fifty miles to procure for his wife something that he knew she much wanted. And the wife, in her turn, knowing how fond the father is of his children, will relate to him, on his return, some little adventures or anecdotes concerning them, that will divert and reward him for all his exertions.

Heckewelder mentions the following anecdote of an aged Indian who had spent much time among the white people in Pennsylvania and New Jersey:—" One day, about the year 1770, he observed that the Indians had a much easier way of getting a wife than the whites, and were more certain of getting a good one—' For,' said he, in his broken English, ' white man court,—court, may be one whole year !—may be two year before he marry ! Well!— may be then get *very good* wife—but may be *not!*—may be very cross !—Well now, suppose cross, scold so soon as get awake in the morning, scold all day, scold until sleep,— all one ; he must keep *him!* * White people have law for- bidding throwing away wife, be *he* ever so cross! must keep *him* always. Well! how does Indian do ?—Indian, when he sees industrious squaw, which he like, he go to *him*, place his two fore-fingers close aside each other, make two look like one, look squaw in the face—see *him* smile— which is all one *he* say *yes!* so he take *him* home—no danger *he* cross! no! no! Squaw know too well what Indian do if *he* cross! throw him away and take another ! Squaw love to eat meat! no husband, no meat! Squaw do everything to please husband, he do the same to please squaw ; live happy !"

DIVORCE.

Whenever an Indian finds it necessary to divorce his wife, it is for some heinous crime, such as adultery; in which case, before the separation ensues, the husband bites off the wife's nose. The children are then equally divided, or if the number happens to be odd, the woman takes the greater number. Intolerable laziness on the part of the woman has also been cause of divorce.

* The pronouns in the Indian language have no feminine gender.

POLYGAMY.

Polygamy once prevailed to a great extent among all the Indian tribes. It was considered lawful for any man to marry as many wives as he could provide for; hence most of the chiefs, brave warriors, and hunters, had a plurality of wives. I have heard of a chief in the West having as many as ten; but I never personally knew any who had more than three, though many who had two. They generally select, if possible, sisters, from an idea that they will be more likely to live together in peace, and that the children of the one would be loved and cared for by the other more than if the wives were not related. Yet, notwithstanding all these precautions, jealousies, as a natural consequence, will arise, which often lead to grievous quarrels and fightings. I once witnessed a fight between the two wives of a chief called Captain Jim. The quarrel arose from the unequal distribution of a loaf of bread between their children. The husband being absent, the wife who had brought the bread to the wigwam gave a piece of it to each child, but the best and largest portion to her *own*. Such partiality immediately led to a quarrel. The woman who brought the bread threw the remainder in anger to the other; she as quickly cast it back again; in this foolish way they kept on for some time, till their fury rose to such a height that they at length sprang at one another, catching hold of the hair of the head; and when each had uprooted a handful their ire seemed satisfied.

Chief John Asance, of Cold Water, at the time of his conversion, in the year 1827, had *three* wives; of whom he used to say to the white people, when under the influence of the fire-waters, " Me very great chief, me got him dree wives, all *broders*,"—meaning they were sisters.

The rule we have adopted with respect to converted

G

Indians who had more than one wife was this.—That, as it was unlawful for any Christian man to have more than one wife at a time, the missionaries were requested to advise all Indians who wished to serve the Great Spirit to put away all excepting the first woman they married. She was considered to be his lawful wife.

This regulation has invariably been enforced, and it is a matter of gratitude to Almighty God that almost in every instance, painful as it was, the Indians have submitted cheerfully. I knew one instance where a chief had a most powerful struggle between his own inclination and his desire to do his duty to his Creator. This man had two wives, the younger of whom was a beautiful woman. The chief loved her very much, and, when told that before he could receive the ordinance of baptism he must put away his young wife, and live only with the old one, whom he had first married, the trial commenced in his mind. He wished to be a Christian, but the thought of parting with his beloved young wife was more than he could then endure ; he told the missionary he must have a little time to consider the subject. He then retired alone into the woods, and was there three days, fasting, praying, and meditating on this important step. At the end of this time he came back and informed the missionary that he had prayed and considered the matter, and that he was now convinced that it would be wrong in him to retain his young wife, and therefore he would put her away; but that he would hereafter call her "*sister*," and that he would help to support her. After this noble conquest over the natural man, the chief, his wife, and his adopted *sister* were baptised. He remained faithful to his promise, and lived with his old wife two or three years, when she died. He then took to himself his beloved adopted sister, the object of his affections.

4

CHAPTER VII.

THEIR RELIGION.

Objects of Worship—Belief in two Supreme Spirits—Subordinate Deities—
Sun, Moon, and Stars worshipped—Animals, Waterfalls, Trees, Rocks,
Thunder—Tradition of Thunder Gods—Personal and familiar Gods—
Mode of making personal Gods, and worshipping them.

THE various tribes of the Ojebway nation scattered
along the shores of the great lakes universally believe in
the existence of one Supreme Being; whom they call
Keche-munedoo, which literally signifies *the Great Spirit*,
or Kezha-munedoo, the Benevolent or Merciful Spirit.
Believing Him to abound in love and mercy towards his
creatures, they suppose him too exalted to concern
Himself with the follies of poor earthly beings, whose
existence lasts only as it were for a day, his chief care
being that of supplying their daily wants. *Munedoo*
means a spirit, either good or bad. In order to designate
the character or nature of the spirit, they use the prefixes,
as in the words above-mentioned.

They also believe in the existence of an evil spirit, whom
they call *Mahje-munedoo*. This spirit, they imagine,
possesses power to injure any who dare to offend him;
and, in order to retain his friendship and appease his
anger, some have been known to offer sacrifice to him, so
that he might not bring upon them death, illness, or bad
luck in hunting.

They, moreover, believe that there are innumerable subordinate deities, or spirits, who have particular control over the affairs of this world. For instance, they believe that there is one god who has the charge of *game*, another who presides over the *fish* and the water, another who controls the winds and the storms, and another who watches over the vegetable world.

These imaginary deities become the objects of their invocations when they are so circumstanced as to require their blessing. For instance, if an Indian wishes for success on a hunting excursion, he will direct his ˹offering and prayer to the god who presides over the deer, the bear, or the beaver, (a wonderful gamekeeper he must be,) that success may attend him ; or, if he desires to catch many fish, or have a prosperous voyage, he will sacrifice to the god of the waters. I have known an Indian kill a black dog and throw it into the lake, that he might meet with no disaster whilst on his voyage. In this way the poor dark-minded Indian ignorantly worships the creatures of his own imagination.

The sun, moon, and stars are also adored as gods. At the rising of the sun the old chiefs and warriors chant their hymns of praise to welcome his return; and, at his going down they thank him for the blessing of light and heat during the day. When a visible eclipse of the sun takes place, the poor Indians are, thrown into the greatest alarm. They call it the sun's dying, and suppose that he actually dies. In order to assist in bringing him to life again, they stick coals of fire upon the points of their arrows, and shoot them upwards into the air, that by these means the expiring sun may be re-animated and rekindled. The moon and stars are reverenced for the light they give by night, enabling the lonely wanderer to travel in the absence of the sun. I well remember, when I was a little

PABOOKOWAIH.

boy, being told by our aged people that I must never point my finger at the moon, for, if I did, she would consider it a great insult, and instantly bite it off.

Besides the superintending gods above mentioned, they hold in great veneration certain animals which they conceive to possess supernatural powers—such as the wolf, fox, and toad, and all venomous snakes. Many of their own brethren are highly esteemed by passing themselves off as pow-wows, or conjurors, and thus, by their cunning art, impose on the credulity of these deluded people. Any remarkable features in natural scenery or terrific places become objects of superstitious dread and veneration, from the idea that they are the abodes of gods: for instance, curious trees, rocks, islands, mountains, caves, or waterfalls.* Whenever they approach these it is with the greatest solemnity, smoking a pipe, and leaving a little tobacco as an offering to the presiding spirit of the hallowed spot. Waterfalls are noted places for their tobacco offerings, from the belief that the gods of the falls are very fond of this plant. In former days, long before the sublime and stupendous Falls of Niagara became a place of fashionable resort, the red man would draw near to this awful cataract with timid steps, invoking most solemnly the blessing of the mighty Spirit, imagining that the *King God* of all other falls must certainly reside here. In fact, everything that strikes the dark untutored mind of the Indian with awe and astonishment becomes to him an object of dread and adoration. No wonder, then, that thunder, being far beyond his comprehension, is regarded as a most powerful deity, and has given rise to many absurd stories. They consider the thunder to be a god in the shape of a large eagle, that feeds on serpents, which it takes from under the earth and the trunks

* *Vide* Appendix G.

of hollow trees. When a thunderbolt strikes a tree or the ground, they fancy that the thunder has shot his fiery arrow at a serpent and caught it away in the twinkling of an eye. Some Indians affirm that they have seen the serpent taken up by the thunder into the clouds. They believe that the thunder has its abode on the top of a high mountain in the west, where it lays its eggs and hatches its young, like an eagle, and whence it takes its flight into different parts of the earth in search of serpents.

The following is a story related by an Indian who is said to have ventured, at the risk of his life, to visit the abode of the thunders:—"After fasting, and offering my devotions to the thunder, I with much difficulty ascended the mountain, the top of which reached to the clouds. To my great astonishment, as I looked I saw the thunder's nest, where a brood of young thunders had been hatched and reared. I saw all sorts of curious bones of serpents, on the flesh of which the old thunders had been feeding their young; and the bark of the young cedar trees pealed and stripped, on which the young thunders had been trying their skill in shooting their arrows before going abroad to hunt serpents."

Another thunder tradition says:—"That a party of Indians were once travelling on an extensive plain, when they came upon two young thunders lying in their nest in their downy feathers, the old thunders being absent at the time. Some of the party took their arrows, and with the point touched the eyes of the young thunders. The moment they did so their arrows were shivered to pieces, as if a young thunder arrow had struck them. One of the party, more wise than his companions, entreated them not to meddle with them, warning them that if they did they would pay dearly for their folly. The foolish young men would not listen, but continued to teaze and finally killed them. As soon as they had done this a black cloud appeared, advancing towards them with great fury. Presently the thunder began to roar and send forth volumes of its fiery indignation. It was too evident that the old thunders were enraged on account of the destruction of their young —soon, with a tremendous crash, the arrows of the mighty thunder-god fell on the foolish men and destroyed them, but the wise and good Indian escaped unhurt.

In addition to their belief in the existence of these general gods, each *pow-wow conjuror* and *medicine man* has his personal or familiar gods, which are of his own imagining.* The method they take to obtain the favour of these is by fasting and watching. The Indian youth from the age of ten to manhood are encouraged by their parents and the old people to fast, with the promise that if they do they will entertain them in the evening by the relation of one of their traditions or tales. Inspired with the hope of gaining favour with some god, and looking forward to the promised reward at the end of the day, they rise before the sun, take a piece of charcoal, which they pound to powder, and with it blacken their faces, the girls only blackening the upper part. During their fast they abstain from all food and drinks; towards sunset they wash their faces and then eat a little broth or soup which has been prepared for them; in this way they go on for several successive days, the longer•

---

* I have in my possession two family gods. One is called *Pabookowaih*— the God that crushes or breaks down diseases. The other is a goddess named *Nahneetis*, the guardian of health. This goddess was delivered up to me by Eunice Hank, a Muncey Indian woman, who with her friends used to worship it in their sacred dances, making a feast to it every year, when a fat doe was sacrificed as an offering, and many presents were given by the friends assembled. She told me she was now restored to worship the Christians' God, and therefore had no further use for it.

the better, and the more *munedoos* they will be likely to propitiate. All this time they notice every remarkable event, dream, or supernatural sound; and whichever of these makes the most impression on their minds during their fast, suggests the particular spirit which becomes their personal *munedoo* as long as they live, and in all emergencies and dangers they will call upon him for assistance. A pious Indian, by the name of Thomas Magee, stated in one of our religious meetings that there was a time when he used to worship a great number of *little gods;* that at one time, when in the danger of perishing in the woods with cold, he prayed to the trees standing around him to save him from freezing to death; but that the trees stood still and made no effort to save him, and had it not been for his own exertions he would certainly have died. He thanked the Great Spirit that he had been brought to know the vanity of idol-worship, and that now he worshipped the one true God. By the agency of these *munedoos* they pretend to possess the power of bewitching one another, performing extraordinary cures, foretelling future events, vanquishing their enemies, and charming the pretty Indian girl they intend to marry. If they chance to dream of seeing a *munedoo* standing on a rock in the lake, they imagine they have obtained the assistance of a powerful god. To dream of seeing an old grey-headed man is taken as a token of long life; or of a pretty woman, that they will be blest with more wives than one. If they happen to dream of sharp-pointed instruments, or anything that is proof against the arrow, tomahawk, or bullet, they fancy themselves proof against the shot of their enemy. When they dream of animals or fowls they imagine they are invested with the power of self-defence as possessed by these creatures. A poor Indian at Lake Huron used to boast that he had obtained the spirit of a bat. The following Ojebway tradition of a war exploit will show the confidence they place in dreams:—

A canoe manned with warriors was once pursued by a number of others, all filled with their enemies. They endeavoured to escape, paddling with all their might, but the enemy still gained upon them; then the old warriors began to call for the assistance of those things they had dreamt of during their fast-days. One man's munedoo was a sturgeon, which being invoked, their speed was soon equal to that of this fish, leaving the enemy far behind; but the sturgeon being short-winded, was soon tired, and the enemy again advanced rapidly upon them. The rest of the warriors, with the exception of one young man who, from his mean and ragged appearance, was considered a fool, called the assistance of their gods, which for a time enabled them to keep in advance. At length, having exhausted the strength of all their munedoos, they were beginning to give themselves up for lost, the other canoes being now so near as to turn to head them, when just at this critical moment the foolish young man thought of his medicine bag, which in their flight he had taken off from his side and laid in the canoe. He called out, "Where is my medicine bag?" The warriors told him to be quiet; what did he want with his medicine bag at this perilous time? He still shouted, "Where is my medicine bag?" They again told him to paddle and not trouble them about his medicine bag. As he persisted in his cry, "Where is my medicine bag?" one of the warriors seeing it by his side took it up and threw it to him. He, putting his hand into it, pulled out an old pouch made of the skin of a *Saw-bill*, a species of duck. This he held by the neck to the water. Immediately the canoe began to glide swiftly at the usual speed of a *Saw-bill*; and

after being propelled for a short time by this wonderful
power, they looked back and found they were far beyond the
reach of the enemy, who had now given up the chase.
Surely this Indian deserved a *patent* for his wonderful propelling power, which would have superseded the use of the
jarring and thumping steam-boats, now the wonder and
admiration of the American Indian. The young man then
took up his pouch, wrung the water out of it, and replaced
it in his bag; telling the Indian that he had not worn his
medicine bag about his person for nothing,—that in his fast
he had dreamt of this fowl, and was told that in all dangers
it would deliver him, and that he should possess the speed
and untiring nature of the *Saw-bill* duck. The old warriors
were astonished at the power of the young man whom they
had looked upon as almost an idiot, and were taught by
him a lesson, never to form a mean opinion of any persons
from their outward appearance.

Another story related by our people illustrates the reli-
ance they place on the power and help of these munedoos:—

Many years ago an old chief had occasion to go to war
with a neighbouring tribe of Indians. He assembled all his
warriors together, and, after informing them of the object
he had in view, called them to him one by one, and inquired
what they had dreamt of during their fast-days, and what
munedoos they could rely on for assistance. Those who had
had dreams, and those who had had none at all, he placed by
themselves. All who had dreamt of wars, or things proof
against the arrow, tomahawk, or bullet, he selected for the
expedition. When he came to the last man and asked him
what he had dreamt of, he replied, with a long whining
tone, "*Ahneed.*" The chief, not understanding what
he meant, repeated the question; the man replied as
before, "*Ahneed.*" "What do you say?" said the chief.

" *Ahneed*" was again the answer. The chief inquired what he meant by *ahneed;* when the warrior surprised him by stating that during his fastings he dreamt of *ahnit,* that is, a spear. The chief asked, " And what good will a spear do you ? " " As the point of the spear is proof against the arrow, tomahawk, and bullet, so is my body against all the shot of the enemy." " Very well," said the chief, " you shall go with me to the war." The chief, with his select warriors, then left for the scene of action ; and, after crossing a river in canoes, they fell upon the enemy, whom they soon conquered, destroying many of them. In all the battles they fought, not one of the old chief's party fell. The success and preservation of this war party was attributed solely to the aid of the munedoos obtained by dreams.

I well remember, in my early days, when I used to blacken my face and fast, in order to obtain the favour of some familiar god, that one day, being thirsty, I took a sip of water. The moment I had done so I remembered I was fasting. The thoughtless act filled me with sorrow, and I wept the greater part of the night, fearing that now no munedoo would ever communicate himself to me.

In all my fastings I never had any vision or dream ; and, consequently, obtained no familiar god, nor a spirit of the rank of a pow-wow. What a mercy it is to know that neither our happiness nor success depends upon the supposed possession of these imaginary gods, but that there is *one* only true and living God, whose assistance none ever did, or ever can, seek in vain !

Many of the white people who have but a partial acquaintance with the Indian character, have imagined that, whilst the Indian follows the *light of nature,* he will be saved by that light, and that he is far happier in that

barbarous state than he would be as a civilised Christian.
They have therefore contended that, as an act of justice
to the poor Indian, the missionary ought not to disturb his
happiness by endeavouring to impart to him that by which
he cannot be benefited. Their constant cry is, "Let the
Indian alone: he is well enough off: do not enhance his
guilt and his misery." Would these objectors wish to
become savages for the sake of bettering their condition?
Perhaps there is not much difference between them and
the wild Indian. I believe that if an Indian avails himself
of the light he has he will be saved, as infants are, through
the merits of Christ's blood. He certainly knows that it
is wrong to murder, quarrel, fight, steal, and commit
fornication and adultery; but I ask, where is the Indian
who ever lived in accordance with this intuitive knowledge
of truth? I know of none, and I have made particular
inquiry of the old men if they ever knew an Indian to
walk so straight as never to break the law of nature. The
answer uniformly has been, "Not a single one." Consequently, if any are saved by the light of nature, the
number must be small. It cannot be expected that the
poor untutored Indian can follow the light, when we consider that "the *light* that is in him is *darkness*," and that
he is under the power and control of the evil spirit, who
worketh in the hearts of all the pagan nations of the
earth. Every enlightened Christian knows that were it
not for the direct aid of the Holy Spirit of God he could
not of himself do any good thing; but that the carnal
mind, which is enmity against God, would predominate,
and lead him to commit all manner of sin. If it be difficult for the Christian to follow the good he knows, what
must be the utter helplessness of the pagan Indian, who is
destitute of all Christian privileges? This much I admit,—

that the state of the red man, previous to the introduction of European vices, and the fire-waters, was superior to what it is now, when the white man's religion has not changed his heart.   But the Indian, unhappily, is more prone to follow the evil than the good practices of the white man.   This proves that he is naturally depraved; and if Christianity has not effected all that is desirable in the suppression of vice, it is the Indian's sin, and not the white man's religion, that ought to be blamed.   I can affirm that the Indian in his natural state is not happy. He has his trials, afflictions, and fears: the worst passions of the human mind bear uncontrolled sway, entailing misery and woe.   " There is no peace, saith my God, to the wicked."   A civilized state, even without religion, is far preferable to paganism.

CHAPTER VIII.

THE Ojebways attach great importance to their religious
feasts and sacrifices. They observe them frequently during
the course of the year, but not at any stated period ; each
person appointing his own time, to suit his convenience or
necessity. The Indians, when approaching their imaginary
gods, never kneel or prostrate their bodies before the
object of adoration, excepting when they enter *Jeesuhkon*,
or the conjuring-house.

Their mode of imploring the favour or appeasing the
anger of their deities, is by offering sacrifices to them
in the following order :—When an Indian meets with
ill-luck in hunting, or when afflictions come across his
path, he fancies that by the neglect of some duty he has
incurred the displeasure of his munedoo, for which he is
angry with him ; and, in order to appease his wrath, he
devotes the first game he takes to making a religious feast,
to which he invites a number of the principal men and
women from the other wigwams. A young man is generally sent as a messenger to invite the guests, who carries
with him a bunch of coloured quills or sticks, about four
inches long.* On entering the wigwam he shouts out

* Indian method of dying porcupine quills :— *White ;* The natural colour.
Red ; Dyed with a roo called *ahdesahwahyon,* and the berries of the sumach,

NAHNEETIS, THE GUARDIAN OF HEALTH

The Breaches were all Annual Presents

Keweekomegoo; that is, "You are bidden to a feast!" He
then distributes the quills to such as are invited: these
answer to the white people's *invitation cards.* When the
guests arrive at the feast-maker's wigwam the quills are
returned to him; they are of three colours, red, green, and
white; the red for the aged, or those versed in the *wah-
buhnoo* order; the green for the *media* order; and the
white for the common people. The guests bring with
them their pouches, pipes, and calumet. When seated on
the ground, around the fire, they soon begin to smoke, in
profound silence, which they continue to do so long as the
food is preparing. The Indian who makes the feast sits
smoking with a solemn countenance, dressed in his best
clothes and ornaments. He then places his medicine-bag,
pouch, and images, by his side. The kettle in which the
meat has been prepared is taken off the fire and placed
before him. The bowls of the guests are then handed to the
person who serves, and returned to the owners with pieces
of meat; giving to the aged such as are most esteemed.
When all are served the remainder is put on the fire as a
burnt offering. Each one also cuts off a piece from his
portion, which he puts on the burning coals. While the
meat is burning, an aged man, previously engaged, offers
up a prayer, consisting of vain repetitions, to the munedoos;
the purport of which is, that as the munedoos are always
pleased with the offerings of their people, this man doth
now come with his offering, and that it may please them to
restore to him their blessings, and cause him his accustomed success in hunting, or as the case may be. At the
conclusion of the prayer all unite in a hearty response, by

called by the Indians *Pahquahnahminzh.* *Blue;* Dyed with blue cloth,
boiled until the dye is extracted. *Yellow;* Dyed with a yellow root, called
oozahwahke. Black; Dyed with the bark of the black walnut tree.

saying *Yoo;* equivalent to the Christian's Amen. After this they proceed to eat; what is left they take away to their own wigwams. The person who makes the feast, and his family, never partake of any.

The gods to whom these feasts are dedicated are various. For instance, if an Indian is visited with sickness, he fancies that he has offended the Master of life; and, therefore, to remove the disease, he makes a feast to that particular god. Should he meet with ill luck in hunting, he imagines he has displeased the god of the game, and the offering is made to him. I have frequently seen the Indians, when on a journey by water, kill a dog and throw it into the lake or river, as an offering to the god of the waters, for a safe and prosperous voyage, or for success in fishing. Tobacco is esteemed a weed peculiarly pleasing to the munedoos, and is used more or less in all their feasts. The *fire-waters,* now so much loved by the natives, have become a common offering, judging the taste of their gods by their own. They consider it the most acceptable sacrifice they can make. Sometimes, an Indian, before he prepares a feast, will sing and beat his *tawaegun* (drum) for a whole night, his object being to make atonement for neglected duty.

In illustrating the nature of the great atonement to my pagan countrymen, I have often made reference to their own sacrifices. This has greatly assisted me in explaining to them the fundamental principles of the Christian religion, —the necessity, value, and efficacy of the oblation presented by our blessed Lord and Saviour for the redemption of transgressors.

The Ojebways have no regularly appointed priests among them. The pow-wows, conjurors, and gifted speakers, act for them, so that any ambitious Indian, by cultivating the

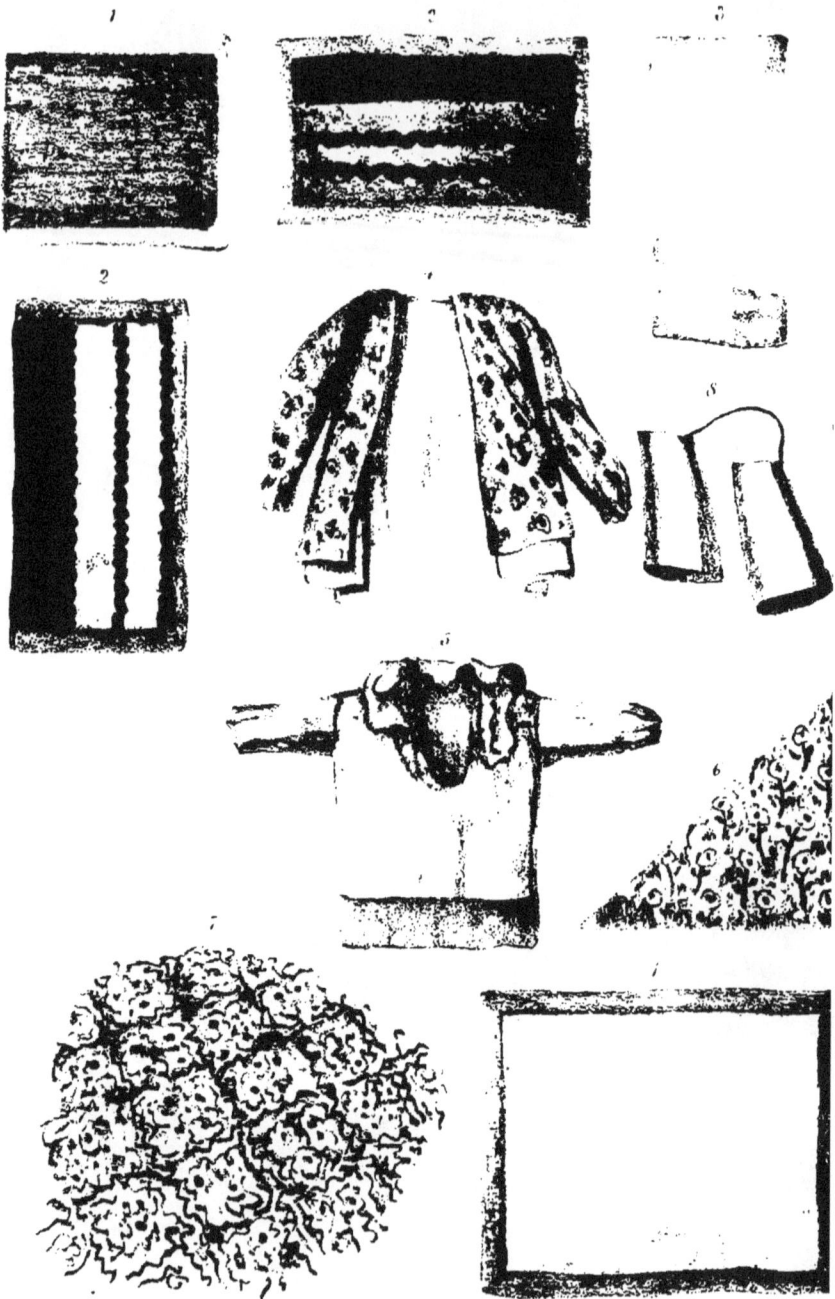

ANNUAL PRESENTS TO NAHNEETIS.

1 Cloth Blankets 2 Cloth Petticoats 3 Piece of Deerskin

talent of public speaking, may become the mouthpiece of his deluded brethren.

There are several kinds of feasts; of these the following are the most important:—

The Painted Pole Feast, or *Sahsahgewejegun*, which signifies the spreading out to view the desires of the supplicants—a term still often used by the Christian Indians in making their wants known to God. When this feast is made a long pole is erected; after the bark is carefully pealed it is painted red and black, and before raising it a bunch of sacred feathers and tobacco is tied near the top. When elevated a shout is raised, after which the meat cooked for the occasion is distributed, part of it being burnt as an offering to the sun, the pole pointing to the object of worship.

Weendahsowin Weekoondewin, The Naming Feast.—This feast is held when a name is to be given to a child. It is prepared by the parents, who invite a number of their relations or neighbours. Representations of the gods to whom the child is to be dedicated are previously prepared, and now laid before it. While the meat is burning, an old Indian offers up a prayer, during which he pronounces the name given to the child, to which the whole company respond by repeating it.

Ooshkenetahgawin, which signifies the offering of the first animal or fowl killed by a boy, and is always turned into a feast. The whole is cooked, and part offered as a burnt offering. These feasts consist of two kinds. The first small game the boy kills, such as a bird, squirrel, or duck, makes the first feast; and the second is when he kills a bear, dear, or buffalo. It is a kind of offering of the first-fruits, and destines the boy to take his place among the braves and noted hunters.

Jeebanahkawin; A feast or offering to the dead.—This ceremony is observed by kindling a fire at the head of the grave, on which a portion of meat is burnt, and a prayer offered to the dead. The *fire-water* was a celebrated offering in this feast, especially if the departed had been fond of it during his earthly career; it was then believed that he would enjoy the pure alcoholic fumes arising from the liquid flames.

Kahgahyeshee, or Crow Feast.—The meat or fish on this occasion is spread on bark trays, around which the party invited take their seats, like a flock of crows round a dead carcase, helping themselves from the abundance placed before them, each trying to outdo his fellow in gormandizing. While eating they now and then raise a noise like a crow. The Indians often say that the white man's table is a complete crow feast.

Uhnemoosh, or Dog Feast, is considered a meritorious sacrifice. After the dog is killed and the hair singed off, it is cooked without breaking a bone. The animal is then divided among the guests, a portion being devoted as a burnt offering. The dog is considered by Indians as an ominous animal, and supposed to possess great virtue.

There are several other minor feasts, unnecessary to detail.

MODE OF BURYING THEIR DEAD.

As soon as an Indian dies his friends proceed to lay him out *on the ground*, putting his best clothes on him, and wrapping his body in skins or blankets. Formerly, coffins were not known, or not used among them. After digging a hole about three feet deep, generally in the course of twelve hours they inter him, with his head towards the west. They then place by the side of the corpse all his

former hunting and war implements; such as his bow and
arrow, tomahawk, gun, pipe and tobacco, knife, pouch,
flint and steel, medicine-bag, kettle, trinkets, and other
articles which he carried with him when going on a long
journey. The grave is then covered, and on the top of it
poles or sticks are placed lengthways, to the height of
about two feet, over which birch bark or mats form a
covering to secure the body from the rain. The relations
or friends of the deceased then sit on the ground in a circle
round the head of the grave, when the usual offering to the
dead—consisting of meat, soup, or the fire-waters—is made.
This is handed to the people present in bowls, a certain
quantity being kept back for a burnt offering. While this
is preparing at the head of the grave, the old man, or
speaker for the occasion, makes a prayer to the soul of the
departed, enumerating his good qualities, imploring the
blessing of the dead that his Spirit may intercede for them,
that they may have plenty of game; he also exhorts his
spirit to depart quietly from them. They believe that the
soul partakes of a portion of the feast, and especially that
which is consumed by fire. If the deceased was a husband,
it is often the custom for the widow, after the burial is
over, to spring or leap over the grave, and then run zigzag behind the trees, as if she were fleeing from some
one. This is called running away from the spirit of her
husband, that it may not haunt her. In the evening of the
day on which the burial has taken place, when it begins to
grow dark, the men fire off their guns through the hole left
at the top of the wigwam. As soon as this firing ceases,
the old women commence knocking and making such a
rattling at the door as would frighten away any spirit that
would dare to hover near. The next ceremony is, to cut
into narrow strips, like ribbon, thin birch bark. These they

H 2

fold into shapes, and hang round inside the wigwam, so that the least puff of wind will move them. With such scarecrows as these, what spirit would venture to disturb their slumbers ? Lest this should not prove effectual, they will also frequently take a deer's tail, and after burning or singeing off all the hair, will rub the necks or faces of the children before they lie down to sleep, thinking that the offensive smell will be another preventive to the spirit's entrance. I well remember when I used to be daubed over with this disagreeable fumigation, and had great faith in it all. Thinking that the soul lingers about the body a long time before it takes its final departure, they use these means to hasten it away.

I was present at the burial of an old pagan chief by the name of *Odahmekoo*, of Muncey Town. We had a coffin made for him, which was presented to his relatives; but before they placed the body in it, they bored several holes at the head, in order, as they supposed, to enable the soul to go in and out at pleasure.

During the winter season, when the ground is frozen as hard as a rock, two or three feet deep; finding it almost impossible to penetrate through the frost, having no suitable tools, they are obliged to wind up the corpse in skins and the bark of trees, and then hang it on the fork of a large tree, high enough to be beyond the reach of wolves, foxes, and dogs, that would soon devour it. Thus the body hangs till decomposition takes place, and the bones, falling to the ground, are afterwards gathered up and buried.

MANNER OF MOURNING FOR THE DEAD.

Immediately after the decease of an Indian all the near relatives go into mourning, by blackening their faces with charcoal, and putting on the most ragged and filthy clothing they can find. These they wear for a year, which is the usual time of mourning for a husband or wife, father or mother.

At the expiration of a year the widow or widower is allowed to marry again. Should this take place before the year expires, it is considered not only a want of affection for the memory of the dead, but a great insult to the relations, who have a claim on the person during the days of the mourning. The first few days after the death of the relative are spent in retirement and fasting; during the whole of their mourning they make an offering of a portion of their daily food to the dead, and this they do by putting a part of it in the fire, which burns while they are eating. I have seen my poor countrymen make an offering of the *fire-waters* to the departed: they deem this very acceptable, on account of its igniting the moment it touches the fire. Occasionally they visit the grave of the dead, and there make a feast and an offering to the departed spirit: tobacco is never forgotten at these times. All the friends of the dead will for a long time wear leather strings tied round their wrists and ankles, for the purpose of reminding them of their deceased relative.

It is a custom always observed by widows, to tie up a bundle of clothes in the form of an infant, frequently ornamented with silver brooches. This she will lie with and carry about for twelve months, as a memorial of her departed husband. When the days of her mourning are ended, a feast is prepared by some of her relatives, at which she appears in her best attire. Having for the first time for a twelvemonth washed herself all over, she looks once more neat and clean.

NOTIONS OF A FUTURE STATE.

The Ojebways, although believers in a future state, know nothing about the blessedness of heaven, as an inheritance

procured by the merits and prepared by the grace of the
Saviour. They have, therefore, no motives to impel them
to a life of holy obedience, and to qualify them for the enjoyment of that world of glory on which the Christian fixes
the eye of faith ; in hope of admission into which he can say :
" *We know* that if our earthly house of this tabernacle were
dissolved, we have a building of God, a house not made
with hands, eternal in the heavens." They are equally
ignorant of a place of torment, as described in the word of
God ; consequently they have no fears of eternal punishment to check their unbridled indulgences, but are left to
act as if there were no hell to escape, and no heaven to
gain. The Indians believe in the existence of the soul
after the death of the body, but their ideas on this subject
are very confused and absurd. The little knowledge they
think they possess is derived from persons who have been
in a trance, and travelled in their dreams to the imaginary
world of spirits, which they say lies towards the sun-setting.
They believe that the souls of brave warriors, good hunters,
the virtuous, and the hospitable, go there and spend an
eternity in carnal pleasures, such as feasting, dancing, and
the like ; but the soul of the coward, the lazy hunter, the
stingy, the liar, the thief, the adulterer, and the unmerciful,
they imagine will wander about in unknown regions of darkness, and be exposed to the continual rage of wolves, bears,
panthers, &c. These are all the ideas the poor Ojebways
have of a future state ; and they can conceive of no greater
degree of felicity or misery as the reward of good and evil.
Some Indians believe, that between this world and the world
of spirits there is a wide, deep, and rapid river, over which
the souls of Indians are constrained to pass on a log or pole
which is placed across it. They think that the souls of the
brave and good encounter no difficulty in crossing, whilst

those of the cowardly and wicked fall off and are carried down by the current into unknown regions.

The following story, which was communicated to me by an Indian named *Netahgawineneh*, will serve to illustrate the source whence they derive their absurd ideas of a future state :—

In the Indian country far west an Indian once fell into a trance, and when he came to life again, he gave the following account of his journey to the world of spirits.

, "I started, said he, my soul or spirit in company with a number of Indians who were travelling to the same spirit land. We directed our footsteps towards the sun-setting. On our journey we passed through a beautiful country, and on each side of our trail saw strawberries as large as a man's head. We ate some of them, and found them very sweet ; but one of our party who kept loitering behind, came up to us and demanded, 'Why were we eating a ball of fire?' We tried to persuade him to the contrary, but the foolish fellow would not listen to our words, and so went on his way hungry. We travelled on until we came to a dark, swollen, and rapid river, over which was laid a log vibrating in a constant wavering motion. On this log we ventured to cross, and having arrived at the further end of it, we found that it did not reach the shore ; this obliged us to spring with all our might to the land. As soon as we had done this, we perceived that the supposed log on which we had crossed was a large serpent, waving and playing with his huge body over the river. The foolish man behind was tossed about until he fell off, but he at length succeeded in swimming to shore. No sooner was he on land than a fierce and famished pack of wolves fell on him and began to tear him to pieces, and we saw him no more. We journeyed on, and by and by came within sight of the town of spirits.   As soon as we made our appearance there was a great shout heard, and all our relatives ran to meet us and to welcome us to their happy country.   My mother made a feast for me, and prepared everything that was pleasant to eat and to look upon ; here we saw all our forefathers ; and game and corn in abundance ; all were happy and contented.

" After staying a short time, the Great Spirit of the place told me that I must go back to the country I had left, as the time had not yet arrived for me to dwell there.   I accordingly made ready to return ; and as I was leaving, my mother reproached me by all manner of foolish names for wishing to leave so lovely and beautiful a place.   I took my departure, and soon found myself in the body and in the world I had left."

The Indians also believe that the soul of the dead lingers about the wigwam or place of the departed for several days, and that it hovers about the body after it has laid in the grave for some time before it finally departs to the world of spirits.   In addition to this belief in the immortality of their own souls, they suppose that all animals, fowls, fish, trees, stones, &c., are endowed with immortal spirits, and that they possess supernatural power to punish any who may dare to despise or make any unnecessary waste of them. When they deify any of these objects, they imagine that they have the aid of their souls, imparting to them the power or destructive quality the animal or thing possesses. In their heathen state they very seldom cut down green or living trees, from the idea that it puts them to pain ; and some of the pow-wows have pretended to hear the wailing of the forest trees when suffering under the operation of the hatchet or axe.

CHAPTER IX.

General Councils—Common Councils—Mode of Electing Chiefs—Government.

GENERAL COUNCILS.

THESE are composed of the chiefs and principal men of the various tribes, met to deliberate on matters connected with their general interests. The head chief of the tribe in whose territory the council is convened, generally takes the lead. The first thing done is to kindle the council fire. This is called the uncovering of the slumbering embers of former councils, and the closing of a council is called the covering of the council fire. From this fire they light their pipes. The council then proceed to the ceremony of smoking the pipe of peace, from which each Indian present takes a few whiffs. This is done in token of their friendship and good-will to all parties. The pipe of peace is generally decorated with coloured feathers, strings of wampum, and ribbons. When the round of smoking is over the ceremony of condolence is repeated,—a specimen of which is the following, delivered by Chief Obwahnowashkung, *alias* John Riley, of the Ojebways, to the Oneidas on their arrival from the State of New York to their new settlement at Muncey Town :—

"*Brothers*,—We thank the Great Spirit for preserving us to meet this day at the time appointed.

" *Brothers*,—It makes our hearts glad to see you all seated with us on this ground.

"*Brothers*,—You have come a long march to settle yourselves down by us.

" *Brothers*,—I raise my hand to heaven and take the

white feather, and brush out your ears, that you may hear us distinctly.

" *Brothers,*—I raise my hand to heaven and take the white linen and wipe out your eyes, that you may see us clearly who we are.

" *Brothers,*—Your journey has been long and tiresome. You have come through dust and mud, and in your hard march have sweat much. I raise my hand to heaven and take the clean white linen, and wipe off all the perspiration and dust from your bodies, that you may be rested and have contentment.

" *Brothers,*—I raise my hand to heaven and take the white linen and make your feet clean, that you may tread softly and take comfort.

" *Brothers,*—We are thankful to the Great Spirit who has brought you here in safety with your women and children. I raise my hand to heaven and take the pure white linen and wipe all your hearts clean, that you may have great happiness in this land of our fathers. Your march is now ended; we meet you as brothers; we shake hands with you all. This is all I have to say."

To this ceremony the assent of "Yah, yah," was responded throughout the whole company of the Oneidas. Having performed this ceremony, they proceed to deliberate on the business for which they have assembled. The leading chiefs of the different tribes rise in succession and deliver their talk, during which the greatest attention is paid by all present, who now and then utter their hearty responses by the word "haahe." At these councils federal unions are formed, war or peace is declared, treaties are made or renewed, and boundaries of territories established. There is no voting among them, but they give their decisions according to the opinions expressed by a majority of the speakers. When a measure is found to be unpopular it is generally dropped :

hence there are seldom any warm discussions. If the same freedom of speech was taken at the Indian Councils which is often witnessed in the Legislative halls of the white man, the scalping-knife and tomahawk would soon be seen glittering in true Lynch style over the heads of the rude Indian law-makers.

COMMON COUNCILS.

These are held in each tribe whenever occasion may require, and are composed of the chiefs and principal men belonging to the tribe. Each person is at liberty to give his opinion on all matters before the council. At these meetings their local affairs are settled, such as the sale and division of their lands, settling disputes, adopting other Indians into their own body, and the transaction of business with the British Government.

MODE OF ELECTING CHIEFS.

The Indian country is allotted into districts, and each section is owned by a separate tribe of Indians. These districts become so many independent states, governed by their own chiefs, one of whom is styled the "head chief." The office of civil chieftainship is hereditary, but not always conferred on the eldest son. When a vacancy occurs, the surviving chiefs and principal men meet in council, and then select the most suitable person out of the family. The eldest son has the first consideration; but if he is deficient in any of the qualifications which they consider necessary, they elect the next best qualified. In some instances this practice has caused bickerings and jealousies in the family, and has been known to lead even to murder. The title of head chief is either hereditary or obtained by the election of the tribe in council assembled. Although the Ojebway nation of Indians is scattered over a vast section of country there is no person among them recognized as king. The office of war chief is not hereditary, but the tribe in council confer this honour on those who have distinguished themselves by bravery and wisdom. Such chiefs always take the lead in their wars, while the civil chiefs manage their general matters at home. Every chief has his attendant, called *mezhenuhway*, who acts as aide-de-camp. It is his duty to deliver the messages of the chief, call a council, and attend to all the necessary preparations. Formerly the chiefs received no emolument for their services. These were purely honorary, except on the division of government presents, when the chiefs got a larger portion than the warriors. Now, however, among some of the civilized tribes the head chiefs receive a small annual allowance out of their payments for lands ceded to the Crown. A universal custom prevails, as far as the influence of the British Government extends, to give to each chief a silver medal, as a mark of recognition of his office. This medal, on all public occasions, is worn suspended round the neck.

GOVERNMENT.

The Indian form of government is patriarchal, after the manner of the ancients. The chiefs are the heads or fathers of their respective tribes; but their authority extends no further than to their own body, while their influence depends much on their wisdom, bravery, and hospitality. When they lack any of these qualities they fall proportionably in the estimation of their people. It is, therefore, of importance that they should excel in everything pertaining to the dignity of a chieftain, since they govern more by persuasion than by coercion. Whenever their acts give general dissatisfaction their power ceases. They have scarcely any executive power, and can do but little without the concurrence of the subordinate chiefs and principal men. They have no written code of laws, nor any power to put their people to death by their own will; but they are taught by their chiefs and wise men to observe a certain line of conduct, such as to be kind and hospitable. They are also encouraged to be good hunters and warriors, and great pow-wows, or medicine men.

The chiefs of each tribe settle all the disputes which arise among the people, watch over their territories, regulate the order of their marches, and appoint the time for their general rendezvous. This generally takes place after sugar-making, or about the first of May, when they have their grand pow-wow dances and various games.

The law with regard to murder was blood for blood, especially if the relatives of the murdered man required the life of the murderer. The manner of pronouncing sentence was the following:—The chiefs and principal men met in council, at which the parties concerned were present, and when the guilt of the accused was proved the head chief pronounced sentence of death. The executioner was the nearest kin to the murderer, and either shot, tomahawked, or stabbed him. It sometimes happened that the relatives of the murdered and his kindred were held responsible for the payment of whatever was demanded.* I knew one instance in which the murderer and his relatives were several years making payment, consisting of clothing, kettles, skins, fire-water, and a horse. This is, in fact, a sort of servitude; for the murderer is not his own, having to exert himself until the injured parties are satisfied. Instances have occurred in which the parties have taken

* *Vide* Appendix H.

upon themselves to punish the offender, instead of sub-
mitting the case to the proper authorities. I was informed
by John Sunday, a well-known Indian Missionary, that
when he was travelling on the south shore of Lake Superior,
the Indians informed him that the tribe who formerly inhabited that part of the country were nearly exterminated
by carrying out this dreadful spirit of revenge. The quarrel
began between two families, which ended in the murder of
one of them. The friends of the murdered killed the murderer, and so they continued to kill one family after another,
till the whole tribe were nearly destroyed. A number of
graves were pointed out to him which covered the remains
of these unhappy victims. Formerly the advice of a chief,
or noted wise man, was implicitly obeyed; but their power
has much decreased since the settlement of the country by
white people. The British Government have taken them
under their paternal care; they have been taught to look
up with reverence to their great Father, the governor, and
the Indian agents. As a consequence, the chiefs have
yielded their authority into the hands of more wise and
powerful guardians. Another cause of their losing their
influence is, the introduction of fire-waters, which have
sadly prostrated the wisdom and dignity of the Indian.

CHAPTER X.

WAR.

War between Ojebways and Nahdoways—Treaty of Peace—Division of Country—General Council held January 17th, 1840—Wars between Ojebways
and Sioux—Treaty between French and Ojebways—British and Ojebways
—Mode of Warfare—Weapons of War—War Song—War Dance—Burying
the Tomahawk.

I HAVE often listened with deep attention to the narration
of Ojebway wars with other tribes, long before the white
man appeared in their country. The Ojebway tradition
states that the greatest and most bloody war their nation
ever waged was with the Nahdoways, a term applied to the
six nations of Indians who originally inhabited territory
now called the State of New York. The Hurons or Wyan-
dots are also called by the same name. At the commencement of their wars the Ojebway country extended eastward
only to the northern shores of Lake Huron, and the
Nahdoways owned all the region east and south of it. The
Nahdoways made the first inroads into the Ojebway country, where they surprised, killed, and scalped many of the
scattered tribes. For some time the Ojebways acted only
upon the defensive ; but, after the war had continued for a
considerable period, during which many were killed on
both sides, the Nahdoways got so exasperated at being
often defeated, that they began to kill and waste, and to eat
all their prisoners. These brutal acts called forth the vengeance of the great Ojebway nation. A general council
was called; the chiefs, prophets, and warriors met; the

council fire was lighted, and the smoke ascended to the abode of the Great Spirit. The meat of the buffalo, deer, bear, and beaver was brought and cooked; sacrifices were offered to the gods of war for success in their contemplated destruction. The prophets predicted certain victory; the sachems made speeches, and exhorted the young braves to signalize themselves by some daring exploit, and thus immortalize their names. The old warriors sung the war song, and the young men danced the war dance. The war whoop was raised, which made the earth quake, the sound echoing like that of thunder from mountain to mountain. The tomahawk, or *puhguhmahgun*, was lifted up, the scalping-knife sharpened, and the bows and arrows made ready. The medicine bags were prepared, and filled with war medicines and emblems of their munedoos. The warriors painted themselves; the women prepared the parched corn and the pemegun. All being in readiness, the war-whoop was again raised, and every warrior breathed vengeance on his enemy. The women saluted their husbands, and, exhorting them to be courageous, wished them a happy return with many scalps. The children wept at the thought that perchance they might never again see the smile of their fathers; but the brave warrior leaves all the endearments of home for the land of the enemy. The first attack they made was on an island on the south shore of Lake Huron. There they fell on a large body of the Nahdoways, who had been dancing and feasting for several nights, and were so exhausted as to have sunk into a profound sleep the night on which they were killed. The island is called Pequahkoondebaymenis, that is, skull island, from the number of skulls left on it. In one of my tours to the north I visited this island, and lodged on it for a night. Its present appearance indicates a place frequented by Indians, the smoothness of its surface being well adapted for a great Indian dance. From this island they extended their conquests to Lakes Simcoe, Ontario, Erie, St. Clair, and the interior parts of the country : wherever they went they conquered, destroying villages, and leaving dead bodies in heaps.

The last battle that was fought was at the outlet of Burlington Bay, which was at the south end of the beach, where the Government House formerly stood. Near to this place a mound of human bones is to be seen to this day ; and also another at the north end, close to the residence of the late Captain Brant. Besides these, there are traces of fortifications at short distances along the whole length of the beach, where holes had been dug into the sand and a breastwork thrown round them. They are about twenty or thirty feet in diameter, but were originally much larger. At this finishing battle the Ojebways spared a few of their enemies, whom they suffered to depart in peace, that they might go and tell their brethren on the south side of Lake Ontario the fate of their nation—that all the country between the waters of the Ontario, Erie, St. Clair, and Huron, was now surrendered into the hands of the Ojebways. After this, the conquering remnant divided into two parties: one went westward, and settled on the banks of the Detroit river ; the other moved eastward, towards the shores of the St. Lawrence. A treaty of peace and friendship was then made with the Nahdoways residing on the south side of Lake Ontario, and both nations solemnly covenanted, by going through the usual forms of burying the tomahawk, smoking the pipe of peace, and locking their hands and arms together, agreeing in future to call each other BROTHERS. Thus ended their wars with the Nahdoways.

The territory conquered was divided among the victorious

I

Ojebways, and the treaty of peace and friendship mentioned has from time to time been renewed at general councils. Yet, notwithstanding this treaty, there has been, and still is, a smothered feeling of hatred and enmity between the two nations; so that when either of them comes within the haunts of the other they are in constant fear. Ever since my remembrance, I have frequently known the Ojebways to be greatly alarmed at the idea of the Nahdoways lurking about in the woods near them, and I firmly believe that nothing but Christianity and a good sound education will ever eradicate this settled hatred.

I shall now give an account of one of the general Councils convened for the purpose of renewing this ancient treaty, which was held at the Credit Mission, U.C., January, 1840.

GENERAL COUNCIL, *Friday, January* 17*th*, 1840.

After singing and prayer the subject of appointing a chairman to preside during the council was discussed. It was stated that our fathers never recognised a presiding chief in their councils; but, as we were imitating the good ways of the white people, it was thought proper to appoint one. It was then proposed by John Sunday that Chief Joseph Sawyer be chosen president of this council. Peter Jones was appointed secretary. The subject of renewing the treaty of friendship with the Six Nations of Indians on the Grand River (whose chiefs intend meeting this council on Tuesday next) was talked over. Joseph Sawyer, Chief Yellowhead, and John Sunday, were named the speakers. Colonel Jarvis, Chief Superintendent of Indian Affairs, met the chiefs in council this afternoon. After smoking the *pipe of peace** with the Colonel, Chief Sawyer proceeded to

* The pipe used on this occasion was the beautiful *pipe tomahawk* presented to Kahkewaquonaby in the year 1838, by Colonel Sir Augustus D'Este, son of the late Duke of Sussex.

inform Colonel Jarvis that the object of convening this council was to talk over various matters which related to their welfare. These were : Firstly, To smoke the pipe of peace with the Six Nations of Indians on the Grand River, and thus renew the treaty formed with them by our fore- fathers many winters ago. Secondly, To thank the British Government for the annual presents and other tokens of friendship shewn to them, and to solicit the continuance of such presents. In reply, the Colonel solemnly assured the council that the British Government had no intention of discontinuing the presents, nor would they ever violate such a pledge as was made between the Indian tribes and the government. Thirdly, To consider whether anything can be done to promote their civilization, forming manual labour schools, &c. Colonel Jarvis expressed his happiness to hear that the attention of the chiefs had been directed to this subject ; thought that they might appropriate part of their annuities to their agricultural pursuits ; and said that the Home Government was now considering what can be done for the central manual labour schools. Fourthly, To renew the application to the government for titles for their lands. The Colonel replied, that he was opposed to the Indians receiving title-deeds ; that this opposition arose from the good-will he had towards them, as he feared if they had deeds many of them would soon dispose of their lands. He also stated that he had recommended a plan to the government, which he thought would answer every pur- pose : this was to give every tribe a map of the reserves, with a full description of it, and the names of the Indians to whom it belongs ; and the said map to contain the seal of the province and the government signature. He added that his Excellency Sir George Arthur had approved of this plan ; and such titles, he thought, would soon be granted

to them. Fifthly, To petition the government to extend
the Indian reserve at the Sangeeny River, for the benefit
of all the Indian tribes who might hereafter wish to emigrate to that place. This subject the Colonel said was
under the consideration of the government. Sixthly, To
enquire of the Colonial Goverument in what relation they
stand to the British Government—whether as subjects or
allies. Colonel Jarvis intimated that all the Chippeway
Indians were considered as subjects, and added that this
question was under consideration. The Colonel before
leaving the council expressed the pleasure which he felt in
witnessing such a large and well-behaved body of people as
he saw before him. He was happy to know that all were
animated by one feeling of attachment to Her Majesty
the Queen, and her government, and thought their de-
mands were quite reasonable.

    Saturday, 18*th January*.—Opened by singing and prayer.
The Muncey chiefs were introduced, and the chairman conveyed to them the salutations of the council, and expressed
their great satisfaction in meeting their grandfathers. Chief
Westbrook, the Muncey chief, replied, addressing his
grandchildren through John Sumeko as interpreter. Peter
Jones enquired of the Muncey chief if they knew the
reason why they called the Ojebways their grandchildren.
Westbrook answered that he did not know exactly, but
what he knew he would tell them. He said that they, the
Munceys, formerly lived towards the sun-rising, whence
their forefathers were driven by the white people; that
when they came to this part of the country they met the
Ojebways; that when the latter had observed their sedate
and quiet disposition, and that they had come from the
east, they said in a council that they would call them their
grandfathers. The designation has continued to this day.

The council disapproved of the conduct of Kandoching and his people, in not attending this assembly after having been notified, and also of their saying that they supposed they were sent for in order to be talked to about the worthless Christianity. During the day the council took into consideration the necessity of making greater exertions in their farming operations. The speakers were Peter Jones, John Asance, John Riley, William Yellowhead, Squire Markin, John Sunday, and John Simpson. John Sunday read and interpreted a communication from Sir Augustus D'Este and Dr. Hodgkin, addressed to the Indians generally in this province, which communication contained much wholesome advice to them. Peter Jones also read a letter to the council from Sir Augustus D'Este. With the contents of these letters the council was highly pleased.*

"*Monday, 20th January.*—After singing and prayer a committee was appointed to draft a statement, embodying those matters which the council wished to lay before the government. The committee consisted of nine of the principal men. Another of sixteen was appointed to consider the propriety of reprinting the old Indian Hymn Book, corrected, and other hymns which Peter Jones may have translated, and to report to this council on the same.

"*Tuesday, 21st January.*—Singing and prayer. The chiefs of the Six Nations of Indians, numbering fifteen, residing on the Grand River, having arrived in the village, were invited to meet their Ojebway brethren in council. Having come, and being seated by themselves, the chairman, Joseph Sawyer, addressed them in behalf of the council to this effect:—That the Great Spirit has brought us together in health and peace. That as they, the Mohawk chiefs, had expressed a wish to meet their Chippeway brethren, he had

* *Vide* Appendix I.

sent for them in order to smoke the pipe of peace together, and thus renew the treaty of friendship which had been made by our forefathers. That the time was when the hearts of our forefathers were black towards each other, and much blood was shed. The Good Spirit inclined the hearts of our forefathers to kindle the great council fires, when the pipe of peace was smoked, the tomahawk buried, and they took each other by the arms, and called each other BROTHERS. Thus their hearts, formerly black, became white towards each other. He had sent for them that the council fire, kindled by our forefathers, might be rekindled by gathering the brand together, as the fire was almost extinguished. He hoped, when it was lighted, the smoke would ever ascend in a straight line to the Great Spirit, so that when the eyes of all our people looked upon it they might remember the treaty of our forefathers. The council fire was then struck with flint and steel, and the pipe of peace having been filled, it was lighted with the new fire, and the Mezhinuway (Aide-de-camp) presented it to each of the chiefs of the Six Nations, then to the Ojebway chiefs, and afterwards to the warriors present. John S. Johnson, one of the Mohawk chiefs, informed the council that the Onondaga chief, who kept the council fire or " *talk* " of the Six Nations, would then speak in their behalf. The purport of this speech was, that, his Ojebway brethren having invited them, they had been brought to meet together ; that they were much pleased with the words contained in the letter sent them; that they were happy to meet their Ojebway brethren, and to hear them speak of the ancient treaties made by our forefathers, and requested to consult among themselves for a short time. This request was granted.

The council again met in the afternoon, when the Onondaga chief, John Buck, made a speech and exhibited the wampum belts, the memorials of the old treaties, and explained the talks contained in them. There were four belts or strings of wampum.

The first contained the first treaty made between the Six Nations and the Ojebways. This treaty was made many years ago, when the great council was held at the east end of Lake Ontario. The belt was in the form of a dish or bowl in the centre, which the chief said represented that the Ojebways and the Six Nations were all to eat out of the same dish; that is, to have all their game in common. In the centre of the bowl were a few white wampums, which represented a beaver's tail, the favourite dish of the Ojebways. At this council the treaty of friendship was formed, and agreement was made for ever after to call each other BROTHERS. This treaty of friendship was made so strong that if a tree fell across their arms it could not separate them or cause them to unloose their hold. The second wampum was given, as the chief stated, where Buffalo is now situated, at which place the original treaty was renewed. The third wampum was given at a great council held at the Maumee River, at which the late Captain Joseph Brant was present. There were a great number of different tribes present, who met the chiefs of the Six Nations for the purpose of forming alliances with each other; but the strangers acted very treacherously, and would have murdered the ambassadors of the Six Nations, had not a noted Ottawa chief, by the name of Agwezheway, honourably protected them, so that they were enabled to effect a treaty of friendship with the Shawneys and other tribes. Agwezheway had formed a confederacy with twenty-one different tribes, whom he could at any time call to his assistance. The fourth and last wampum was given by the Ojebways and Ottawas in confirmation of the treaties of our fathers. This council took place at Wellington Square

about twenty-five years ago. After this chief had rehearsed
the talks contained in the wampums in his possession, one
of the Mohawk chiefs, John Johnson, addressed the council
to this effect :—That it was their intention to renew treaties
of peace and friendship with all the Indian tribes in the
dominions of Her Majesty the Queen : that the interests of
all the Indians were one : that they had always supported
the British Government, as they were strongly attached to
it, and if even that attachment should be lessened, it would
not be their fault, but the fault of the government, in not
keeping faith with the Indians : that all the Indian tribes
ought to unite in obtaining titles to their lands, as all
Indians stood in the same situation with regard to their
lands : that the government and the white people were
taking away their lands by fair promises : that they called
the Governor brother, and not father, as the Ojebways do.
The reason why they called the Governor brother was,
that they might feel themselves equal with the Governor,
and so speak more freely with him, which they could not
do if he was their father : that they called the ministers
who preached to them fathers only in spiritual things.

Wednesday, 22nd January.—The council being constituted, proceeded to business. Chief Yellowhead made a
speech, exhibiting the great wampum belt of the Six
Nations, and explaining the talk contained in it. John
Sunday next addressed the chiefs of the Six Nations, and
replied to the several particulars related yesterday by the
Onondaga chief, and concluded by stating that they (the
Ojebways) a few years ago were very poor and miserable,
but the Great Spirit had been pleased to smile upon them,
and now they had begun to have their eyes opened to see
what was for their good, and hoped that their brothers, the
Six Nations, would now look upon them as having risen
from their former wretchedness and degradation.

The Ojebway chiefs having closed their talk concerning the renewal of the treaties, the wampum belts were returned to the Onondaga chief, with the salutations of all the Ojebway chiefs, their warriors, women, and children.

John S. Johnson, one of the Mohawk chiefs, next addressed the council. He informed the Ojebway chiefs of the relation existing between the Six United Nations. " The Mohawks," he said, "are considered the head nation—next to them the Onondagas and the Senecas, who are their brothers. The Oneidas, the Cayugas, and the Tuscaroras were their children, who were also three brothers. The Tuttelees, Nanticokes, Mantuas, and Delawares were their nephews, who dwell in their bosoms." Johnson then explained the emblems contained in the wampum belt brought by Yellowhead, which, he said, they acknowledged to be the acts of their fathers. Firstly, the council fire at the Sault St. Marie has no emblem, because then the council was held. Secondly, the council fire as Mamtoulni has the emblem of a beautiful white fish; this signifies purity, or a clean white heart—that all our hearts ought to be white towards each other. Thirdly, the emblem of a beaver, placed at an island on Penetanguishew Bay, denotes *wisdom*—that all the acts of our fathers were done in wisdom. Fourthly, the emblem of a white deer placed at Lake Simcoe, signified *superiority;* the dish and ladles at the same place indicated abundance of game and food. Fifthly, the eagle perched on a Fall pine tree at the Credit denotes *watching*, and *swiftness* in conveying messages. The eagle was to watch all the council fires between the Six Nations and the Ojebways; and being far-sighted, he might, in the event of anything happening, communicate the tidings to the distant tribes. Sixthly, the sun was hung up in the centre of the belt, to show that their acts were done in the face of the sun, by whom they swore that they would for ever after observe the treaties made between the two parties.

Mr. Johnson also informed the Ojebways that they would, at some future day, desire to hold another council with all the Ojebways and Ottawas, and that they would let the eagle know that he may take the message to the white deer, who would decide when the council should be held. Yellowhead presented the Six Nations with two strings of white wampum, as a memorial or pledge of this council, and of what had been transacted between the two parties. The chiefs of the Six Nations then returned the wampum belt to Yellowhead, and so parted, shaking each other by the arm; which method was adopted by our forefathers when the treaty of friendship was first formed. Thus ended the renewal of the treaty, with which all present were much pleased.

The committee appointed to report on the subject of reprinting another edition of the old Ojebway hymns met this evening (January 22nd), J. Sawyer in the chair. After a good deal of discussion on the subject, the following motion passed:—Yeas, 14; Nay, 1.

"That this committee recommend to the general council to reprint the old hymns revised, with such other as our brother Peter Jones may translate, at the expense of the several Ojebway tribes."

Thursday, 23rd January.—In the evening of this day the duties of the chiefs to their people and property, and the duty of warriors to their chiefs, were discussed; when many of the chiefs who had given way to drink solemnly promised that they would never again be overcome by the fire-waters.

Friday, 24th January.—The council being constituted, the secretary, Peter Jones, read the following Address to the Governor-General, and moved its adoption. This was carried unanimously by a rising vote :—

"To our Great Father the Right Hon. CHARLES PAULETT
THOMSON, Governor-General of British North America, &c., &c.

"The Address of the Ojebway Nation of Indians residing
at River Credit, Aldersville, Rice Lake, Mud Lake, Balsam
Lake, Nanows, Snake Island, Coldwater, Sangeeny, St.
Clair, and Muncey Town, in general council assembled.

"*Father,*—We, the children of the great Mother, the
Queen, who sit beyond the great waters, beg leave most
respectfully to approach you, our great Father, for the
purpose of congratulating you.

"*Father,*—We are the original proprietors of this country,
on which your white children have built their towns, and
cleared their farms.

"*Father,*— Our people were once numerous, free, and
happy, in the enjoyment of the abundance which our
forests, lakes, and rivers produced.

"*Father,*—When the white man came into our country,
our forefathers took him by the hand, and gave him land
on which to pitch his wigwam. Ever since that time he
has continued to flow to our shores; and now the white
man is greater and stronger than your red children.

"*Father,*—For many years we have been made very
poor on account of the introduction among us of the fire-
waters and other evils, which have killed or ruined many of
our fathers.

"*Father,*—About sixteen years ago the words of the
Great Spirit were preached to us by the Methodists. We
opened our ears, and the Good Spirit opened our hearts,
to receive the Gospel; and we are happy to inform your
Excellency that great changes have taken place among our
people. We have forsaken our old ways and evil habits,
and are trying to live like good Christians and good far-

mers. We have churches, school-houses, and fields. These things make our hearts very glad.

"Father, — The presents we receive from our good Mother, the Queen, are of great benefit to us and our people, and we beg to convey to her Majesty, through your Excellency, our unfeigned gratitude for the same, which we hope may ever be continued.

"Father,—We rejoice to assure your Excellency that we are perfectly satisfied and contented to live under the good and powerful protection of the British Government, who have already proved, by repeated acts of kindness, that they are the true friends of the red man ; and we shall ever hold ourselves in readiness to obey the calls of our Great Mother the Queen to defend this country.

"Father,—We are also glad to state that the fame of British generosity has spread far to the west, and many of our red brethren living within the territory of the United States have experienced a desire to come and settle in the dominions of our great Mother the Queen.

"Father,—As her Majesty has been pleased to send a chief of your exalted station and wisdom for the purpose of arranging and settling the affairs of these provinces, we lift up our hearts to the Great Spirit above that he may bless your important undertaking, and make you a great blessing both to the white and red men of this country ; so that our children after us may rise up and call you blessed.

"Father,—We now shake hands with you in our hearts, in which all our warriors, women, and children unite.

"This is all we have to say.

(Signed)　　　Joseph Sawyer.
"In General Council,　　　Peter Jones.
River Credit, Jan. 24th.　　　John Jones.
And thirty-six other chiefs from different tribes."

Peter Jones moved the adoption of the following petition to the Queen, through his Excellency the Governor-General. Carried unanimously :—

" To our Great Father, the Right Hon. CHARLES PAULETT THOMSON, Governor-General of British North America, &c., &c.

"The Ojebway (Chippeway) Nation of Indians, in general council assembled, beg leave most respectfully to approach your Excellency.

"*Father,*—We have heard that a union of Upper and Lower Canada is about to take place, and that in all probability the great council fire which was lighted at Menecing (now called Toronto) will be removed farther towards the sun-rising.

"*Father,*—We beg to inform you that the great body of your red children reside towards the sun-setting, from Menecing, or Toronto.

"*Father,*—Your red children have been happy and contented to live within sight and reach of the smoke of your great council fire, to which our forefathers and ourselves have resorted for wisdom, protection, and assistance.

"*Father,*—It fills our hearts with fear and sorrow when we think of the difficulties and expense of such a journey by your red children, when any of them may desire to see their great Father.

"*Father,*—We, your red children, humbly pray that our beloved great Mother, the Queen, may be graciously pleased to allow the great council fire of our great Father to remain at Toronto. And we, as in duty bound, will ever pray.

"*In General Council,*   [SIGNED AS THE FOREGOING
  River Credit, Jan. 24th."   ADDRESS.]

Peter Jones moved the adoption of the following address. Carried unanimously.

"To our Great Father, Sir GEORGE ARTHUR, Lieutenant-Governor of Upper Canada, &c., &c.

"*Father,*—We, the chiefs representing the different Indian settlements in this province, in general council assembled, beg leave most respectfully to address your Excellency.

" *Father,*—It is with great pleasure that we have learned from the Chief Superintendent of Indian Affairs that your Excellency's attention has been directed to those matters which relate to our prosperity and happiness, and that your Excellency has put them in such a train as will bring about their final accomplishment.

" *Father,*—We thank your Excellency for the readiness which you have always manifested in promoting our welfare, and we hope your Excellency will continue still to look after the interests of your red children, and to secure to us and to our children, as soon as convenient, the lands on which we reside, as expressed in Lord Glenelg's despatches.*

" *Father,*—We all unite in praying to the Great Spirit, that he may bless your Excellency with health and peace. We also send our good wishes to her Ladyship and family.

" *Father,*—All our warriors, women and children, join us in shaking hands with you in our hearts. This is all we have to say.

" *In General Council,*   [SIGNED AS THE FOREGOING
River Credit, January, 24th."   ADDRESSES.]

Peter Jones moved the adoption of the following petition to the government, through the Chief Superintendent of Indian Affairs. Carried unanimously.

* *Vide* Appendix J.

"To our Father, Col. S. P. Jarvis, Chief Superintendent of Indian Affairs.

"*Father*,—We, the chiefs representing the Indian settlements in this province, in general council assembled, beg, leave most respectfully to submit, through you, to our Great Father the Governor, the following matters for consideration.

"*Father*,—Being convinced of the necessity of making greater exertions in our agricultural improvements, and in the attainment of useful trades, we are willing to adopt any measures which our Great Father may recommend for the accomplishment of these objects.

"*Father*,—It is our earnest desire that one or more manual labour schools should be established at some of our settlements for the religious education of our children, and at the same time to train them up in industrious and domestic habits. And we beg to state that if our Great Father would render assistance in the formation of such schools, we are willing ourselves to appropriate part of our land payments for these objects.

"*Father*,—We would again humbly solicit our Great Father to secure to us and our descendants for ever the lands on which we reside.

"*Father*,—It is our wish to be informed of the relation which your red children sustain to the British Government : whether as subjects or allies.

"*Father*,—Having considered the future welfare of our children, and anticipating the time when your red children will be so crowded by your white children, as to be compelled to leave their present settlement and seek a home elsewhere : we therefore humbly pray that our beloved great Mother the Queen may be graciously pleased to rescue a sufficient tract of land in the vicinity of the Sangeeny River, as the future home of all your red children.

"*Father,*—We wish to be informed whether the white people have power to prevent the Indians from hunting on their wild lands. We ask this question on account of our people having repeatedly been ordered from the woods when they had gone to hunt, and in some instances have had their venison taken away, by white men.

"*Father,*—We have taken into consideration the practice of our people removing from one tribe to another, and in order to have a proper understanding on the subject, we have agreed that any of our people leaving their tribe shall forfeit their portion of the land payments, and on presenting a certificate from the chief or chiefs to whom they belonged shall henceforth become one of the tribe to which they remove, and be entitled to all the allowances received by them. It is further agreed that when any of our people leave their tribe, they shall be paid for the buildings they may have put upon the land where they have resided; and after having left their tribe and been adopted into another, they shall not be allowed to return to their former residence without the sanction of the chiefs in council.

"*Father,*—Last winter an act was passed by the Parliament of this country for the preservation of game and for the better observance of the Sabbath day, imposing fines and penalties upon any person or persons shooting game on the Sabbath. It is our desire that our Great Father may be pleased to recommend that the said Act may be so amended as to impose the same fines and penalties upon any person or persons fishing on the Lord's day.

"*In General Council,*   [SIGNED AS THE FOREGOING
River Credit, January 24th."   ADDRESSES.]

There is a tradition among the Ojebways, that many generations ago their fathers made extensive war excursions in the country of the Flat-head Indians beyond the Rocky Mountains; but with what success I have not learned. For many years past a wasting war on a small scale has been kept up between the Ojebways and Sioux or Nahdo-waseh Indians. This originated in encroachments made by either nation upon the hunting-grounds of the other. When any hunter was found trespassing, he was imme-diately killed and scalped. This called for revenge on the part of the relatives of the person killed, who would pursue the murderer until they had satisfied the calls of their friend's blood. This warfare is still kept up; it is both trea-cherous and cruel; every year they are thinning each other's numbers; and the author sincerely wishes that the British and American Governments would unite to put it down.

I have been informed that when the French came to this country, a treaty of friendship was made between them and the Ojebways. This treaty bound their hands together by a steel chain. But when the English conquered the French in Canada, they broke this steel chain, and entered into a treaty of friendship with the Ojebways, stating to them that the chain which had bound their hands with the French was one that would soon rust and break, and was of little value; but the chain that they (the British) would use should never rust nor break, and would be of great value. This would be a silver chain, and this chain has kept their hands bound together to this day.

During the last American war the Ojebways, as well as other Indian tribes, rendered the British great assistance in fighting the Americans. In that war many of our fathers fell, sealing their attachment to the British Government with their blood. As to the wars of other Indian tribes, I

K

am not prepared to give an account. Many historians have
noticed the wars of the Six Nations, and their conquests.
The following are the names of the chiefs who distinguished
themselves during the Indian wars:—King Philip, Pontiac,
Captain Joseph Brant, Tecumseh, Black Hawk, Osceola,
and Yellowhead.

MODE OF WARFARE.

In their war excursions the war chiefs take the lead, and
act as captains over their respective warriors. These chiefs
direct the order of the march and mode of attack, and are
men who have distinguished themselves for their bravery,
and consequently obtain the confidence of their tribe. The
civil chiefs, who in general inherit their chieftainship by
descent, are not expected to go to the field of action. They
seldom, however, neglect a good opportunity of displaying
their wisdom, skill, and bravery, and often accompany their
people and engage in the conflict. The more scalps they
take, the more they are revered and consulted by their
tribe. Their mode of action is entirely different from that of
civilized nations. They have no idea of meeting the enemy
upon an open plain face to face, to be shot at like dogs, as
they say. Their aim is to surprise the enemy by darting upon
them in an unexpected moment, or in the dead of night.
They always take care, in the first place, to ascertain the
position of the enemy. When they find them unprepared
or asleep, they creep up slowly and stealthily, like panthers
in pursuit of their prey; when sufficiently near, they simul-
taneously raise the war whoop, and before the enemy awake
or have time to defend themselves, the tomahawk is rattling
over their heads. When a village, a wigwam, or a party
is thus surprised, there is seldom any mercy shown either
to age or sex: all are doomed to feel the weight of the
tomahawk and the deep incision of the bloody scalping-

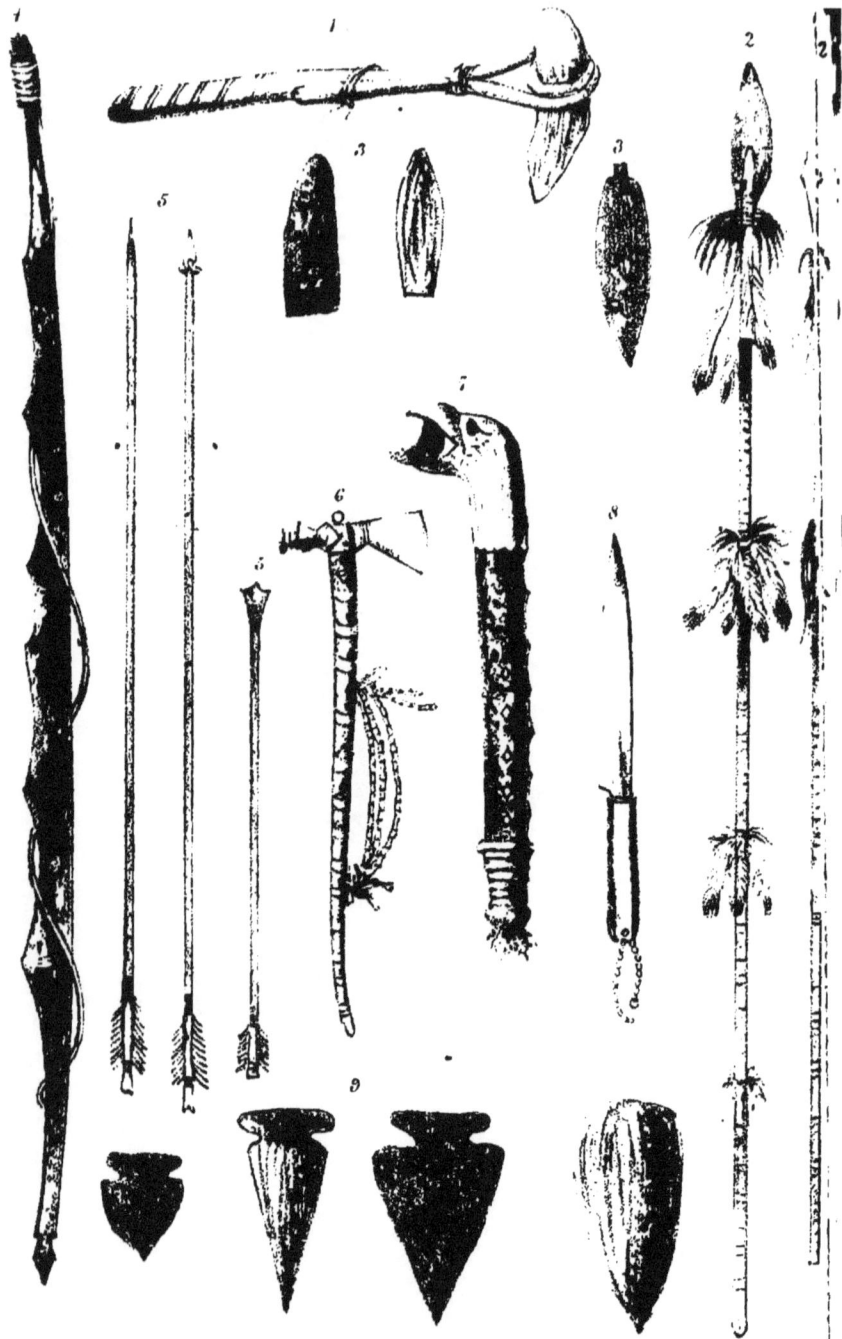

1 Ancient Axe. 2. Spears. 3. Axe and Spear heads. 4. Bow. 5. Arrows. 6. Tomahawk and pipe of Peace. 7. Ornamented War Club. 8. Skalping Knife. 9. Arrow heads.

knife. Such close battles, if they may be so called, seldom last long, not more than a few minutes.* If they have a regular pitched battle, they endeavour to get behind the trunks of trees, whence they shoot the enemy. Sometimes a few are taken captives and conveyed home, where they are adopted by some family who have lost a relative in the war. The prisoner then either becomes like a member of the family, enjoying perfect freedom, or is doomed to serve as a slave. If the captive is not thus adopted, he is com pelled to undergo the most painful death, by being burnt alive either at the stake or tree, when a war dance is gene- rally performed. It is stated that the Indian victims thus burnt have never betrayed any weakness in complaining of the severity of their punishment by shedding a tear, or uttering a groan ; but, on the contrary, when undergoing the greatest suffering, have been known to upbraid their tormentors, telling them that they did not know how to give pain ; that they were not men, but a set of old women.

WEAPONS OF WAR.

Before the introduction of guns, swords, &c., by Euro- peans, their weapons of war consisted of *bows and arrows.* These are too well known to require description. *Spears :* These are about eight or nine feet long, pointed with sharp stone, flint, or bone. *Tomahawk :* This instrument was made of hard grey stone, sharpened at one end, and fastened into a wooden handle. The pipe tomahawk now in use among the Indians, is of recent date, being made by Europeans.

* Carver says—"The greatest blemish in the Indian character is that savage disposition which impels them to treat their enemies with a severity other nations shudder at. But if they are thus barbarous to those with whom they are at war, they are friendly, hospitable and humane in peace. It may in truth be said of them, that they are the worst enemies and the best friends of any people in the world."

K 2

It is of iron, steel, or silver. At one end is a pipe; the other serves as a hatchet. It is, therefore, used for three purposes—war, luxury, or husbandry. The handle is of wood, and is pierced from end to end that the smoke may escape. Some of these are fantastically ornamented. *Puhguhmaguns* or war clubs: One kind is cut out of a solid piece of wood which had a knot in the end of it; the other is made of a flat piece of hard wood in the shape of an obtuse angle; and to this is fastened a sharp flint or bone. *Scalping knife:* This originally consisted of a sharp flint or bone, but those now in use resemble a large butcher's knife pointed and sharpened. When scalping any one, they take hold of the hair of the head, making an incision with the knife round the head to the skull, and then jerk off the scalp. This must be a very painful operation when performed on a living person, yet some have survived. I have seen an Indian woman at Lake Huron, who had been both tomahawked and scalped by the Sioux. She had recovered from her wound when I saw her, but was obliged to wear a wig of cloth. The scalps are stretched on round hoops and carefully dried. They are then painted, and decorated with wampum beads and ribbons.

WAR WHOOP.

This is a sudden raising of the voice to its highest pitch, repeated in rapid succession, sometimes causing a vibration by beating the hand against the mouth. When the voices of a hundred brave warriors are thus raised, it is indeed a terrific sound, well calculated to strike terror into the hearts of their enemies.

WAR SONG.

This is what is used at their war dance. The words refer to their invincible bravery, and the manner in which they will treat their enemies. They invoke their gods, rehearse their war dreams, and exhort their women not to weep for them.

WAR DANCE.

The war dance is designed to kindle the passion for war in every breast; and certainly, when we consider their war song, painted bodies, war implements, and the warriors' antics performed on such occasions, nothing could be better calculated to rouse the feeling to the highest state of excitement. A smooth piece of ground is chosen for the exhibition, in the centre of which a pole is placed. The singers take their seats and begin to beat on their drums, to which they keep time by singing in a most monotonous tone. The warriors, fully equipped, dance round and round the pole, brandishing their tomahawks, throwing their bodies into all sorts of postures, and raising at intervals the hideous war whoop. A warrior will occasionally strike the pole, which is a signal that he is about to make a speech. On a sudden the dancing and singing cease, and all attention is given to the speaker while he relates his war exploits, and receives the hearty responses of the assembly. At these dances they also have a sham fight, in which they exhibit the manner of surprising the enemy—tomahawking, scalping, and drinking the blood of the foe.

BURYING THE TOMAHAWK.

This is a figurative speech, signifying the cessation of hostilities, and the entering into a treaty of peace and friendship, so that past differences are forgiven and forgotten.

CHAPTER XI.

Dancing—Foot Races—Ball Playing—Bow and Arrow—Bowl Plays—Jumping and Leaping—Smoking—Mode of keeping Time—Toodaims—Wampum.

DANCING is a favourite amusement, in which both men and women participate. The men begin with a slow step, and quicken their motions as the singing and beating rise, till every muscle is strained to its greatest tension, stamping and shaking most violently. The women scarcely ever raise their feet from the ground, but glide along sideways.

The Ojebways have two kinds of drums. One, called *mahdwauhkoquon*, is made from the trunk of a hollow tree, about two feet long, having one end headed with a board, and the other covered with undressed deer-skin, on which they strike. These drums are used principally for sacred purposes. The other kind, called *tawaegun*, is made in the form of English drums. These are used on festival occasions and at amusements. They have no other musical instruments, except a rude kind of flute, which makes a monotonous sound.

Foot races, in which they show much swiftness, are common among them. *Ball playing* is another favourite amusement. Their principal play during the winter season is the *snow snake*, which is made of hard smooth timber, about six feet long, having eyes and mouth like a snake. The manner of playing is to take the snake by the tail, and throw it along the snow or ice with all their strength. Whoever sends his snake the farthest a certain number of

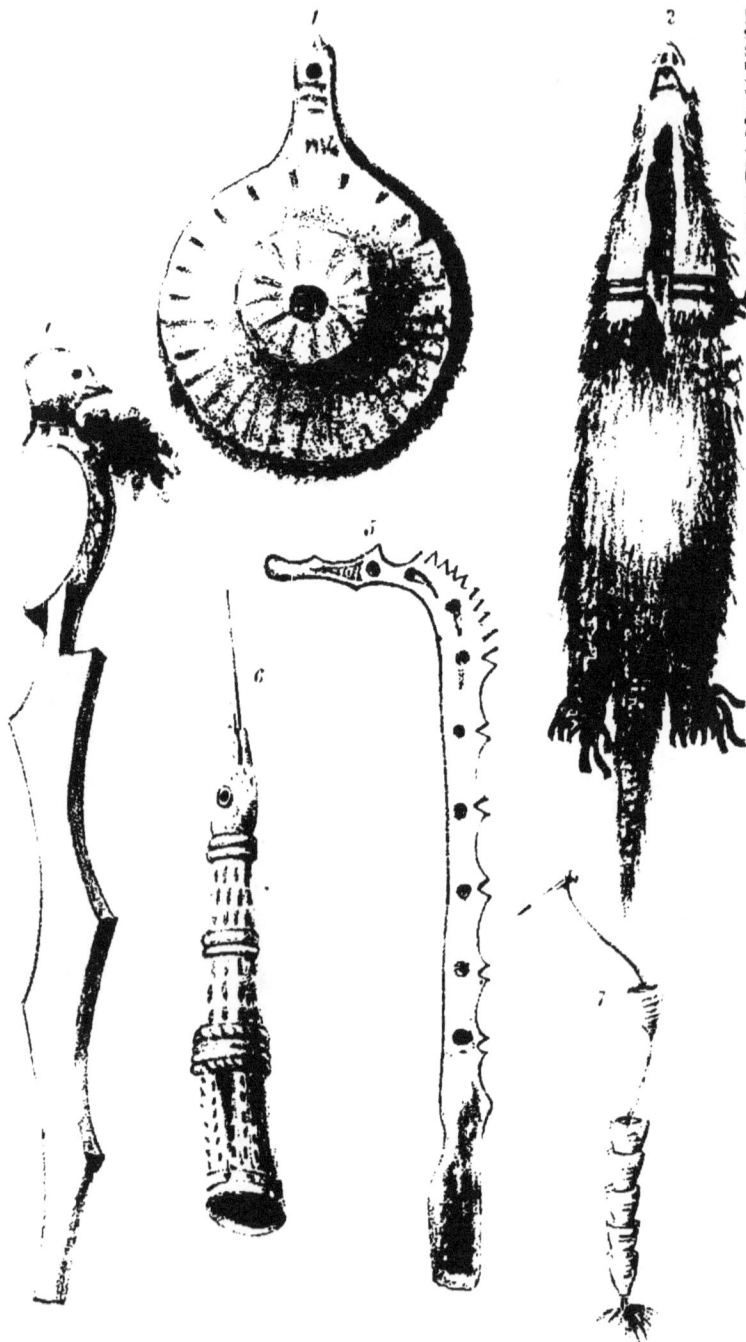

1 Drum   2 Tobacco Pouch   3 Snow Snake   4 Pawnee Rattle   5 Drum stick

times gains the prize. *Shooting with bow and arrow* forms the first amusement of little boys, who grow up, as it were, with bows and arrows in their hands. They shoot at marks, birds, and squirrels, and in this way become good marksmen. They have also their *swimming and diving races*, and are in general good swimmers, thinking nothing of crossing a river a mile wide. In their *bowl plays* they use plum stones. One side is burnt black, and the other is left of its natural colour. Seven of these plums are placed in a wooden bowl, and are then tossed up and caught. If they happen to turn up all white, or all black, they count so many. This is altogether a chance game. *Wrestling, jumping*, and *leaping* are practised by the young people. The women have a game called *uhpuhsekuhwon*, which is played with two leathern balls tied with a string about two feet long. These are placed on the ground, and each woman, with a stick about six feet long, tries to take up *uhpuhsekuhwon* from her antagonist, throwing it in the air. Whichever party gets it first to their respective goals or stakes counts one. *Smoking the pipe* is a very favourite occupation of the men. They mix the tobacco with sumach leaves or red willow bark, which greatly sweetens the fragrance. The old men are passionately fond of their pipes, and oftentimes spend many hours in the course of the day in raising the smoke. While thus employed they think a great deal of their munedoos, which causes them to attach a kind of sacredness to this practice, as if it were pleasing in their sight.

MODE OF KEEPING TIME.

Indians divide the year into four quarters, which they designate *seegwun* (spring), or the sap season ; *neebin* (summer), or the abundant season ; *tuhgwuhgin* (autumn), the fading season; and *peboon* (winter), which signifies cold freezing weather.

They also reckon by moons, the names of which are as follow:—

January moon—*Keche Munedoo keezis* (the Great Spirit moon).

February—*Nuhmabene keezis* (the mullet fish moon).

March—*Neke keezis* (the wild goose moon).

April—*Omuhkuhkee keezis* (the frog moon).

May—*Wahbegwunee keezis* (blooming moon).

June—*Odœmin keezis* (strawberry moon).

July—*Mesquemene keezis* (red raspberry moon).

August—*Meen keezis* (huckleberry moon).

September—*Ahtabuhgah keezis* (fading leaf moon).

October—*Penahqueewene keezis* (falling leaf moon).

November—*Kuhshkuhdene keezis* (freezing moon).

December—*Munedoo keezis* (Spirit moon).

They have no division of time into weeks or days of the month, nor have they any knowledge of the number of days in a year. They divide the day into morning, noon, and afternoon. Morning commences at sun-rising, and ends at noon; when afternoon begins, and ends at sun-setting. They divide the night into evening, midnight (which they know from the position of certain stars), and dawn of day. Having no timepieces, they are quite ignorant of hours, minutes, and seconds. They reckon their ages by the number of winters they have passed since certain remarkable events happened; and the time of the year by some particular circumstance, such as planting-time, hoeing, or gathering Indian corn, the time when the different fruits of the country are ripe, the croaking of the frogs in spring, the falling of the leaf, and the snow or cold of winter. Mothers often number the days of their

children's ages by cutting a small notch each day on some
part of the infant's cradle, but they seldom keep up this
register beyond two or three months, and from that time
reckon by moons and winters. It is a notorious fact that
very few Indians know their exact age, and when asked,
"How old are you?" will reply, "I do not know; I
cannot remember when I was born." I once asked an
Indian of about fifty how old he was. He replied, "I do
not know." "Are you fifty?" "A great way beyond
that; I think I am more than one hundred." I heard of
a young man about twenty who positively declared he was
one hundred years old. This ignorance is not at all
surprising when we consider they have no correct standard
for computing time. When our Indians were first converted to Christianity we were obliged to make a sort of
hieroglyphic almanac for them, so that they might know
when the Sabbath returned. We did this by making six
marks alike, to represent working or hunting days, and the
seventh different, thus: 0 0 0 0 0 0 +   These they took
with them, and, as each successive week-day returned, they
pierced a hole, until it reached the Sabbath mark. In this
way the Christian Indians, far in the wilderness, kept
holy day, and worshipped the Christian's God.

As to the value of time, it never enters their thoughts
that it is a gift which every human being ought to make
a good use of, and endeavour to improve, both for his own
benefit and that of others. The poor Indian lives as if he
were to remain on this earth for ever,—as though each day
would necessarily supply all his wants. It may truly be
said of the Indians that they are "careful for nothing."
Indians can count to any number, but have no idea of
arithmetic, figures as well as letters being quite unknown
to them.

OF THEIR TOODAIMS.

Their belief concerning their divisions into tribes is, that many years ago the Great Spirit gave his red children their toodaims, or tribes, in order that they might never forget that they were all related to each other, and that in time of distress or war they were bound to help each other. When an Indian, in travelling, meets with a strange band of Indians, all he has to do is to seek for those bearing the same emblem as his tribe ; and having made it known that he belongs to their toodaim, he is sure to be treated as a relative. Formerly it was considered unlawful for parties of the same tribe to intermarry, but of late years this custom is not observed. I have remarked that when the English speak of the different *nations* of Indians they generally call them *tribes;* which term is quite erroneous, as each *nation* is subdivided into a number of tribes or clans, called "toodaims," bearing some resemblance to the divisions of the twelve tribes of Israel mentioned in Scripture; and each tribe is distinguished by certain animals or things, as, for instance, the Ojebway nations have the following toodaims : — the Eagle, Reindeer, Otter, Bear, Buffalo, Beaver, Catfish, Pike, Birch-bark, White Oak Tree, Bear's Liver, &c., &c. The Mohawk nation have only three divisions, or tribes—the Turtle, the Bear, and the Wolf.

The tribe to which I belong is the Eagle, called by us *Messissauga,* a term commonly used by the English when speaking of the Indians residing at the River Credit, Rice Lake, Grape Island, Mud Lake, and those in the vicinity of Kingston, but it is incorrect when applied to them as a body, for in these bands are found remnants of almost all the tribes existing among the Ojebways; and the Eagle tribe, or Messissauga, does not form more than about one quarter of the whole number of Indians residing at the above-mentioned places. Another common mistake is, that the Messissauga Indians are distinct from the Ojebways, whereas they are a part of that nation, and speak the same language.

From the great number of tribes, or toodaims, found among the different nations, many of which are now extinct, there is no doubt that they were once far more numerous than they are now.

It is my opinion that the origin of the toodaims might, were it possible, be traced back to the time when our forefathers first came into the continent of America, and that it has been handed down from one generation to another from time immemorial. Coming into a vast wilderness country, and fearing that in their wanderings they might lose their relationships to each other, they probably held a general council on the subject, agreeing that the head of each family should adopt certain animals or things as their toodaims, by which their descendants might be recognized in whatever part of the world they were found, and that those of the same tribe should ever be considered as brethren or relations.

WEEGIS, OR WAMPUM.

Wampum was first introduced at Plymouth, New England, as an article of commerce, by Isaac De Razier, a Dutch merchant, in the year 1627. It was made by the Indians residing on the sea coast. The following is extracted from the " History of Plymouth," p. 70 :—" Wompompagne," says Mr. Gookin, " is made artificially of a part of the wilk's shell; the black is double the value of the white. It is made principally by the Marraganeet and Long Island Indians. Upon the sandy flats and shores of those coasts the wilk-shells are found." In Roger William's Key, wampum is considered as the Indian money, and is described in the twenty-fourth chapter of that interesting work. "One fathom of this thin-stringed money is worth five shillings. Their white money they call wampum, which signifies white; their black, suckaw-hook; suki signifying black." The editor of the memorial says he received from the late Professor Peck a reply to some inquiries on this subject. He was satisfied that wampum was made from the shell of the paquawhock or quahog. A traveller in this country in the year 1760, describing his journey from Newark to New York, by the way of Staten Island, has the following remark :—" In my way I had an opportunity of seeing the method of making wampum. It is made of the clam-shell; a shell consisting within of two colours, purple and white, and in form not unlike a thick oyster-shell. The process of manufacturing it is very simple. It is just clipped to a proper size, which is that of a small oblong parallelopipedon; then drilled, and afterwards ground to a smooth round surface and polished. The purple wampum is much more valuable than the white, a very small part of the shell being of that colour."

CHAPTER XII.

DISEASES.

Original—Introduced by Whites—Pow-wows and Medicine Men—Mode of performing Cures—Opposition to the Missionary—Interesting Conversion of a Pow-wow—A strange story, by Captain Anderson—Another—Jesuhkon, or Conjuring-house—Medicines—Great variety in their Woods—Minerals—Medicine Bag—Hunter's Medicine—Warriors' Love Powder.

THE diseases most common among the aborigines of America before the landing of the Europeans were few, in comparison with those now debilitating their constitutions, and so rapidly thinning their numbers. There is a saying among our people, that our forefathers were so exempt from sickness, that, like the cedar which has withstood the storms of many ages, and shows the first signs of decay by the dying of the top branches, so the aged Indian, sinking under the weight of many winters, betokens, by his gray hairs and furrowed cheeks, that life is declining.

The diseases most common to the Indians were, consumption, fever, pleurisy, cough, worms, and dysentery. The measles, small-pox, hooping-cough, and other contagious disorders, were unknown to them before the landing of the white man. But now they are subject to all these maladies, and suffer greatly from them, not knowing their nature. Being also much exposed to winds and storms, they are very liable to colds, which increase the virulence of the complaint, and thus hurry thousands off the stage of life. I am happy to say, however, that the small-pox does not now make such havoc as it did on its.

first appearance. The English Government have from time to time sent medical gentlemen to vaccinate the Indians; and this, under the blessing of God, has tended much to check the progress of that loathsome and fatal distemper. Blessed be the memory of Dr. Jenner, the discoverer of this valuable antidote, by which thousands of lives, not only among my own people, but in all parts of the world, have been prolonged. Oh that it may be to show forth the praise of Him in whom we live, move, and have our being!

The Indians die of inflammation of the lungs and consumption, more frequently than of other diseases. The seeds of them are often sown in the constitution when they are young, owing, partly to insufficient or unwholesome diet, and partly to exposure to all kinds of weather. Many of them linger but a short time; others gradually waste away till they are reduced to skeletons, and at length the little spark of life quits the enfeebled and emaciated frame. Other existing causes are, the fatigues which they often undergo in chasing the deer; sometimes using the utmost exertion for a whole day, before they can tire out the animal, and then, when enduring the extremes of heat and thirst, taking large draughts of cold spring water. Another injury arises from the carrying of heavy burdens, which often causes inward strains. I have known some Indians carry a whole deer, weighing about 200 lbs. on their backs for several miles. Then, again, their exposure to frost and cold during a state of intoxication, and the wounds and internal injuries they receive by fighting when in this sad condition, are frequent causes of mortality.

It is painful for me to relate, that of all the children that have been born among those tribes with which I am acquainted, more than one half die before even reaching the period of youth; it is only those who have the strongest constitutions that survive the shocks and exposures to which they are subjected during infancy and childhood. The poor mothers are very ignorant of the nature of the diseases common to children, and of the proper treatment of them; sometimes their clothing is very scanty, at other times they are almost smothered in blankets. The food which they eat is often injurious, and thus disease is generated by the very means used to subdue it. These evils can be remedied only by the benign influence of the gospel, the precepts of which teach men to be sober and industrious, to cultivate the earth, and provide for their families. By these means they would soon possess everything necessary for the supply of their temporal wants, and at the same time be inspired with gratitude to the bountiful Giver of all good.

POW-WOW, OR MEDICINE MEN.

Each tribe has its medicine men and women,—an order of priesthood consulted and employed in all times of sickness. These pow-wows are persons who are believed to have performed extraordinary cures, either by the application of roots and ' herbs, or by incantations. When an Indian wishes to be initiated into the order of a pow-wow, in the first place he pays a large fee to the *faculty*. He is then taken into the woods, where he is taught the names and virtues of the various useful plants; next he is instructed how to chaunt the medicine song, and how to pray: which prayer is a vain repetition offered up to the master of life, or to some munedoo whom the afflicted imagine they have offended.

The pow-wows are held in high veneration by their deluded brethren; not so much for their knowledge of medicine, as for the magical power which they are supposed to possess. It is for their interest to lead these credulous people to believe that they can at pleasure hold intercourse with the munedoos, who are ever ready to give them whatever information they require.*

I am acquainted with a noted medicine man, a chief residing at the River St. Clair, who, by his subtle art and cunning, has impressed with fear all the Indians who know him, insomuch that the other chiefs never undertake anything of importance without consulting him. If he approve, it is well; if not, the object is abandoned. This chief is quite like a patriarch among his people, and may be considered a rich pagan Indian, as he possesess many horses, which run wild on the plains, and are only caught as he wishes to use or sell them. It is said that he has obtained most of his possessions by his pow-wowism on the sick, and by curing those who are bewitched. The pow-wows are generally paid well for their performances, either by a gun, kettle, blanket, coat, or a gallon or two of whisky. When the last article is demanded and paid, the performance of the pow-wow is sure to be crowned by a drunken frolic, in which the doctor joins with his companions for a whole night, singing, yelling, and beating a drum, much to the annoyance of the afflicted person, whose sufferings are aggravated and his death hastened by this barbarous custom. I have visited this chief and his people three or four times for the purpose of introducing the Gospel among them; but, like Elymas the sorcerer, he has by subtlety and mischief resisted our endeavours and prevented his tribe from embracing the truth.

The greatest opposition which missionaries encounter in the spreading of the Gospel is from these medicine men and conjurors, who well know that if the Indians become Chris--

* *Vide* Appendix K.

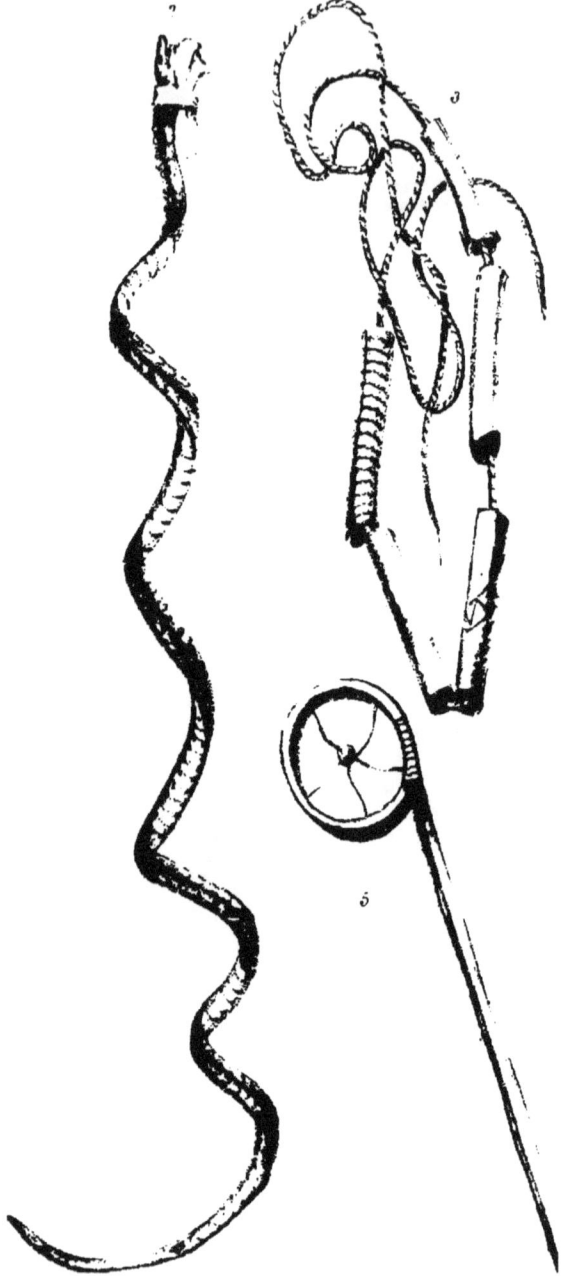

1 Warden God 2 Snake Skin God medecine tied up in a weasel skin at its head 3 Bo

tians there will be an end to their craft and gains. In reading the Acts of the Apostles we find that their preaching was greatly opposed by the same sort of persons, and for similar reasons.*

WITCHCRAFT.

As the pow-wows always unite witchcraft with the application of their medicines, I shall here give a short account of this curious art.

Witches and wizards are persons supposed to possess the agency of familiar spirits, from whom they receive power to inflict diseases on their enemies, prevent the good luck of the hunter, and the success of the warrior. They are believed to fly invisibly at pleasure from place to place ; to turn themselves into bears, wolves, foxes, owls, bats, and snakes. Such metamorphoses they pretend to accomplish by putting on the skins of these animals, at the same time crying and howling in imitation of the creature they wish to represent. Several of our people have informed me that they have seen and heard witches in the shape of these animals, especially the bear and the fox. They say that when a witch in the shape of a bear is being chased, all at once she will run round a tree or a hill, so as to be lost sight of for a time by her pursuers ; and then, instead of seeing a bear, they behold an old woman walking quietly along, or digging up roots, and looking as innocent as a lamb. The fox witches are known by the flame of fire which proceeds out of their mouths every time they bark.

Many receive the name of witches without making any pretensions to the art, merely because they are deformed or ill-looking. Persons esteemed witches or wizards are generally eccentric characters, remarkably wicked, of a

* *Vide* Appendix L.

L

ragged appearance and forbidding countenance. The way in which they are made is either by direct communication with the familiar spirit during the days of their fasting, or by being instructed by those skilled in the art. The method they take to bewitch those who have offended them is this :—The necromancer in the first place provides himself with a little wooden image, representing an Indian with a bow and arrow. Setting this figure up at a short distance before him, he will name it after the person whom he wishes to injure ; he then takes the bow and arrow and shoots at the image, and wherever the arrow strikes, at that instant, they say, the person is seized with violent pain in the same part.

The causes that urge them to take revenge by witchcraft often arise from quarrels, or from supposed injuries done to them, and not unfrequently has it led to murder. A relative of the person thought to be bewitched will go secretly and put the necromancer to death. Many instances, which have come under my own observation, have arisen out of disappointments in marriage. If the witch or wizard is denied the object of his or her desire, then the poor creature in request is immediately threatened with some severe disease, and from fear of being bewitched they are often induced to give their consent to marry. In this way it is that many of the old noted conjurors obtain more than one wife. Frequently, when I have enquired the cause of a disease, the reply has been that it originated in offence given to some witch or wizard.

I have been informed that formerly, when any notorious necromancer was suspected of having bewitched any one, they were often condemned by the councils of the different tribes to execution ; but this was always done with great caution, lest the conjuror should get the advantage over them, and thus bewitch the whole assembly.

I have sometimes been inclined to think that, if witchcraft
still exists in the world, it is to be found among the aborigines of America. They seem to possess a power which, it
would appear, may be fairly imputed to the agency of an
evil spirit.

The conjurors not only pretend to have the powers
already specified, but they profess also to have the gift of
foretelling future events. The following curious account
on this subject I received from a respectable gentleman who
has spent most of his life in the Indian country, and who
is therefore well acquainted with their character and pretensions. He is now one of the Government Indian Agents
in Upper Canada. He thus relates :—

" In the year 1804, wintering with the Winebagoes on
the Rock river, I had occasion to send three of my men to
another wintering house, for some flour which I had left
there in the fall on my way up the river. The distance
being about one and a half day's journey from where I
lived, they were expected to return in about three days.
On the sixth day after their absence I was about sending
in quest of them, when some Indians, arriving from the
spot, said that they had seen nothing of them. I could
now use no means to ascertain where they were : the plains
were extensive, the paths numerous, and the tracks they
had made were the next moment covered by the drift snow.
Patience was my only resource ; and at length I gave them
up for lost.

" On the fourteenth night after their departure, as
several Indians were smoking their pipes, and telling
stories of their war parties, huntings, &c., an old fellow,
who was a daily visitor, came in. My interpreter, a
Canadian named Felix, pressed me, as he had frequently
done before, to employ this conjuror, as he could inform me

L 2

about the men in question. The dread of being laughed at
had hitherto prevented my acceding to his importunities;
but now, excited by curiosity, I gave the old man a
quarter-pound of tobacco and two yards of ribbon, telling
him that if he gave me a true account of them, I would,
when I ascertained the fact, give him a bottle of rum. The
night was exceedingly dark and the house situated on a
point of land in a thick wood. The old fellow withdrew,
and the other Indians retired to their lodges.

" A few minutes after, I heard Wahwun (an egg) begin
a lamentable song, his voice increasing to such a degree
that I really thought he would have injured himself. The
whole forest appeared to be in agitation, as if the trees were
knocking against each other; then all would be silent for a
few seconds; again the old fellow would scream and yell,
as if he were in great distress. A chill seized me, and my
hair stood on end; the interpreter and I stared at each
other without power to express our feelings. After remaining in this situation a few minutes the noise ceased, and we
distinctly heard the old chap singing a lively air. We
expected him in, but he did not come. After waiting some
time, and all appearing tranquil in the woods, we went to
bed. The next morning I sent for my friend Wahwun to
inform me of his jaunt to see the men.

" ' I went,' said he, ' to smoke the pipe with your men
last night, and found them cooking some elk meat, which
they got from an Ottawa Indian. On leaving this place
they took the wrong road on the top of the hill; they
travelled hard on, and did not know for two days that they
were lost. When they discovered their situation they were
much alarmed, and, having nothing more to eat, were afraid
they would starve to death. They walked on without
knowing which way they were going until the seventh day,

when they were met near the Illinois river, by the Ottawa before named, who was out hunting. He took them to his lodge, fed them well, and wanted to detain them some days until they had recovered their strength; but they would not stay. He then gave them some elk meat for their journey home, and sent his son to put them into the right road. They will go to Lagothenes for the flour you sent them, and will be at home in three days.' I then asked him what kind of place they were encamped in when he was there? He said 'they had made a shelter by the side of a large oak tree that had been torn up by the roots, and which had fallen with the head towards the rising sun.'

" All this I noted down, and from the circumstantial manner in which he related every particular,—though he could not possibly have had any personal communication with or from them by any other Indians,—I began to hope my men were safe, and that I should again see them. On the appointed day the interpreter and myself watched most anxiously, but without effect. We got our suppers, gave up all hopes, and heartily abused Wahwun for deceiving us. Just as we were preparing for bed, to my great joy the men rapped at the door, and in they came with the flour on their backs. My first business was to enquire of their travels. They told me the whole exactly as the old Indian had before stated, not omitting the tree or any other occurrence; and I could have no doubt but the old fellow had got his information from some evil or familiar spirit.

" Not long after this I had another opportunity of trying Wahwun's witchcraft, which was shewn in the following occurrence :—I had occasion to send my interpreter Felix to Millwurkie, a distance of about ninety miles. He was to have returned on the fourth day. On the seventh I got very uneasy about him, and applied to my friend Wahwun, to tell me what had become of him. I paid him as I had done before, but heard nothing of the noise which had so terrified me on the former occasion. At daylight the next morning the old fellow came in, and, making a great noise, woke me up, and said :—'Tell the cook to put on the kettle quick and get something ready for Felix to eat; he is close by and is very hungry. Make some broth for him; he has not eaten anything for two days.' The tea-kettle had scarcely time to boil when in came Felix. He told me that they—himself and another man—had started from Millwurkie with a gallon of rum, of which they drank pretty freely during the first day's march. At night they got very drunk, and whilst a drop remained they continued in the same encampment, and, like all improvident men, they ate, drank, and were merry, as long as their means lasted. The tea, broth, &c., were not spared; and indeed it required no small quantity to replenish the void made by a two-days' fasting."

On the 9th of August, 1828, I was engaged in preaching to the Indians at Lake Simcoe, at which time the Great Spirit began in a very powerful manner to convert them from paganism to Christianity. During the day some of the Christian Indians informed me that a certain pagan pow-wow had intimated his intention of consulting his munedoos, to ascertain from them whether it was right for Indians to forsake the religion of their fathers, and take hold of the white man's religion. I requested them to let me know when he would begin his performance, as I wished to go and hear him for myself. Shortly after dark they brought me word that the pow-wow had gone towards the pine-grove to commence his incantations. I immediately accompanied them in that direction, and we soon heard the rattling of his conjuring wigwam, called in Ojebway *jeesuhkon;* which is made by putting seven poles in the ground to the depth of about a cubit, in a circle of about three or four feet in diameter, and about six feet high, with one or more hoops tied fast to the poles, to keep them in a circle. The sides were covered with birch bark, but the top was left open. Into this the pow-wow had entered, and was chaunting a song to the spirit with whom he wished to converse. The *jeesuhkon* began to shake as if filled with wind. Wishing to see and hear his performance without his knowing we were present, we proceeded towards him as softly as we could, and placed ourselves around the *jeesuhkon.* On our approach we heard the *muttering talk* of one of the *familiar spirits,* in answer to questions he had put to him. This spirit told him that it was right for Indians to become Christians, and that he ought to go to the meetings and hear for himself. The next spirit he invoked spoke decidedly against Indians becoming Christiains, and exhorted him to adhere to the religion of his fathers. The third spirit spoke nearly as the first ; with this addition, —that he, the conjuror, was quite wrong in supposing the Christian Indians to be crazy, as if they were under the effects of the fire-waters; that they were not as they appeared to be, but that all the time they were crying and praying, they were in their right minds and worshipping the Great Spirit in their hearts, and according to His will. The fourth spirit informed him that shortly one of his children would be taken from him by death. One of the Christian Indians standing near whispered to me, saying, " If we kneel down and begin to pray to the Great Spirit, his enchantment will be broken, and all his devils will have to fly." I replied, " We had better not disturb him," as I wished to hear the end of it. My friend then in a low whisper prayed that the Great Spirit would have mercy on this poor deluded Indian. That very instant the *jeesuhkon* ceased shaking, and the muttering talk stopped, as if the evil spirits had all been put to flight.

The juggler then spoke to himself: "I suppose the Christian Indians are praying at my wigwam?" He then began to sing with all his might, and presently his jee-suhkon was filled with wind, and began again to shake as if it would fall to pieces. Then a grumbling voice spoke and said, "The Christian Indians are standing all around you." Upon this the conjuror came out of his *jeesuhkon.* We then asked him what news the spirits had communicated to him? He replied, "Some have forbidden me to become a Christian, and encourage me to live as my forefathers have done; but others inform me that it is perfectly right to be a Christian, and that I ought to go and hear the missionaries for myself; this I shall now do, and to-morrow I shall go and hear you at your meetings."

I have now stated what came under my own observation in this one instance, and I leave the reader to form his own judgment as to the power by which these deluded Indians perform their incantations. This Indian, according to promise, attended worship the next day.

Another story of a conjuror I received from John Sunday.*

THEIR MEDICINES.

In describing the medicines used by the North American Indians, I am led to admire the wisdom and goodness of the Almighty, in supplying them with such a variety of remedies every way applicable to the diseases common to their country and climate. Their forests abound with medicinal plants; so that the pow-wow who has obtained

* *Vide* Appendix M.

a knowledge of the virtue of roots and herbs is never at a loss for a supply during the summer season, when he lays up a store for winter use. I doubt not that our woods, plains, and marshes, could furnish a specific for every disease, if the virtues of the plants were better known; for, even with the limited knowledge which the pow-wows possess, they are enabled to perform wonderful cures. I have known instances of persons who had been given up by regular physicians, being restored to health by the simple administration of Indian medicines; and many of the white people, who have great confidence in their beneficial effects, will travel miles to place themselves under the care of an Indian doctor.

The following are some of the principal medicinal plants in common use:—

Of Roots:—Sassafras, spignet, Seneca snake,* alecampaine, wild turnip, coltsfoot, skunk cabbage, lady slipper, poke-root, gold thread, liverwort, white root, milkweed, white pond lily, thistle, sassafrilla.

Of Herbs:—Pennyroyal, lobelia or emetic herb, balm, winter green, Oswego bitters.

Of Barks:—White oak, butternut, elder, hemlock, spotted alder, red willow, wild cherry, iron-wood, slippery elm.

Of Leaves:—Beech, sumach, hemlock, basswood.

Of Minerals:—Gypsum, and native lead.

They also use yellow ochre, and other substances, which they find in the crevices of steep rocks and mountains, and mix with other medicines. There are several poisonous plants; the most noted is the wild parsnip, generally resorted to when an Indian wishes to poison either his enemy or himself. Many of the healing plants are held in

---

* A sure remedy for the bite of the rattlesnake.

religious veneration; so much so that even the *muhshke-mood*, or medicine-bag, is considered to possess supernatural power to injure any who may dare to examine its sacred contents. So afraid are the Indians of it, that it might lie for months in the wigwam without being touched. The pow-wows are very careful to instil this feeling of dread and veneration for the bag and its contents, that they may the more easily work upon the credulity of their subjects.

There are also roots, which the Indians term medicines, and suppose to act as charms.

First. *The hunter's medicine.*—This is held in great esteem by all hunters. It is made of different sorts of roots, which he takes with him on his hunting excursions, a little of which he puts into his gun, that it may make the first shot take effect. He will also place a small portion of it in the first deer or bear's track he meets with, supposing that if the animals be two or three days' journey off, they will come in sight of it in a short time, the charm possessing the power of shortening the journey from two or three days to two or three hours. To render the medicine more effectual he will frequently sing the hunter's song; and I have known many a hunter sit up all night beating his tawagun, and then at daylight take his gun and go in quest of the game. This is generally done when an Indian imagines he has displeased the god of the game, by not paying him that reverence which secures his success in the chase. The first animal he takes he then devotes to the god of the game, making a feast, and offering part in sacrifice, by which he thinks to appease his wrath.

Secondly. *The warrior's medicine.*—This the Indians highly esteem, and never fail to take with them when they go out to war, believing that the possession of this medicine renders their bodies invulnerable to the bullet, the arrow, and the spear.

Thirdly. *Love powder.*—This is a particular kind of charm which they use when they wish to obtain the object of their affections. It is made of roots and red ochre. With this they paint their faces, believing it to possess a power so irresistible as to cause the object of their desire to love them. But the moment this medicine is taken away, and the charm withdrawn, the person who before was almost frantic with love, hates with a perfect hatred.

CHAPTER XIII.

INDIAN NAMES.

Fairies—Waindegoos, or Giants—Indian Names—Derivation—Specimen of Indian Names—Ojebway Words in common use, and their signification.

THE heathen Indians all believe in the existence of those imaginary little folks called *Fairies*. The Ojebways call them *Mamaywasewuy*, the hidden or covered beings. They believe them to be invisible, but possessed of the power of showing themselves. Many old Indians affirm that they have both seen and talked with them. They say that they are about two or three feet high, walk erect, and have the human form, but that their faces are covered over with short hair. The following are some of the stories related concerning them :—

A hunting party were once encamped near a river; finding that their powder and shot gradually decreased every night, and being unable to account for the fact, one of the party determined to lie awake, in order, if possible, to discover the thief. Sometime after midnight, as the fire was going out, a fairy entered the wigwam, and began very softly to help herself to the powder and shot. The Indian then made a noise, upon which the little elf ran towards the door, but as she was passing over the legs of the Indian he raised them suddenly, and she tripped up. The moment she found herself caught she covered her face with the blanket belonging to the Indian, and could not be prevailed upon to show it until he promised to give her a quantity of powder and shot. When she uncovered her face he saw that it was grown over with short soft hair, and it was on this account that the fairy was so reluctant to disclose her countenance. After keeping her a prisoner for a short time, and receiving a promise that good luck should attend him in hunting, he released her, and she soon vanished out of sight, According to agreement, success attended him.

The Indians say that fairies are very fond of shooting, and that they frequently hear the report of their guns. How they obtain them is a mystery, unless they steal them from the hunters, or take them from the graves of the dead.

Several places have been pointed out to me as their residence before the white people became numerous. One is a large pond near Burlington Bay, where the old Indians say they frequently saw them in a stone canoe. When pursued they would paddle to a high bank; and the moment the canoe struck the bank all would disappear, and nothing be heard but a distant rumbling noise. The Indians supposed they had their abode inside the bank. Another tribe of fairies were said to have formerly resided on the east bank of the River Credit, about a mile from the lake, where they often showed themselves.

They are reported to be extravagantly fond of pieces of scarlet cloth and smart prints; and whenever they appear to an Indian, if he can only bestow some such gaudy present upon them, however small, the giver is sure to be rewarded either with long life or success in hunting. In all my travels through the wilderness I have never been favoured with a visit from these invisible beings.

The following story is related of fairies on the River St. Clair :—In the year 1824, a Scotch family, residing on the banks of the River St. Clair, were visited by some strange invisible agencies. The first attack was made on their

poultry, which were taken as if with fits, and soon died ;
then the cattle, pigs, and horses were seized in the same
manner, and died. After this the house was attacked,
and stones and pieces of lead were thrown against the
windows, breaking them and entering the house. The pots
and kettles were then moved from their places without any
one being near them. An attempt was next made to burn
the house. Live coals of fire were found tied up in tow
and rags in different parts of the chambers, which were
extinguished as soon as discovered; but eventually the
house was burned down. While these occurrences were
taking place, a vigilant watch was kept up by the family
and neighbours, who flocked in to witness these strange
scenes; but no clue could be discovered as to the cause.
It was finally declared to be the work of *witchcraft.*
Accordingly, a celebrated witch doctor, by the name of
Troyer, residing near Niagara Falls, was sent for, to expel
all the witches and wizards from the premises. Being on a
missionary tour to the Walpool Island Indians at the time
these incidents were going on, I went to the enchanted
house, and preached the ever-blessed Gospel; but the mis-
chievous spirits were all very quiet, so that I saw nothing
out of the common order of things. But the Rev. R.
Phelps was more fortunate, for he told me that when he
visited the family, and attempted to preach, they kept throwing in small stones and bits of lead, one of which struck
his body. This he picked up, and showed to me. On my
return from the St. Clair, I met an old man who, from his
appearance, wearing a long flowing beard, I judged must
be the witch doctor. I therefore asked him if he were Mr.
Troyer. He replied, "I am." He then positively stated
that he knew the whole affair was witchcraft, and that he
would soon make a finish of the witches. I was after-

wards informed that he began to expel them by firing off
guns loaded with silver bullets, which he stated were the
only kind of weapons which could take effect upon a
witch. Whilst he was in the midst of his manœuvring,
the neighbouring magistrate, hearing of what was going
on, issued a warrant to take him into custody. The
great doctor, being apprised, quickly made his escape to his
own quiet home. Thus ended the whole affair of the
supposed witches and fairies.

In conversation with a noted pow-wow chief, *Pashegee-
ghegwaskum* of Walpool Island, I asked him what he thought
of these strange occurrences among the white people. He
replied, " O, I know all about it. The place on which the
white man's house now stands was the former residence of
the *Mamagwasewug*, or fairies. Our forefathers used to see
them on the bank of the river. When the white man came
and pitched his wigwam on the spot where they lived, they
removed back to the poplar grove, where they have been
living for several years. Last spring this white man went
and cleared and burnt this grove, and the fairies have again
been obliged to remove; their patience and forbearance
were now exhausted; they felt indignant at such treatment,
and were venting their vengeance at the white man by
destroying his property." The old chief uttered these
words as if he fully believed in the existence of these
imaginary beings, and in their power to harm those who
dared to disturb their habitations.

GIANTS, OR WAINDEGOOS.

In my early days I have often listened with wonder and
deep attention to the stories related of the *waindegoos*, or
giants. They are represented as beings tall as pine trees,
and powerful as the munedoos. In their travels they pull

down and turn aside immense forests, as a man would the high grass he passes through. They are said to live on human flesh, and whenever they meet an Indian are sure to have a good meal; being also invulnerable to the shot of an arrow or bullet, they are the constant dread of the Indians. Persons who have been known to eat human flesh from starvation are also called *waindegoos*, after the giants.

INDIAN NAMES.

The Indians have but one name, which is derived either from their gods or some circumstance connected with their birth or character. Many of their names are taken from the thunder gods, who, they suppose, exist in the shape of large eagles. My Indian name *Kahkewàquonàby* belongs to this class, and signifies "*Sacred Feathers.*" This name was given me by my grandfather when I was a few days old. I was named after my mother's brother, who died at the age of seven. These feathers plucked from the eagle represent the plumes of the supposed thunder god, by which it flies from one end of the heavens to the other. When my name was given me, a bunch of eagles' feathers was prepared for the occasion. It was considered sacred, as it represented the speed of the thunder and the eagle. At the same time I received a war-club, to which they tied a little bunch of dried deers' hoofs, denoting the power with which I should be invested by the thunder to become a brave and mighty warrior; and a little canoe, to show that I should have success in crossing the waters.

Their names are generally derived from the following objects,—the sun, moon, stars, sky, clouds, wind, lakes, rivers, trees, animals, fowls, snakes.

As the wise and aged Indians have the best knowledge of

the ancient names of their forefathers and are the most capable of inventing new ones, the office of giving names is generally invested with them.

When a child is to be named, the parents make a feast, and invite all the old people to come and eat at their wigwam. A portion of the meat is offered as a burnt sacrifice. During the time this is burning, the giver of the name makes a prayer to the god to whom he is about to dedicate the child, and towards the close proclaims what it is to be. There is no particular time observed for this ceremony to take place; it is left with the parents, who some-times have their children named when a few months old, at other times not till they are two or three years of age.

Almost every young person receives a nickname either characteristic or arising from some peculiarity; these names they often retain after they have arrived at maturity. It is the custom of the Indians on extraordinary occasions to change their names. For instance, if a sick person, or his friends, suppose that the grim monster Death has received a commission to come after an Indian bearing a certain name, they immediately make a feast, offer sacrifices, and alter the name. By this manoeuvre they think to cheat Death when he comes for the soul of the Indian of such a name, not being able to find the person bearing it.

The following are specimens of Indian names, with their literal translations:—

Nawahjegezhegwabe, masculine; the sloping sky.

Pepoonahbay, m.; the god of the north, who makes the winter.

Manoonooding, m.; the pleasant wind.

Kezhegoowinene, m.; sky man, or man of the sky.

Pamegahwayahsing, m.; the blown down.

Sahswayahsegog, m.; the scattering light by the sun or moon.

M

Mahyahwegezhegwaby, m. ; the upright sky.
Kanahwahbahmind, m. ; he who is looked upon.
Oominwahjewun, m. ; the pleasant stream.
Naningahsega, m. ; the sparkling light.
Pahoombwawindung, m.; the approaching roaring thunder.
Ahzhahwahnahguahdwaby, m. ; the cloud that rolls beyond.
Madwayahshe, m. ; the whistling wind.
Oozhahwahshkoogezhig, m. ; the blue sky.
Shahwundais, m. ; the god of the south, who makes the summer.
Wahbegwuhna, m. ; white feathers.
Wawanosh, m. ; the beautiful sailor.
Wahbahnoosay, m. ; morning walker.
Nahwahquayahseya, m. ; the noon-day, or shining sun.
Kechegahmewinene, m. ; man of the lake.

The female names are distinguished from the males by the feminine termination, *quay*, or *gooquay*. Any of the above names can be rendered feminine ; for example :—

Naningahsegaquay, f. : the sparkling light woman.
Oozhahwahshkoogezhigooquay, f. ; the blue sky woman.
Oogenebahgooquay, f. ; the wild rose woman.
Mesquahquahdooquay, f. ; the red sky woman.

A singular fancy prevails among the Ojebways with respect to mentioning their own names. When an Indian is asked his name he will look at some bystander and request him to answer. This reluctance arises from an impression they receive when young, that if they repeat their own names it will prevent their growth, and they will be small in stature. On account of this unwillingness to tell their names, many strangers have fancied that they either nave no names or have forgotten them. Husbands and wives never mention each other's names, it not being in accordance with Indian notions of etiquette.

I received the following letter from Thomas G. Ridout, Esq., of Toronto, requesting some Indian names for places. As it gave me great pleasure to furnish them, I take the liberty of inserting his communication, wishing more places in Canada were named after the aborigines of this great country.

" *Bank of Upper Canada,*

" TORONTO, 24*th March*, 1855.

" MY DEAR SIR,

"There is to be a station of the Great Western Railway Company's line on some land that I own on the River Thames, in the township of North Dorchester; and as it is on the site of an ancient Indian town, I have a great desire to give the place an Indian name, and so perpetuate some landmark of that noble and ancient race, who for ages past were the rightful owners of this great country. May I beg of you to inform me the Chippewa name of the River Thames, or some other appropriate name? Perhaps you may know the name of some Indian town on the banks of the Thames, which would please the ear, and be easily spoken. . . . .

" Yours most truly,

"THOMAS G. RIDOUT."

" The Rev. PETER JONES."

In answer the following names were sent:—

As-kun-e-See-be ; the Horn River, or Chippewa name for the River Thames.

Wau-bun-o ; * the morning light.

Torn-e-co ; the name of the head chief of the Chippeways of the River Thames.

O-je-bway ; the proper name for Chippewa.

* Name of a celebrated chief—my grandfather.

M 2

O-da-nuh ; the name of any town.

Ta-kuh-mo-say ; he who walks over the water.

The following Ojebway words being in common use among the white settlers in Canada, it may be deemed interesting to give their signification :—

As spelt in English.	As pronounced by Indians.	Signification.
Chippewa.	Ojebway	The puckered moccasin people
Messissaga	Ma-se-sau-gee..............	The eagle totem, clan, or tribe
Etobicoke..........	A-doo-pe-kog	Place of the black alder
Esquesing	Ash-qua-sing	That which lies at the end
Nassagaweya......	Nan-zuh-zau-ge-wa-zog ...	Two outlets, 16-mile creek
Chinguacousy	Shing-wau-koons-see-be...	Young pine river
Schoogog	Wuh-yau-wus-ke-wuh-gog	Shallow muddy lake
Otonabee.	O-doon-ne-be	Mouth-water
Napanee	Nau-pau-na..	Flour
Saugeen	Sau-geeng.	Mouth of a river
Manitoulin.	Mun-e-doo-me-nis.	Spirit Island
Manitouwanning.	Mun-e-doo-wah-ning	The abode of a spirit god
Manito.	Mun-e-doo	Spirit, or god
Moccasin.	Muh-ke-zin	Indian shoe
Penetanguishene.	Pe-nuh-dau-wung-o-sheeng	Caving sandbank
Notawasaga.......	Nau-do-wa-sau-ge.........	Mohawk outlet
Oshawa............	Au-zhuh-wuh	Ferry him over
Tecumseth	Ta-kuh-mo-sah	He who walks over water
Shebenaning	Shee-ban-o-nau-ning	Straight narrow passage
Gananoque.........	Gau-nuh-nau-queeng	Place of residence
Squaw *	Equa	Woman
Consecon	O-gons-e-kong	Place of small pickerel (fish)
Toronto	A Mohawk word............	Looming of trees
Brantford	Brant's ford	Capt. Brant's place of crossing
Mackinaw.	Mesh-e-ne-mah-ke-noong	The great turtle

* The Indians generally consider this word a term of reproach.

CHAPTER XIV.

Indian Fur Companies and Traders.

THE intercourse which has long subsisted between the red man and the white man has to a great extent changed the character of the former as regards native simplicity, moral habits, language, and dress. Some of the aged relate that their forefathers informed them that previously to the arrival of the white man in America the Indians were far more virtuous than they are now, and that the fire-waters have tended to demoralize them in every respect. Indeed, every traveller who has written on the condition of the Indians affirms that their intercourse with Europeans has sadly corrupted their morals and lowered their dignity.

Carver states:—"The southern tribes, and those that have held a constant intercourse with the French and English, cannot have preserved their manners or customs in their original purity. They could not avoid acquiring the vices with the language of those they conversed with ; and the frequent intoxications they experienced through the baneful juices introduced among them by the Europeans, have completed a total alteration in their character."

The reason is obvious. The first adventurers into the Indian territory were, in general, destitute of moral principle, " neither fearing God nor regarding man." Such persons would naturally introduce vice instead of virtue ; and I have every reason to believe that had they then inculcated the holy principles of the pure word of God, my countrymen would long since have become prosperous and happy. A circumstance which happened in my early days will prove that their dark minds were at that time ready to receive the light of the gospel had there been any one to instruct them.

Our wigwam was pitched by the shore of Lake Ontario, and our little band consisted principally of poor Indian women, who got their living by making baskets and brooms, which they sold to the white people then settled in the country. One evening, after the return of the women, they began to relate what some white woman had been telling them about the Son of the Great Spirit.—"A long time ago the Great Spirit sent his Son into this world, in order, as they understood, to make the white people good and happy, but that the wicked people hated him, and after he had been here a little while, they took him and killed him. While this was being related, all in the wigwam listened with deep attention, when one of them spoke with a heavy sigh, and said—"*O, that the Son of the Great Spirit had not been killed, for had he lived till this day he might have had compassion on us poor Indians, as well as on the white people, but now we are so poor.*"

Mr. Harman states, as to the whites corrupting the Indians: "The tribes that are the most enlightened, and that have advanced the farthest towards a state of civilization, are the Sauteux, or Chippeway, the Muskagoes, and the Crees, or Knisteneux. The white people have been among the above-mentioned tribes for about 150 years. To this circumstance it is probably to be attributed that the knowledge of these Indians is more extensive. But I very much question whether they have improved in their character or condition by their acquaintance with civilized people. In their savage state they were contented with the mere necessaries of life which they could procure with considerable ease; but now they have many artificial wants, created by the luxuries which we have introduced among them; and as they find it difficult to obtain these luxuries, they have become, to a degree, discontented with their condition, and practise fraud in their dealings. A half-civilized Indian is more savage than one in his original state. The latter has some sense of honour, while the former has none. I have always experienced the greatest hospitality and kindness among those Indians who have had the least intercourse with white people. They readily discover and adopt our evil practices; but they are not as quick to discern and as ready to follow the few good examples which are set before them."

I shall now state some of the evils introduced by the white people.

First. *Drunkenness.*—This was the polluted source whence flowed poisonous waters that contaminated, and deadened every good feeling of the heart. No people, as a body, can be more addicted to this crying sin than the natives of America. Previously to the introduction of Christianity among them, I have often seen such scenes of degradation as would sicken the soul of a good man; such as husbands beating their wives, and dragging them by the hair of the head; children screaming with fright, the older ones running off with guns, tomahawks, spears, knives, and other deadly weapons, which they concealed in the woods to prevent the commission of murder by their enraged parents; yet, notwithstanding this precaution, death was not unfrequently the result. Dr. Schofield related—" That when he first settled in Canada, there were many Indian families who gradually disappeared. He knew twelve children perish in one drunken frolic, their mothers being too intoxicated to take care of them." When an Indian gets a taste for the *fire-waters*, his craving appetite knows no bounds, and in order to get them he will part with anything which the white trader will receive from him. I knew an Indian woman named Nawich, who, when drunk, would sell her little daughter for a quart of whisky! because she had nothing else wherewith to procure what her soul thirsted after.

Second. *The habit of taking the name of God in vain*, is another evil taught the Indian by his white brother. In their own language they have no words by which they can blaspheme the name of the Lord; but I have often observed, that among the very first things which they learn in English or French, is to swear. There is this, however, in their favour,—that many of them do not know the meaning of the words they utter.

Third. *Introduction of contagious diseases*, such as small-pox, measles, whooping cough. In P. J. De Smet's "Sketches" we have the following notice of a nation nearly destroyed by small-pox :—" Next day we crossed the forest, the winter quarters of the Gros Ventres and Arikaras, in 1835. It was there that those unfortunate tribes were nearly exterminated by the small-pox. We saw their bodies wrapped up in buffalo robes, tied to the branches of the largest trees. It was truly a sad and mournful spectacle. Two days later we met the miserable survivors of these unhappy tribes."

Fourth. *Dishonesty, lying, and deception*, are too often taught them by the traders. Cases have often occurred where the Indian has received credit from a trader ; but should another trader meet him, in order to save some skins for the one to whom he is indebted, he will conceal part of them, and then say he has no more. Their furs are often taken from them by force, or a very poor remuneration paid for them. When an Indian first arrives at a trading-post with his pack of skins, he will begin by asking a fair price for his peltries. The trader, knowing wherein his weakness lies, will appear indifferent about closing the bargain, and treat him with some rum. No sooner does the Indian taste the *fire-waters* than his thirst becomes insatiable; so that the trader, by a little manœuvring, will get all the skins he wishes at his own price.

Fifth. *The loss of their country and game*, for a trifling remuneration. This the poor Indian feels keenly, and often has he thirsted for revenge on his encroaching neighbour. This has been seen lately in the south, in the case of the Seminoles struggling in vain against the power of the United States. The warrior may raise the war whoop, whirl the tomahawk, and brandish his scalping knife; but how can a handful of braves compete with a well conducted army? They may annoy and slaughter their intruders for a time, but ruin and degradation will be the result of these unequal struggles, and the poor Indians will be obliged to lay down the tomahawk with shame and disgrace. ' Every traveller in the Indian country has borne ample testimony to the fact that injury after injury has been inflicted on the red man by the adventurers who first penetrated the American forests.

INDIAN FUR COMPANIES AND TRADERS.

History informs us, that soon after the discovery of America by Europeans, the adventurous traders penetrated far into the interior, for the purpose of procuring furs from the Indians; in exchange for which they gave them trinkets, guns, ammunition, clothes, prints, knives, whisky!

The French were the first who established regular trading-posts along the chain of the great lakes in Canada. After its conquest by the English the Honourable Hudson's

Bay Company was formed, which has been in successful operation ever since, and I have been informed that they have amassed great wealth. A celebrated person in New York has made an immense fortune by his Indian trade. It is reported that he commenced business a comparatively poor man, but that now he is one of the richest men in New York, and owns the famous Astor House in Broadway. Persons acquainted with the enormous profits made on these skins are not at all surprised that so many get rich in this trade. A beaver skin worth eight hundred dollars is often bought for one hundred dollars, and so in proportion.*

* *The Poor Indian.*—In the splendid regions of the " far west " which lie between Missouri and the Rocky Mountains, there are living at this moment on the prairies, various tribes who, if left to themselves, would continue for ages to live on the buffalo which cover the plains. The skins of these animals, however, become valuable to the whites, and accordingly this beautiful verdant country and these brave and independent people have been invaded by white traders, who by paying them a pint of whisky for each skin, (or " robe," as they are termed in America,) which sell at New York for ten or twelve dollars, induce them to slaughter these animals in immense numbers, leaving their flesh, the food of the Indian, to rot and putrify on the ground. No ambition or caution can arrest for a moment the propelling power of the whisky ; accordingly, in all directions these poor thoughtless beings are seen furiously riding, under its influence, in pursuit of their game, or, in other words, in the fatal exchange of food for poison. It has been attentively calculated by the traders, who manage to collect about 150,000 buffalo skins per annum, that at the rate at which these animals are now disposed of, in ten years they will be killed off. Whenever that event happens, Mr. Catlin very justly prophecies that 250,000 Indians, now living in a plain of nearly three thousand miles in extent, must die of starvation, and become a prey to wolves ; or they must either attack the powerful neighbouring tribes of the Rocky Mountains ; or, in utter frenzy of despair, rush upon the white population, in the forlorn hope of dislodging it. In the two latter alternatives there exists no chance of success ; and we have, therefore, the appalling reflection before us, that these 250,000 Indians must soon be added to the dismal list of those who have already withered and disappeared, leaving their country to bloom and flourish in the possession of the progeny of another world !—*Quarterly Review.*

The American Fur Company have also extended their operations far to the west; and I am happy to state that, as far as my information goes, with respect to the conduct pursued by these companies towards the Indians, it is now as honourable as circumstances will permit; and I rejoice to add, that since they have seen the evils occasioned by the fire-waters, they have abolished them as an article of traffic. This speaks loudly for their humanity.

Many of the factors are now taking an active part in assisting the missionary to civilize and christianize the Indians within the bounds of their territory. The factors and servants of the Fur Company have almost universally adopted the custom of marrying Indian wives, from whom a numerous offspring of half-breeds have sprung up. These intermarriages have produced a kind of half civilization, which, without importing the religion of the Bible, only makes the poor Indian " ten times more the child of the devil than he was before," his superior worldly knowledge enabling him to be a skilful worker in all kinds of iniquity. The traders exert a powerful influence over the Indians, who invariably get greatly indebted to them, and thus become subservient to their creditors.

Their servants, who are mostly Canadian French, profess the Roman Catholic religion, and have their priests in different parts of the western wilderness. These missionaries are most persevering and self-denying men; they will compass sea and land to make proselytes to their faith. The ceremonies and gaudy show connected with the services of the Romish Church, resembling much his own heathen rites and ceremonies, are well calculated to strike the untutored mind of the Indian. Hence he readily adopts the Papist religion in preference to the Protestant, which requires the renunciation of idolatry, witchcraft, and drunkenness. No barbarous people will forsake their old customs and manners till the rays of Divine revelation dissipate the mists of ignorance, and, by enlightening the conscience, show them the vanity of Pagan worship. Then, and not till then, will they "cast their idols to the moles and to the bats." I have never discovered any real difference between the Roman Catholic Indian and the pagan, except the wearing of crosses.

As the country becomes peopled by the whites, the Indian traders disappear, the game is destroyed, and what little fur may be taken the Indians dispose of to the shopkeepers or merchants.

Desirous of the welfare of our Christian Indians, I have often longed for the time when the game and fur shall be so destroyed as to leave no inducement for them to abandon their farms and houses. This, coming from the pen of an Indian, may appear strange; but I have good reasons for saying so. No one acquainted with the hunting propensities of Indians will deny that the little game now left is rather a source of injury than benefit to them. It induces them to leave their homes, and fosters indolent and lounging habits. So long as they depend upon this precarious mode of subsistence they must continue in wretchedness and want. The sooner, therefore, they abandon hunting the better. They will then from necessity be compelled to devote their attention to the more primitive, healthy, and profitable employment of man, and become tillers of the ground.

CHAPTER XV.

Indians' love for the Fire-waters before conversion—Firmness in resisting after.

THE Rev. S. Waldron, when missionary at Muncey Town, stated, at a missionary meeting, that Rufus Turkey was so fond of the fire-waters that he went by night to the still-house, and when he could not get in at the door or window climbed upon the roof, thinking to descend by the chimney; but when he got half-way down he stuck fast, and was obliged to remain there till morning. The whisky-maker, when he came to make his fire, heard an unaccountable noise of groaning; and, looking up, he saw the Indian, who was almost suffocated. He flogged the intruder, and sent him away. Poor Rufus soon after died.

An Indian, who was a notorious drunkard, on one occasion, after taking a dram of the fire-waters, exclaimed, " O that my throat were two miles long, that I might have tasted it all the way as it went down !"

An Indian came to an agent at Mackinaw, and began to beg for a dram of fire-water. The agent said to him he never gave drunken Indians any drams. The Indian then said, "Me very good Indian." The agent replied that good Indians never asked for drams, and it was only bad Indians who drunk or asked for whisky. The Indian replied, " Den me be d—— rascal."

FIRMNESS OF THE INDIANS IN RESISTING THE FIRE-WATERS,
AFTER THEIR CONVERSION.

Shortly after the work of God commenced among the
Indians of Schoogag Lake, an Indian trader bought a
barrel of whisky to sell to them.   The Indians requested
him to take it away, as they were resolved not to purchase
any.   He persisted in offering it.   The brave Christian
Indians then went in a body to the trader, and demanded
the barrel, which he reluctantly delivered.   They rolled it
to the lake, cut a hole through the ice, into which they
tumbled it, sinking it to the bottom.

A similar circumstance occurred to my mother when returning from Toronto in a canoe, in company with other
Indian women.   She informed me they were overtaken
by a boat-load of white men, who came alongside, and then
pulled out a bottle of whisky, asking them to drink.   The
women told them that they did not drink; but the men
were urgent, saying, " Surely a little will do you no
harm."   The former still refusing, and the latter persisting,
my mother held out her hand, saying, " Hand me the
bottle."   This being done, the white men thought they had
prevailed.   But, instead of that, my mother poured out
the liquid fire on the opposite side of the canoe into the
lake, and then returned the bottle empty to their tempters.
The white men laughed and applauded, saying they had
done perfectly right.

The Rev. Thomas Hurlbert informed me that four Indians
from Muncey Town went to the white settlement to trade.
The trader tempted them to drink some whisky, but they
refused, saying they were Christians.   Finding he could
not succeed, he thought perhaps they were afraid lest some
one should see them drink and tell the missionary, and

that if they could take it slily they would drink as formerly. Knowing the road they would return home, he put a small keg of whisky by the side of the Indian path, at the edge of a sloping bank, and hid himself in the bushes beneath, thinking to enjoy the sport of seeing them drink when all alone. At length they came along following in Indian file; when, suddenly, the first one stopped, and exclaimed, " O, mah-je-mun-e-doo sah-oomah ahyah:—Lo! the evil spirit (the devil) is here." The second, on coming up, said, " Aahe, nebejemahmahsah :—Yes, me smell him." The third shook the keg with his foot, and said, " Kaguit, nenoondahwahsah :—of a truth me hear him." The fourth Indian coming up, gave the keg a kick, and away went the fire-waters tumbling down the hill. The four Indians went on their way like brave warriors, leaving the mortified *white* heathen to take up. his keg and drink the devil himself.

The Rev. Elijah Hedding mentions the following incident occurring just before his visit to the Grape Island Mission, W. C., which shows how strong had become their hatred of whisky drinking :—" A Christian Indian had gone out in the bay in a canoe, and been driven off in a storm; and in his danger had been picked up by a steam-boat. The poor Indian was almost exhausted, and the captain of the steam-boat made him drink a glass of whisky. When he came back to the village the Indians were so afflicted that he should, under any circumstances, drink whisky, that they took up a discipline with him; and for one whole afternoon and evening, alternately, one would exhort him, and another pray for him, and then they would make him promise that he would drink no more whisky."

A CURIOSITY.

Our red brothers, the Indians, are curious people—very. The extract below is an illustration in point.

" *Memorial of the Onondaga Nation in favour of the Maine Law.*

" *To the Senate and House of Representatives, Albany, N. Y.*

" Dear Fathers and Brothers:—We understand that you are at the great Council House at Albany, and that the great council fire is now burning, and that our white brothers all over the State are sending wood to put on the council fire, but we 'fraid the council fire will not burn bright and clear without more help; so we send this to make it burn. Now brothers, what we want to say is this:—We hear about our brothers in the State of Maine— we hear that they find Great Rogue—this Rogue he gets folks' money, sometimes he burns houses, sometimes he kill people, sometimes he make a family very poor, sometimes he take 'way senses, sometimes he make 'em very cross and ragged and dirty, and sometimes he freeze 'em to death.

" Now, we hear our brothers there—they try to stop it— they try talk about it, see if can stop it little—but he won't stop it. We hear at last our brothers wont bear it no longer—so they make law to knock him on the head, anywhere they find him—in barrel, or jug, or bottle; in tavern, grocery, or barn: anywhere—knock him on the head. Now we want to tell you brothers, that this big *Rogue* has been here to Onondago; he has made us great trouble. Some of our people would be very good if this bad fellow would keep away. We try—our people try some, but he will not. Now what we ask you is to make us laws—such as our brothers in the State of Maine have made. We have tried to coax him, but he wont be coax ; we try scare—he wont scare much ; he still make great deal trouble ; we think better make law to knock him on head—then he make us no more trouble. We Christian party ask it, and Pagan too—most all ask it—you make this law.

" Now brothers, our people sold our land to white people, and white people make treaty—he say he be good to Indian. But he let this *Rogue* trouble us most too long. Now, brothers, we was one great people, and we have gone to war for our white brother ; but now we are few, and our white brothers are strong. We want you help us—we want you make this law, so when we find this *Rogue* we will keep him. We see him great many times, but we mean to be good and peaceable, and so he got away ; but if you make this law then we kill him, and then we live happy and friendly—no more cross—no more ragged—no more fight, but raise corn, wheat, oats, beans, cattle, horses, and some children too ; no more get drunk— no more freeze to death—work and get good things like white men.

" DAVID HILL,   ⎫
" DAVID SMITH, ⎬ *Chiefs.*
            ⎭

" And 61 more of the Onondagas."

CHAPTER XVI.

Two Roots—Peculiar Construction—Capable of being arranged grammatically
—Specimen of Conjugations—Lord's Prayer in Ojebway.

AFTER minute observation on the various Indian dialects I have heard spoken, I have only discovered *two* distinct or leading languages, and have come to the conclusion that all others bear affinity to them both in sound and idiom. These two roots I should call the *Ojebway* and the *Mohawk*, which are entirely different from each other. The former comprehends the following tribes, viz. :—*Ojebway, Odahwah; Potawahduhmee; Minoomenee; Kenistenoo,* or *Cree; Delaware; Muncey; Saukie; Kicapoo; Muskeeyoo; Mohegan*, backwoods men ; *Miskwukeeyuk*, red earthmen, from wearing red blankets; *Juskwaugume; Weah; Shawnee; Miamee; Peoria; Aubinaukee; Kaskaskia;* and *Piangeshaw.* The Rev. Thomas Hurlbert, who has travelled extensively in North America, has met with large tribes whose nationality and language is entirely distinct from the above-mentioned, for instance :—Saux ; Assinebwaunuk; Osage ; Kansas; Quaupaw ; Oto ; Pawnee ; and Omuhaw.

The Mohawk includes the *Oneida; Onondaga; Seneca; Cayuga; Tuscarora; Wyandot; and Cherokee.*

It is allowed by all travellers in the Indian country, that the Ojebway is the most extensive of any of the North American languages, being understood and spoken by all the tribes found on both sides of the lakes Huron, Michigan, and Superior, and so on to the head-waters of the Mississippi and Red River. It is true that some of the tribes find it difficult to understand each other when they first meet, but after a short intercourse they are enabled to converse with one another. This establishes the fact that there is one common origin to the different dialects of the Ojebway and Mohawk languages. The following are some examples : [See pp. 180-1.]

All the Indian languages abound in polysyllables, and, owing to the affixes and prefixes, some of the words are enormously long. A whole sentence is often expressed by one compound word, as for example :—

Ki-ku-we-un-too-tu-mau-ga-tu-mo-wau-nau-nik.

We will desire to ask alms for those persons.

Ki-ku-we-ni-ta-wau-bu-mau-nau-nik.

We will try on the way to be in time to see them.

The following is a definition of the word Conscience in Ojebway:

Kekandahmauwin; knowing, or knowledge.

Kekanedezowin; knowing one's self.

Mooshetumowin; internal feeling or consciousness.

The Ojebway language is capable of being arranged into grammatical order. It possesses great strength, and is full of imagery, as the words express the nature, use, or resemblance of the things spoken of. On this account it makes a deeper impression on the mind of both speaker and hearer than a language composed of arbitrary or unmeaning sounds. I shall now give a specimen of the conjugation of an Ojebway verb. (This verb was left unfinished by the Rev. P. Jones, but it is deemed proper to insert it as his production. At the same time the editor is greatly indebted to the Rev. Thomas Hurlbert for his kindness in furnishing a complete verb, which with his observations on the intricacies

English	Ojibway.	Odahwah.	Poodawahduhwae.	Delaware.	Munsee.	Cree.
Man	E-ne-ne	E-ne-ne-za	Enin-uh	Lin-noh	Lin-oowh	Eyc-new
Woman	E-qua	E-qua	E-qua	Oorh-qua	Oorh-quaiwh	Isk-wao
Child	Uh-be-noo-jeeh	Uh-be-noo-jeeh	Uh-ba-na-ja	Um-ce-minz	Um-ee-minz	O-wau-sis
Boy	Quee-we-zans	Quee-we-zans	Ko-kah-bn	Pee-lowh-waiz	Skah-in-zoowh	Nau-ba-sis
Girl	E-qua-zans	E-qua-zuns	Keeg-yug-koons	Orh-qua-chy	Oorh-qua-zis	Es-kwa-sis
Earth	Uh-ke	Uh-ke	Uh-ka	Kuk-keh	Uh-ko	Us-keo
Sky	Kee-zhig	Koe-zhig	Koo-zheeg	Pa-mah-pun-eek	Keesh-koowh	Kc-se-kook
Sun	Kec-zis	Kee-zis	Kee-zas	Kee-shoorqh	Koo-shoorqh	Pe-sin
Moon	Te-bik-kee-zis	Te-bik kee-zis	Tc-bik-zas	Nee pau shoorqh	Nee-pau kee-shoorqh	Tc-pis-kow-pe-sim
Star	Uh-nung	Uh-nung	Uh-nung	Uh-lun-qua	Uh-lon-qua	Uh-ju-kosu
God	Kezha-munedoo	Kezha-munodoo	Kezhamunadoo	Pahtum-owhwoz	Pah-tumowhwoz	Ko-sn-mu-ni-too
Heaven	Ish-pe-ming	Ish-pe-ming	Ish-poo-ming	Owhwossahkuma	Owhwozuhkuma	Is-pi-mik
Water	Ne-bo	Nee-beesh	Na-beesh	Ne-bi	Ne-be	Ne-po
Lake	Ko-oho-guh-mo	Ko-che-guh-me	Ko-che-gum-mee	Me-no-paigh	Ne-bee-zis	We-ni-pag
River	Sec-be	Sce-be	See-ba	Soo-poh	See-poowh	Se-peo
Tree	Me-tig	Me-tig	Me-tig	Hit-tuqh	Me-tuqh	Mis-tik
House	Wee-ge-waum	We-ge-waum	We-gee-waum	Week-wuhm	Week-wuhm	Waus-kah-e-gun
Bear	Muh-quuh	Muh-quah	Mah-koo	Marqk	Marqk	Mus-kwu
Deer	Wah-wah-shka-sho	Wah-wah-shke-she	Suk-ko-cee	Uh-toowh	Uh-toowh	
Dog	Uh-ne-moosh	Un-ne-moosh	Uh-na-moosh	Mwah-kun-a	Mwah-kun-a	Utim

English.	Mohawk.	Cayuga.	Onondaga.	Seneca.	Oneida.	Tuscarora.
Man	Rongwe	Hongwe	Hengwe	Hengwe	Longwo	Rongwe
Woman	Yongwe	Ahgongwe	Ahgongwe	Yagongwe	Akonheti	Kaneaweah
Child	Exaah	Exaah	Exaah	Exsaah	Exah	Ekatsah
Boy	Raxaah	Haxaah	Haxsaah	Haxsaah	Lanigeatreh	Rotsughwes
Girl	Exaah	Exaah	Exsaah	Exsaah	Ehyatase	Etyatshayea
Earth	Ohwensia	Ohwenjah	Onwenjah	Yowenjah	Oghwonja	Ofna
Sky	Karenya	Kaonhyate	Kaonhya	Kaonhyate	Karoya	Orealiyo
Sun	Karaghgwa	Kaabgwa	Kaabgwa	Kaagwaa	Wenteka Wehuita	Oshoeakeha Igus
Moon	Eghnita	Ennita	Wennita	Wennitaa	Wasontekhah Wenita	Hihte
Star	Ojistok	Ojisonta	Ojistanyogwa	Ojisontaa	Ojistohgwa	Onihseareh
God	Niyoh	Hawenniyoh	Hawenniyoh	Hawenniyoh	Raweaniyoh	Yeweaniyoh
Heaven	Karoghyage	Kaonyageh	Kaonhyageh	Kononyage	Kalonyageh	Orcahyagch
Water	Oghneganos	Oghneganos	Oghneganos	Oneganos	Oghneganos	Aweah
Lake	Kanyatare	Kanyataeh	Kanyatach	Kanyaeh	Kanyatale	Kanyature
River	Kaihohah	Konhyate	Konhyonhate	Kenhato	Kisheahataly	Kinea
Tree	Kerhite	Kraet	Kechah	Keet	Kerhit	Keshih
House	Kaneasote	Kanohsot	Kanonsayen	Kanensot	Kaneasot	Oneasoh
Bear	Oghquarih	Nyagwai	Ohgwaih	Nyagwaih	Oghgwalih	Oghireah
Deer	Oskononto	Tewahontes	Skennonton	Neogen	Oskononte	Awkweh
Dog	Erhahr	Sowas	Iihah	Iiyrah	Elhahl	Hahjis

of the Indian verb will give a more satisfactory insight into the peculiarities of the language. Much difficulty has been found in writing the Ojebway with the English Alphabet from the fact that there are many sounds between b and p, d and t, g hard and k, ch and j, s and.z. The writer often interchanges these letters in writing the same word. It will be observed that the orthography of the following verbs differs in this respect.)

CONJUGATION OF THE VERB TO WALK, *Chebemosung.*

INDICATIVE MOOD.

PRESENT TENSE.

Singular.	*Plural.*
1. Nebomosa.........I walk.	1. Nebemosamin.........We walk.
2. Kebemosa.........Thou walkest.	2. Kebemosam ....Ye walk.
3. Bemosa............He walks.	3. Bemosawug............They walk.

PAST TENSE.

1. Ningeebemosa ...I walked.	1. Ningeebemosamin ...We walked.
2. Kegeebemosa ...Thou walkedst.	2. Kegeebemosam ......Ye walked.
3. Keebemosa ......He walked.	3. Keebemosawug ......They walked.

FUTURE TENSE.

1. Ninguhbemosa ...I shall walk. ·	1. Ninguhbemosamin ... We shall walk.
2. Keguhbemosa ...Thou shalt walk.	2. Keguhbemosam ...Ye shall walk.
3. Duhbemosa ....He shall walk.	3. Duhbemosawug ...They shall walk.

PERFECT TENSE.

1. Ningeebemosanahbun...I have walked.	1. Ningeebemosaminahbun.We have walked
2. Kegeebemosanahbun ...Thou hast walked.	2. Kegeebemosamwahbun..Ye have walked.
3. Keebemosabun............He has walked.	3. Keebemosabuneeg.......They have walked.

POTENTIAL MOOD.

PRESENT TENSE.

Singular.
Plural.

1. Nindahbemosa..I may walk.
1. Nindahbemosa ....We may walk.
2. Kedahbemosa. .Thou mayest walk.
2. Kedahbemosam...Ye may walk.
3. Dahbemosa......He may walk.
3. Dahbemosawug...They may walk.

PAST TENSE.

1. Nindahgeebemosa ...I might walk.
1. Nindahgeebemosamin.We might walk.
2. Kedahgeebemosa...Thou mightest walk.
2. Kedahgeebemosam....Ye might walk.
3. Dahgeebemosa.........He might walk.
3. Dahgeebemosawug.....They might walk.

PERFECT TENSE.

1. Nindahgeebemosame-dook...I may have walked.
1. Kedahgeebemosaminah-doog...We may have walked.
2. Kedahgeebemosame-dook...Thou mayest have walked.
2. Kedahgeebemosamwah-doog...Ye may have walked.
3. Dahgeebemosadoog... He may have walked.
3. Dahgeebemosadooya-nug ....They may have walked.

SUBJUNCTIVE MOOD.

PRESENT TENSE.

1. Bemosawahnan ...If I walk.
1. Bemosawungwan .....If we walk.
2. Bemosawuhnan ...If thou walkest.
2. Bemesawagwan........If ye walk.
3. Bemosagwan ....If he walk.
3. Bemosawahgwan .....If they walk.

IMPERATIVE MOOD.

2. Bemosan ....Walk thou.
2. Bemosayook...—..........Walk ye.

(Thus ends the verb unfinished by the Rev. Peter Jones.
The following is furnished by the Rev. Thomas Hurlbert:—)

SPECIMEN OF AN OCHEPWA VERB.—*Root*, Waubi, He sees.

Waubing ....To see. Infinitive
Waubim.................To see. Infinitive absolute.

INDICATIVE MOOD.

PRESENT TENSE.

Singular.	*Plural.*
1. Niwaub ....I see.	1. Niwaubimin...We see, exclusive of the party addressed.
	1. Kiwaubimin...We see, inclusive of the party addressed.
2. Kiwaub ....Thou seest.	2. Kiwaubim......You see.
3. Wauhi ....He sees.	3. Waubiwug .....They see.
4. Waubiwun* ......Him or his sees.	4. Waubiwun ....Them or theirs see.

PAST TIME, OR IMPERFECT TENSE.

1. Niwaubinaubun...I saw.	1. Niwaubiminnaubuu..We saw, exclusive of the party addressed.
	1. Kiwaubiminnaubun..We saw, inclusive of the party addressed.
2. Kiwaubinaubun...Thou sawest.	2. Kiwaubimwaubun....You saw.
3. Waubebun ......He saw.	3. Waubebunneg ......They saw.
4. Waubebunen ......Him or his saw.	4. Waubebunen ....Them or theirs saw.

PERFECT TENSE.

1. Ninkewaub. ..I have seen.
2. Kikewaub ...Thou hast seen.
3. Kewaubi ....He has seen.
4. Kewauwun ...Him or his has seen.

Note.—There are no pronouns in the third and fourth persons in the Intransitive Verbs.

Ninkewaubinaubun	I had seen.
Ninguwaub	I will see.
Ningukewaub	I will have seen.
Nintauwaub	I may or can see.
Niwewaub.................................	I wish to see.
Nimpewaub	I come seeing.

---

* Anomalous as it may seen, this language has four persons. For want of pronouns in the English we cannot express it better than above.

Niwepewaub...............................	I wish to come seeing.
Ningunipimon ....`.........	I will go walking.
Ninguniwaub	I will go seeing.
Nintaukewaub	I should have seen.
Nintawaub.................................	I am able to see.
Niwetawaub	I wish to be able to see.
Ninguwepetawaub	I will desire to be able to come seeing.

SUBJUNCTIVE MOOD.

PRESENT TENSE.

Singular.	*Plural.*
1. Waubiyaun.........If I see.	1. Waubiyaung..If we see, exclusive of the party addressed.
	1. Waubiyung...If we see, inclusive of the party addressed.
2. Waubiyun ....If thou seest.	2. Waubiyag ...If you see.
3. Waubit ....If he see.	3. Waubiwaud...If they see.
4. Waubinit...........If him or his see.	4. Waubinit......If them or theirs see.

Chiwaubiyaun	That I may see.
Wewaubiyaun	If I wish to see.
Piwaubiyaun	If I come seeing.
Kauwaubiyaun	When I had seen.
Chiwewaubiyaun	That I may desire to see.
Chipewaubiyaun	That I may come seeing.
Chitawaubiyaun	That I may be able to see.
Chiwetawaubiyaun	That I may desire to be able to see.

PASSIVE VERBS.

1. Niwaubumigoo .....I am seen.	1. Niwaubumigoomin ......We are seen, exclusive of the party addressed
	1. Kiwaubumigoomin ......We are seen, inclusive of the party addressed.
2. Kiwaubumigoo......Thou art seen.	2. Kiwaububigoom .....You are seen.
3. Waubumau ....He is seen.	3. Waubumauwug ......They are seen.
4. Waubumimaun......Him or his is seen.	4. Waubumimaun......Them or theirs are seen.

SUBJUNCTIVE MOOD.

1. Waubumigooyaun	If I am seen.
2. Waubumigooyun	If thou art seen.
3. Waubumint	If he is seen.
4. Waubumimint	If him or his is seen.

(&c.)

Ni wewaubumigos	I am desirous of being seen.
	I show myself.

(&c.)

Niwaubumigoowiz	I am providentially, fortunately, or luckily seen.

(&c.)

Niwaubumawiz	The same as above.
Niwaubikauz	I pretend to see.
Okimaukauzo	He pretends to be a chief.
Niwaubundis	I see myself.
Niwaubuntimin	We see each other.
Niwaubunjiga	I see, I look on.
Niwaubuntumau	I see, it is not dark.

TRANSITIVE VERBS.

Singular.	*Plural, transitive object.*
Niwaubumau ......I see him.	Niwaubumaug............I see them.
Niwaubiau ....I cause him to see.	Niwaubiaug...............I cause them
Niwaubunduau.....Icause him to see it.	to see.
Niwaubundumowau ......I see it with or for him.	

INVERSE TRANSITION.

1. Niwaubumik	He sees me, or rather him sees I.
2. Kiwaubumik	He sees thee.
3. Owaubumigoon	He sees him, or him sees he.
4. Owaubumigoni	This form implies the return action from a second transitive object to which the first objective case is nominative, thus—

3   4   5`
He   Him

	3 4
Owaubumaun	He sees him
Omaubumaune	4 Him sees. No. 5.

•

The form above is the inverse or return action from No. 5 to 4. To attempt to express these inflections by using English pronouns, obscures instead of elucidating the subject.

Niwaubumigoog	They see me.
Niwiwaubiigoog	They cause me to see.
Niwaubunduigoog	They cause me to see it.
Niwaubundumaugoog...................	They see it with or for me.

TRANSITIVE OBJECT INANIMATE.

Niwaubundaun	I see it.
Niwaubundaunun	I see them.
Niwaubumigon	It sees me.
Niwetookaugon	It assists me.
Ninoojimoigon...........................	It cures me as a medicine.
Ninoojimoigowaun	His medicine cures me.
Nimetookaugowaun	They assist me.

I have given the most important forms of conjugation. The inflections arising from one root amount to many millions. This language has more moods of time than the Greek, and more pronouns and forms of conjugation than any other known language.

Thos. Hurlbert.

None of the North American Indians, when first visited by Europeans, had any written language; consequently, they were entirely destitute of anything like literature, Some years ago, a Cherokee Indian, named George Guess, invented an alphabet for that language, which has been adopted by the nation. The following is an account of this singular fact:—

"The Cherokees," said John Ridge, in his late speech, "are the only modern nation who can claim the honour of having invented an alphabet. George Guess, a Cherokee Indian, who did not understand a single letter within a few

years, had invented an alphabet in which a newspaper is
published in the Cherokee nation, and their children taught
to read and write.   He was a poor man, living in a retired
part of the nation, and he told the head men one day that
he could make a book.   The chiefs replied it was impossible, because, they said, the Great Spirit at first made a
red and a white boy ; to the red boy he gave a book, and
to the white boy a bow and arrow, but the white boy came
round the red boy, stole his book, and went off, leaving
him the bow and arrow, and therefore an Indian could not
make a book.   But George Guess thought he could.   He
shut himself up to study ; his corn was left to weeds, and
he was pronounced a crazy man by the tribe.—His wife
thought so too, and burnt up his manuscripts whenever
she could find them.   But he persevered.   He first
attempted to form a character for every word in the Cherokee language, but was forced to abandon it.   He then set
about discovering the number of sounds in the language,
which he found to be sixty-eight, and for each of these he
adopted a character, which forms the alphabet, and these
characters combined like letters form words.   Having
accomplished this he called together six of his neighbours,
and said, 'Now I can make a book.'   They did not believe
him.   To convince them, he asked each to make a speech,
which he wrote down as they spoke, and then read to
them, so that each one knew his own speech, and they then
acknowledged he could make a book, and from this inven-
tion of this great man, the Cherokees have become a
reading people."

With regard to the Ojebway language, I was the first
person who attempted to reduce it to a written form ; and,
in so doing, I made use of the Roman characters.   I first
translated the Lord's Prayer, the Apostles' Creed, and the

Ten Commandments. After this I wrote a small spelling-book, and then translated a few of Wesley's and Watts' hymns, with the following portions of Holy Scripture :— Genesis, Matthew, and John. In these I was assisted by my brother Mr. John Jones, and others.

Dr. James and John Tanner have translated the whole of the New Testament into the Ojebway; but, owing to an imperfect knowledge of the language, I regret to say they have not given correct translations.

The Rev. S. Hall, and George Copway, Indian missionary, have translated the Gospel of St. Luke. In the year 1851 I translated additional hymns for the use of our missions. The late Rev. James Evans, and George Henry, Indian, also translated a number of hymns, which have been printed by the Canada Missionary Society. There are a few other minor translations which have been printed. A translation of the Lord's Prayer, in Ojebway, may interest some of my readers.

| Noo-se-non | ish-pe-ming-a-yah-yan ; | tuh-ge-che-e-nain-dah-gwud |
| Our Father | in heaven who art ; | supremely adored |

| ke-de-zhe-ne-kah-ze-win. | Ke-doo-ge-mah-we-win tuh-be-tuh-give-she-noo-muh- |
| be thy name. | Thy kingdom let it come. |

| gud. A-nain-duh-mun o-mah uh-keeng tuh-e-zhe-che-gaim, te-be-shkoo go |
| Thy will here on earth let it be done, as it |

| n-zhe-uh-yog e-we-de ish-pe-ming. Meen-zhe-she-nom noong-com kee-zhe-guk |
| is yonder in heaven. Give us this day |

| ka-o-buh-qua-zhe-gun-e-me-yong. Kuh-ya wa-be-nuh-muh-we-she-nom e-newh |
| that which will be our bread. And forgive us |

| nim-bah-tah-e-zhe-wa-be-ze-we-ne-nah-nin, a-zhe ko wa-be-nuh-muh-wung- |
| our sins, as we forgive |

| e-dwah e-gewh ma-je-doo-duh-we-yuh-min-ge-jig. Ka-go ween kuh-ya |
| them who have done us evil. Do not (and) |

| uh-ne-e-zhe-we-zhe-she-kong-ain e-mah zhoo-be-ze-win-ing ; mah-noo suh |
| lead us into temptation ; but do |

go   ke-de-skee-we-ne-she-nem.   Keen mah ween   ke-de-bain-don   ewh

thou   deliver us from evil.   For thine is   the

o-ge-mah-we-win,   kuh-ya   ewh   kuh-shke-a-we-ze-win,   kuh-ya   ewh

   kingdom,   and   the   power   and   the

pe-she-gain-dah-go-ze-win,   kah-ge-nig   kuh-ya   kah-ge-nig.

     glory,   for ever   and   for ever.   Amen.

The Mohawk Indians have had portions of the Word of God in their language for many years, such as the Gospels of Mark and John, and a few chapters in Genesis, with some Psalms in metre; also portions of the Church of England service. St. Mark was translated by Captain Joseph Brant, and St. John by Major John Norton.

It cannot be expected that any of these are perfect. After more mature experience and knowledge, I see many defects in my own translations. I have, however, this satisfaction, that I did my best, and I am happy to say that the errors are not of vital importance; but, were I to revise them, many improvements could be made both in translation and orthography. It is my opinion that if it be desirable to form a written standard of the language, new characters should be invented, something like the Cherokee.

Some years ago the Rev. J. Evans and Rev. T. Hurlbert commenced a syllabic character for the Ojebway, which they have since applied to the Cree language at Hudson's Bay, and I am informed that it is well adapted for that language, being both easy and simple. All that the Indian has to do is to learn the characters, and when he has done so he can read and write the language.

CHAPTER XVII.

Indians' Desire and Capacity to Receive Instruction—Illustrations—Indian Eloquence, Wit, and Shrewdness.

As "facts are stubborn things," the best method of establishing our position is, to relate facts. Those who read the statement of them will be able to decide, whether the Indian has not the same capacity to learn as the white man. All that is wanting is, the proper means of instruction. William Wilson, an Indian youth of superior abilities, was sent to Cobourg College, and whilst there, stood at the head of the first-class. He made rapid progress in the classics, and wrote poetry with great ease. On leaving College, he went to New York, where he was seized with small-pox, which terminated fatally.

The following respecting him is taken from the *Christian Guardian*, dated *May* 23rd, 1838 :—

" INDIAN IMPROVEMENT.

" On our first page will be found an original poem, on 'England and British America.' The author, William Wilson, is an Indian youth, whose educational opportunities have been exceedingly limited, but whose praiseworthy assiduity is as creditable to him and to his too much despised countrymen, as it is gratifying to his friends and instructors. The poem is far from being faultless, but we hazard nothing in saying that it exhibits an incipient genius which deserves cultivation, and which, under due religious influence, may yet be of essential service to a people who are nobly desirous to emerge from the barbarism and wretchedness in which they have long been enveloped."

ENGLAND AND BRITISH AMERICA.

BABEL ! whose primal empire erst did rise
In peerless pomp 'neath fair and fervid skies,
Where now thy lofty tower, whose summit proud
Attempted heav'n, and pierc'd the ambient cloud ?
Assyria where ? against whose vices bold
The prophet's ire in dread denouncement told,—
Along whose streets betimes his warnings swept,
And o'er her doom in plaintive accents wept,—
Till, loudly echoing, flash'd the bolts of heav'n,
Launch'd by Jehovah's arm in thunder giv'n,
And dire revenge from giant slumber burst,
Hurling her smitten fabrics to the dust !
Where Carthage now ? against whose rival coast
Triumphant Rome led forth her conquering host,
Ere warring Scipio bends her prostrate walls,
And Romans shout exulting as she falls !
Where do the myriad spires of Egypt gleam
Along the banks of Nile's extended stream,—
Rearing aloft her monumental pyre,
Whose cloudy top would fain to heaven aspire ?
And where her halls by learned Magi grac'd,
Whose gifted minds the path of science trac'd ?
Where too her sceptred kings that proudly shone
In pomp barbaric on th' empurpled throne,
Commanding nations far, by stern decree,
In adoration low to bend the knee ?
And Greece ! oh where that mighty empire now
That bade the Perse with trembling homage bow ?
Bright clime of that immortal bard, whose name
With deathless hues shall live in brightest fame,
Who tun'd his hallow'd harp, all wild and free,
To rapturous strains of heav'nly harmony,—
Of him whose thunder did the forum shake,
And made the throne of haughty Philip quake,
While rude Oppression from his seat was hurl'd
And Freedom's banner o'er his corse unfurl'd !

Where now her classic field, her sylvan grove,
Made vocal with the muses' lays of love ?
Arcadia where, where sacred Science dwelt,
At whose fair shrine exalted sages knelt ?
Alas ! the lamp that brightly shone of yore
On her its light effulgent sheds no more ;
No more with her doth Genius rear his throne,
And fondly view a realm from zone to zone :
For lo ! her sons by Moslem tyrants fall,
And slavish chains their captive minds enthrall.
Where is the mighty Alexander now,
Who fought the world to deck ambition's brow,
Who dar'd in arms to match all-conquering Jove,
And boldly spurn the laws of Heaven above ?
Rolling his chariot fierce to realms afar,
And with rebellious arms wag'd dastard war ;
While nations wild with consternation stare,
And groans of slaughter'd millions fill the air ;
Until he made, by more than mortal skill,
A fated world obsequious to his will.
Th' Eternal City where, imperial Rome,
Whose standard proudly wav'd o'er realms unknown,
And through the earth her battling legions bore,
To glut their madden'd ranks with human gore ?
Where now those rock-built tow'rs that darkly frown'd
In mystic awe o'er Tiber's stream profound,
And rear'd their impious heads in height sublime,
Scowling defiance 'gainst the blasts of time ?

To this bless'd land I turn from Empires' fall,
O'er which stern fate has stretch'd oblivion's pall, —
Have fled like ocean's spray before his nod,
That dar'd the brunt of his relentless rod.
Here would the muse kneel at Apollo's shrine,
In votive strains t' invoke the tuneful Nine,
Perchance t' imbibe alike th' enlivening fire
Of him who did the early bards inspire.
But Britain first behold, that " sea-girt isle,"
With pow'r and wealth as boundless as the Nile,
With genius, learning, art, and science bless'd,
And reason's nobler ray at her behest ;
Her sons, the first in glory's hallow'd field,
The last in battle's darker hour to yield,

O

Behold, in firm recluse from tyrants' shock,
Around the standard of their country flock,—
A formidable front to despots show,
While to the field they dare the angry foe :
Contentment, peace, and good their steps attend,
Their sacred hearths from ruthless vice defend ;
To them each genial year its charms renews,
The fruitful earth their thousand wants pursues ;
For them wing'd commerce wafts from distant climes
The treasures of their land and richest mines ;
Harmonious laws their kindred hearts unite,
And wisdom's ways their nobler thoughts delight.
Behold her red-cross flag unfurling far,
Victorious Wellington directs her car ;
Triumphant too at Waterloo he rode,
Beneath its wheels the vain tricolor trode,—
Inglorious bade the proud usurper bow,
And own his conqu'ring arm in suppliance low.
Behold, 'midst yonder deep and princely hall,
Where godlike Justice sits in awful pall,
Where Freedom's matchless champions mutual join
To shield the laws, and for their rights combine,
Immortal Pitt with conscious boldness rise ;
Destructive lightning flashes from his eyes ;
Now threat'ning vengeance sits upon his brow,
His glowing cheeks bespeak his fervour now ;
Through all his frame th' inspiring god is seen,
And all his pow'rs with mingled terror gleam.
Hark ! through the long-drawn aisle his voice resounds,
And dreadly now re-echo back the sounds ;
Like when th' Olympian sire in thunder pours
His vengeful wrath, and arrowy tempests showers :
On schemes corrupt he wreaks his fell desire,
And fiercely vents his all-devouring ire,
While round the pompous heads of tyrant kings
Aloud his dread denunciation rings,—
In thunder loud his vengeance flings retort,
While heaven and earth revere the dread report.
Before his voice now brazen discord shrinks,
Now lordly guilt in meek submission sinks ;
Insatiate ease now startles from his couch,
In frantic terror factious minions crouch :

The sable sons of Afric gladly hear
His welcome voice, and lend a list'ning ear ;
He bids the captive slave from bondage flee—
He fondly sets the iron-bound pris'ner free.
Amid the crowd of patriots, heroes, view,
That grace proud Albion's clime with bright halo,
The train of star-eyed Science' devotees,
Who to her altar bow with suppliant knees.
On learning's pinions proud they take their way,
And through the maze of latent myst'ries stray ;
Far as imagination's piercing ken
With philosophic eye their flight they wend ;
Stay with firm hand the planets in their course,
Direct the pathless comet, trace its source.
Chief to her bards is due the meed of praise,
Though feebly giv'n in low discordant lays :
High on Parnassus' cliffs they glorious stand,
They strike the lyre with more than mortal hand ;
Melodious sounds retreat on heav'nly wings,
As sweet the muse in pensive sorrow sings,
And o'er romantic vales and distant plains
In fitful echoes die the mystic strains.
But first enroll'd on list of genius' throng,
Who scal'd the proudest heights of lofty song,
With dazzling rays, as shines the morning star,
Her Milton stands on fame's dread mount afar,
And gently beckons the aspiring muse,
As o'er his soul his sacred beams diffuse.

The clime of Canada in fondness gleams,
And western wilds awake more pleasing themes :
From where the eagle gluts his hungry beak
On Labrador's far coast of barren peak,
To where the Rocky Mountains sternly rise,
O'erlook the land, and half invade the skies,
Its fair and undulating soil extends,
And to the eye its bright enchantment lends.
Here Nature's God in matchless splendour rears
His living fane, and in wild pomp appears.
Here placid lakes like molten silver beam,
The full-orb'd sun reflects the glassy stream,—

o 2

Alluvial mountains lift their verdant heads,
And on the prairies prone their influence spreads.
Here fertile vales their rich luxuriance show,
Where nature's works in loveliest beauty glow ;
From whose retreats, or sounds the woodman's hymn,
Far from the bustling throng of madd'ning din,
Or 'mid their haunts aërial spirits stray,
While to the breeze they chaunt their roundelay.
Here cataracts vast the echoing forests wake,
And all the ground with quick vibrations shake ;
Where dread Niagara in thunder roars,
As o'er the rocky steep his deluge pours,—
Along whose banks the lonely Indian wound,
And in the scene his kindred spirit found.
Here boundless plains in fragrant verdure stretch,
Bright landscapes there invite the artist's sketch ;
Here forests dark their stately branches wave,
And rivers there in solemn silence lave.
But though this land with ev'ry good is crown'd,
And choicest gifts on ev'ry hand surround,—
Though Nature here has wrought her grandest plan,
Yet does the mind deplore the fate of man.
Those lordly tribes that lin'd these mighty lakes
Have fled, and disappear'd like wintry flakes.   .
Lo ! on the mountain-tops their fires are out,
In blithesome vales all silent is their shout ;
A solemn voice is heard from ev'ry shore,
That now the Indian nations are no more,—
A remnant scarce remain to tell their wrongs,
But soon will fade to live in poets' songs.

    Hail to thee, Canada ! the brightest gem
That decks Victoria's brilliant diadem ;
Thine is the happy seat, the blissful clime
Where art and nature form one vast sublime ;
Where temp'rate skies effuse their golden rays,
The fertile land the labourer's toil repays;
Plenty and peace at ev'ry footstep smile,
And sunny scenes to gentler thoughts beguile.
A voice is heard upon thy mighty floods,
A voice resounds throughout thy trackless woods,—
Heard in the plaintive rill and cataract's roar,
Heard in the whisp'ring breeze on ev'ry shore :

Tis Freedom's voice ; 'tis on thy rivers roll'd,
That in their course the sacred theme have told,
And bid the dwellers on the mountains swell
The choral strain, and wake the joyful knell, —
Till all mankind shall hear the gladd'ning sound,
Rouse from the trammel yoke of sleep profound,
And o'er the earth Britannia's banner wave,
Each foeman crush'd—unshackled ev'ry slave.

THE BIRCH BARK ALPHABET.

About the year 1827 I made a missionary tour to Lake Simcoe, Mahjedushk, Sahgeeng, St. Clair, and Muncey Town. At Sahgeeng the Indians received the Gospel very gladly. On departing, we left one of our party, (Keche-jeemon,) to labour among them. He continued to tell them all he knew about the Christian religion. One day some of the young people inquired if he could not teach them to read in the white man's book. Keche-jeemon told them he could not read himself; all he knew was a, b, c. They then said, "Teach us a, b, c." The next difficulty was, he had no book containing the alphabet. At length, he thought of making the letters on *birch bark ;* so he went into the woods, got the bark, and then with charcoal formed the letters a, b, c. When the missionary went to establish the mission in that region, he found all the young people knew the a, b, c.

An Indian lad, named Joseph Quenchenau, belonging to the Credit tribe, showed great love for his books, and was very punctual and attentive at school. But best of all, he loved his Saviour, and regularly, night and morning, offered up his private prayer to God. In the twelfth year of his age he was taken ill,' when he committed himself into the hands of his Maker, saying he was not afraid to die, for he knew God would take him to heaven. After he was dead, his friends placed all his books, consisting of his Bible, Indian hymn-book, and spelling-book, on the top of his coffin, because he had loved them so much. I was very sorry to lose such a promising boy from our little society ; but God saw best to take him, and therefore we must bow to His sovereign will.

THE MORMON BOOK AND AN INDIAN.

Soon after the conversion of the Indians on the Bay of Quinty, as a converted Indian was passing through the white settlement, he heard preaching in a school-house, and, being anxious to learn more about the words of the Great Spirit, he turned in, and took his seat near the door. He listened ; but, instead of hearing about the good old Bible, the preacher was extolling another book he called the Mormon Bible, which he said was much better and plainer than the old one. He then entered into an explanation as to its origin, telling how Joe Smith had dug it up out of the ground, and was inspired to translate it. When the preacher had finished his discourse, he gave permission for any of the congregation to say what they thought of the things they had heard. All sat still, and, as no white man was found to speak for the good old Bible, the Indian at length rose up and said, " May Indian speak ?" The Mormon preacher replied, "Yes, Indian may speak." The Indian then said, " A great many winters ago, the Great Spirit gave his good book Bible to the white man, over the great waters. He took it, and read it, and it make his heart all over very glad. By-and-bye, white man come over to this country, and brought the good book with him. He gave it to poor Indian. He hear it, and understand it, and it make his heart very glad too. But when the Great Spirit gave his good book to white man, the evil spirit

Muhje-munedoo try to make one too, and he try to make it like the one the Good Spirit made, but he could not; and then he got so ashamed of it, he go into the woods, dig a hole in the ground, and then he hide his book. After lying there many winters, Joe Smith go and dig it up. This is the book this preacher has been talking about. I hold fast on the good old Bible, which has made my heart so happy. I have nothing to do with the devil's book."

CAPTAIN JOHN AND HIS BIBLE.

Captain John, or Wageezhegome, was one of the most intelligent chiefs of the Credit tribe. In his early days he went for a short time to school, and learnt to read a little in English; but afterwards, mingling in Indian life, he soon forgot all he had learnt at school. Some time before his conversion Mrs. Small, of Toronto, made him a present of a Bible, which he kept for her sake. Soon after the work of God commenced on the Grand River, Captain John went up there, where he was made a partaker of the grace of God. He no sooner found the Lord than he began to learn to read the Bible the lady had given him, and by perseverance was soon able to understand its contents, so as to become a teacher of righteousness to his people. He made one or two visits to the Credit at his own expense, for the express purpose of inviting his people up to the Grand River, to hear for themselves the wonderful things of God; and I am happy to state that his labours were not in vain. After adorning the Gospel of our Saviour a few years, he died, praising God, and exhorting his people to cleave to Him with all their hearts.

In John Sunday we have a remarkable instance of the capability of an Indian to receive instruction. John was about thirty years old when he was converted from the depths of Paganism to the knowledge of the true God. In a letter lately received from him he writes :—" It took me only half an hour to learn the alphabet, and it was not many months after I began to read a little. The first word that I spelled was b, a, g, bag, and by-and-bye I knew the word G, o, d, and I thought I learned a great thing then, and at last I began to read, but when I began to write it was very difficult to me. When I try to make a straight mark I make a mink,* and after a while I began to write."

The late Bishop Hedding mentions the following fact as coming under his own observation when on a visit to the River Credit Mission, C.W., in 1827 :—" I saw among these nations an Indian, named John Crane, who could read quite well, especially in the New Testament. He said, and others confirmed it, that he did not know his letters. I found, on inquiry, that he had been so anxious to learn to read that he carried a New Testament with him constantly, and asked every boy or girl he met with what was the name of any particular word he would point out. Thus, he learned the word by its shape, just as a child learns the name of a chair, a spoon, or a hat, before it learns its letters."

Extract of a Letter to PETER JONES, *from an Indian Youth desiring more instruction.*

" I am wishing to come to your school, Muncey Town, if possible. I have been to school here, Wesleyan Seminary, Albion, but my time will be out next spring. My people are very poor, and have not the means to assist me. I belong to the Chippewa tribe. Half of us are in

---

* Mink was the *toodaim*, or tribe, to which he belonged, the representation of which he made as a signature.

Canada, and the remainder, to whom I belong, are in
Michigan. I wish to know if you could assist me to come
to school, as it would enable me to instruct our ignorant
brethren. I wish to have a little more instruction in the
English language. I know you can assist me anywhere to
go in your schools. I would endeavour to make it a lasting
benefit to our poor people, by teaching them the way of
life. Please send an answer.

" Yours truly,

"JOSEPH RUCKY,

" *Alias* O-SHE-NAH-WA-GE-SHIEK."

" *January 8th,* 1852.

" To Rev. PETER JONES."

Extract of a Letter from the Rev. MATTHEW RICHEY, M.A.,
dated March 20th, 1845.

" Our missionary meeting at Hamilton took place on
Wednesday evening, the 29th. John Sunday was particularly happy in his address at this meeting, and, towards the
close, thrilled and astonished all present by the ingenuity
and power of his appeals. I wish I were able to present
you with a correct report of his entire speech. Connecting
with the perusal of it your vivid recollection of his mental
idiosyncrasy,—never so fully developed as when he becomes
animated on a missionary platform,—I am sure you would
be delighted above measure. His closing words I can give
you with substantial—I think I may say, with verbal—
accuracy; and they are too good to be suppressed. ' There
is a gentleman,' said Shawandais,—' There is a gentleman,
I suppose, now in this house; he is a very *fine* gentleman,
but he is very *modest.* He does not like to show himself.
I do not know how long it is now since I saw him, he
comes out so little. I very much afraid he sleeps a great

deal of his time, when he ought to be going about doing good. His name is *Mr. Gold.* Mr. Gold, are you here to-night? or are you sleeping in your iron chest? Come out, Mr. Gold! Come out, and help us to do this great work, to preach the gospel to every creature! Ah, Mr. Gold, you ought to be ashamed of yourself, to sleep so much in your iron chest! Look at your white brother, *Mr. Silver.* He does a great deal of good in the world while you are sleeping. Come out, Mr. Gold! Look, too, at your *little* brown brother, *Master Copper. He everywhere!* Your little brother running about all the time, doing all *he* can. Why don't you come? *Come out,* Mr. Gold! Well, if you *won't* come out, and give us *yourself,* send us your shirt, that is, a *Bank Note.*'"

At a meeting of the Canada Conference Missionary Society, at which Bishop Hedding was present, one of the speakers narrated the following incidents, with a view to show the eagerness with which the natives receive instruction:—

"An Indian chief, residing in the neighbourhood of 'Lake Simcoe, came to solicit missionary aid. After unfolding their needy state, he observed that they did not wish the labours of the missionary for nothing. They would hunt deer, beaver, &c., and each one would lay aside some skins, and appropriate the avails of them to the support of the mission. As a demonstration of this generous disposition, and of their ardent desire to have their children instructed, the women stripped themselves of their nose and ear jewels, brooches, and breastplates, which had been given them by Government, and sent them to the missionary to purchase books for the school; and these were exhibited on the occasion, as an evidence of their devotion to this sacred cause."

We give only another proof of their general mental capacity, in their talent for music in particular. A book of Indian melodies, by Thomas Commuck, a Narragansett Indian, was published in New York, in 1845. The tunes in this little book are named after noted Indian chiefs, Indian names of places, &c., &c. The author remarks: "This has been done as a tribute of respect to the memory of some tribes who are now nearly, if not quite, extinct; also as a mark of courtesy to some with whom he is acquainted." The book contains 120 new tunes.

The Rev. G. Cole, who is regarded as naturally and scientifically a good judge, thus speaks of it:—" In the first strain of the first tune there is something worthy of Handel, and in the whole there is something equal to anything we ever saw in the productions of Haydn. In the next, there is something strikingly original. The third, as sweet as the gentle flowings of Kedron. The fourth, rather tame, but suited to a solemn train of thought. The fifth is bold, rich, and joyous. The sixth is in the style of Leach's 'Watchman, S.M.,' but greatly superior. The hearer, when he hears a good tune, thinks that he could make as good an one himself. We have tried this principle with regard to the tunes before us several times, and in every case our auditor has shown, by unequivocal signs, that he felt as if he could do the like himself, if he only had the ability."

SPECIMENS OF INDIAN ELOQUENCE, WIT, AND SHREWDNESS.

At the negotiation for peace, in 1774, after the Battle of the Kanhawa, the great " Mingo chief," Logan, refused to appear at the council. He was in favour of peace, but his proud spirit scorned to ask for it; and he remained in his cabin, brooding in melancholy silence over his own wrongs.

Of so much importance was his name considered by Lord Dunmore, that a special messenger was despatched to ascertain whether he would accede to the articles of peace. This conference took place in a solitary wood, and, at its close, he charged him with the celebrated speech to Lord Dunmore, which has become familiar wherever the English language is spoken.*

"I appeal to any white man to say if he ever entered Logan's cabin hungry, and he gave him not meat; if ever he came cold and naked, and he clothed him not. During the course of the last long and bloody war Logan remained idle in his cabin, an advocate for peace. Such was my love for the whites, that my countrymen pointed, as they passed, and said, 'Logan is the friend of the white man.' I had even thought to have lived with you, but for the injuries of one man. Colonel Cresass, the last spring, in cold blood and unprovoked, murdered all the relations of Logan, not even sparing my women and children. There runs not a drop of my blood in the veins of any living creature. This called on me for vengeance. I have sought it; I have killed many; I have fully glutted my vengeance. For my country, I rejoice at the beams of peace; but do not harbour the thought that mine is the joy of fear. Logan never felt fear. He will not turn on his heel to save his life. Who is there to mourn for Logan? Not one!"

WIT AND SHREWDNESS.

It is related that two chiefs came from the far West to the city of Washington, on business with the government. While they were there, a gentleman invited them to dinner. They went,—and being seated for the first time at a white man's table, they began to eat such things as were set before

* Life of Brant.

them, and to help themselves to such as were within their reach. One of them seeing some yellow-looking stuff (mustard,) took a spoonful, swallowing the whole. Tears soon ran down his cheeks. His brother chief, seeing him weep, said, "Oh! my brother, why do you weep?" The other replied, "I am thinking about my son who was killed in such a battle!" Presently the other chief took a spoonful of the same stuff, which caused his eyes to weep as did his brother's; who in return asked him, "Why do you cry?" Upon which he replied, "Oh! I weep to think you were not killed when your son was."

Once the Rev. W. Case took John Sunday with him to visit the United States, for the purpose of raising funds for the Canadian Missions. John one day received an invitation to dine with a minister. At table this good man was talking to John about religion, feeling truly thankful to see a converted Indian. Among other eatables before him was a dish of finely-scraped horseradish: John, not knowing what it was, and supposing it might be something very sweet, took a spoonful of it into his mouth; presently tears came into his eyes; the minister observing them, and supposing John was weeping for joy at what was the topic of discourse, began to shout, "Glory! glory! glory!" John, as soon as he could, raised his hand, and pointing to the dish of horse-radish, said, "O, it is that,—it is that!"

From this anecdote we may see that tears are not always to be depended upon; and also the difference between a pagan and a Christian Indian's veracity.

A hunting Indian one day called at a farm-house for some food. The good woman of the house began asking him all sorts of questions. At length she pointed to a

shaking aspen tree, and asked the Indian, " What do you
call that ?" He replied, " Me call it woman's tongue."
" Why do you call it woman's tongue?" was the next
question. The Indian then said, " You see those leaves
always shaking, never stand still; so me call it woman's
tongue."

An Indian and a white man agreed to hunt in partner-
ship. At the end of three days they were to divide equally
what they had killed. The white man killed a *buzzard*,
and the Indian a *turkey*. The white man then said, " It
would be a pity to cut the birds in two, therefore you may
take the buzzard and I will take the turkey ; or else I will
take the turkey and you may take the buzzard." The
Indian replied, " You say white man take turkey twice, you
no say Indian take turkey once."

In J. Long's travels the following story is related :—" An
old American savage, being at an inn at New York, met
with a gentleman who gave him some liquor, and, being
rather lively, boasted he could read and write English.
The gentleman willing to indulge him in displaying his
knowledge, begged leave to propose a question, to which
the old man consented. He was then asked who was the
first circumcised ?—the Indian immediately replied, ' Father
Abraham'—and directly asked the gentleman who was the
first Quaker ? He said it was very uncertain,—that people
differed in their sentiments exceedingly. The Indian
perceiving the gentleman unable to solve the question,
put his fingers into his mouth, to express his surprise, and
looking steadfastly, told him that Mordecai was the first
Quaker, for he would not pull off his hat to Haman."

CHAPTER XVIII.

OPINION OF THE INDIANS RESPECTING THE SOVEREIGN AND PEOPLE OF GREAT BRITAIN.

Patriotism—Re-interment of Captain Brant—Enjoy no Political Rights—
Considered by the Colonial Government as Children—Opinion as to their
capability to use their rights as British Subjects—Opinions of the
Americans ; of the Negroes—Letter from an Indian in Paris—P. Jones's
impression of England and English customs on his first visit.

THE ideas entertained by the Indians generally of the
King of England, with regard to his power, riches, and
knowledge, are most extravagant. They imagine his power
to be absolute, and his authority unlimited ; that his word
is law, to which all his subjects bow with implicit obedience ; that his wigwam is the largest in the world, and
decorated with the most gorgeous trappings ; that he sits
upon his throne, clothed in robes of many colours, surrounded by his officers of state ; and that heralds are
always in attendance, to proclaim his mandates to the
people from day to day.

They also consider that his riches and benevolence are
unbounded, the whole resources of the kingdom being at his
command, a portion of which he grants to those of his subjects who are needy. With regard to his wisdom, they
conceive that he knows everything that is going on in the
world ; that even the speech or talk of an Indian chief
delivered to a Superintendent of Indian Affairs in the wilds
of Canada is made known to him.

On the eve of my visiting England in the year 1831,

Chief Yellowhead of Lake Simcoe came to me, and said, " I shake hands with our Great Father over the great waters ; when you see him tell him my name ; he will know who I am, as he has often heard of me through our fathers the governors and Indian agents, who have sent my messages to him. Tell him I am still alive." This chief delivered his talk with the utmost gravity and sincerity, and with the fullest assurance that the king knew all about the great chief Yellowhead. In short, the simple-minded Indians believe that the whole management of public affairs devolves upon the Sovereign, and that everything is done under his supervision and with his cognizance.

They designate a king *Ningeche Noosenon*, that is, " Our Great Father ;" and a Queen *Ningahnon*, " Our Great Mother." A noted chief at Walpool Island, on the river St. Clair, by the name of *Pashegeezheywashkum*,—the meaning of which is " he who makes footsteps in the sky,"—once delivered a speech to me in which he had occasion to mention the king of England and the President of the United States. The former he styled " Our Great Father," and the latter " Our *Step-father*." This was the first time I had ever heard the Great Chief of the *Keche Mookomon*, or *Big Knives*, called *Step-father*. This chief had formerly resided in the United States ; but, having stepped over the boundary line, he transferred the " great" to the King of England, and left only his " *step*" on his former father.

It has been well said by a certain writer,* that the attachment of the red men of the forest to the British Government and people borders on veneration : there are none in their estimation equal to them for wisdom, power, and benevolence. They have the highest opinion of the prowess of the British soldiery, whom they designate *Maskokonahyad*, or *red coats*.

* Sir F. B. Head.

Mohawk Church Grand River, U.C. The oldest Episcopal Church in Canada Here Peter Jones was baptized.

In the American Revolution, the greater portion of the famous Six Nations of Indians, with other tribes, took up the tomahawk in behalf of Great Britain ; and by so doing lost their beautiful and rich country on the Mohawk River. During the war of 1812 between England and America, all the Indians in Canada, and many of the western tribes, rallied round the British standard; and it is generally believed, that had it not been for their efficient and timely aid, Canada would have been wrested from the crown of Great Britain. It is also well known that during the late rebellion in Canada, the Indians were not slow in assisting to suppress the insurrection. In these wars many of our fathers fell and mingled their blood with the brave sons of Britain, whose bones now lie side by side.

I mention these facts to shew the devotion of the Indian tribes to the Sovereign of Great Britain. As a further manifestation of their patriotic feelings it may be interesting to mention the noble manner in which they came forward and subscribed to the rebuilding of General Brock's Monument, after it had been destroyed by some unprincipled wretch. The following speeches, selected from many that accompanied the donations of the chiefs, will show their loyalty as British subjects.*

Another illustration of the devotion of the Indians to the British Government, is furnished by the account of the re-interment of Brant, taken from the *Brantford Herald* of November 27th, 1850 :—

" On Monday last the remains of Thayendenegea, which had been previously exhumed, were placed in the tomb at the Mohawk that had recently been prepared for their reception. This was done with no small degree of pageantry. The vast multitude of people who had as-

* See Appendix N.

sembled from different quarters, went in procession from the town of Brantford to the Mohawk village. . . . .
" Addresses were delivered by the Rev. A. Nelles, Rev. P. Jones, Sir A. McNab, D. Thorburn, Esq., and others; among whom was an American gentleman whose father had, many years ago, been most generously treated by Brant. After the speaking was concluded, the interment took place, when three volleys were fired over the grave of the brave and faithful Indian soldier, Captain Joseph Brant." . . . .

The following speech, delivered on the occasion by Kahkewaquonaby (the Rev. Peter Jones), and published at the time by request, is here subjoined :—

An Address delivered on the occasion of the re-interment of the celebrated CAPTAIN JOSEPH BRANT, *by* KAHKEWA-QUONABY (*Rev.* PETER JONES), *Chief and Missionary.*

"MY CHRISTIAN FRIENDS.—In offering a few remarks on the occasion for which we are this day assembled, I may be allowed, in the first place, to express my own personal interest in the history of him whose bones we are now about to re-commit to their resting-place. This deep interest arises from the fact that my late father, Augustus Jones, and Joseph Brant, maintained the closest friendship to the day of Brant's death. By mutual consent, Brant settled at the northern extremity of the Burlington Bay beach, now called Wellington Square, and my father at the southern extremity, now called Stony Creek—the beautiful smooth beach forming a delightful natural sand-road, over which they travelled backwards and forwards in visiting and sharing each other's hospitality. At the birth of my late brother, John Jones, Brant, from his deep attachment to my father, gave his own Indian name, ' Thayendenagea,' by which name he was always known among the Indians. This second Thayendenagea afterwards became the husband of one of Brant's grandaughters, whose name was Christiana Brant, daughter of the late Jacob Brant. I would also state, that on the arrival of Captain Brant and his people in Canada, after the loss of their territory in the United States, they applied to my own people, the Messissaugas or Chippeways of the river Credit (of whom I am one of their chiefs) to purchase a portion of their lands. Our people replied in council :—

" ' Brethren—The whole country is before you, choose you a tract for yourselves, and there build your wigwams and plant your corn.'

" The Six Nations then selected this splendid Grand River tract, which they said was very much like the country on the Mohawk river in the State of New York, which they had lost. They offered pay to our nation, but the Chippeways would not take any. From this time Captain Brant and his people became much attached to the Credit Indians, to whom they have lately manifested their good will in a noble manner. The Credit Indians, at their old reserve, being crowded on every side by the whites, resolved to emigrate ; and whilst they were in search of a suitable location, the Six Nations, in remembrance of the former kind and generous reception they had received from the original owners of this fine tract of country, sent a message to the Credit Indians, inviting them to come and share their reserve, and nobly made a free grant of a large tract of land in Tuscarora, where the Credit Indians are now settled. I may also be allowed to say that I feel myself *connected* with Brant's people, as I was adopted into their nation, and received the name of *Sagondensta ;* so that I may be proud of the honour you are paying to the departed

P 2

warrior and his mourning and lonely people. In regard
to the attachment of Joseph Brant to the British nation,
and his numerous exploits during the Revolutionary war, I
feel incompetent to do justice, and must leave this to
others. I would only say, that from all I can learn, his
adherence to Great Britain was strong and sincere ; and in
consequence of that attachment the Six Nations lost their
extensive fertile country, now the garden of the State of
New York. No one can dispute his bravery. In Indian
language it may be said of him as was said of the lamented
General Brock: ' His eye was like the eagle's — his
motions like arrows from the bow—his enemies fell before
him as the trees before the blast of the Great Spirit.' The
shout of victory echoed from tribe to tribe.—The tomahawk
was then buried and peace proclaimed. The loyalty of
Brant's people, the same spirit of devotion to the Crown
of England, has been deeply infused into the veins of the
Six Nations, who, during the last war, flew, with other
Indian nations, to the help of the British ; and I have
heard it stated by good judges, that had it not been for the
help of the Indians, Canada would have been wrested from
Great Britain. At a general council held at the river
Credit a few years since, the chiefs of the Six Nations
informed their Chippeway brethren that they had always
been strongly attached to the British Government, and
that if that attachment was ever lessened it would not be
their fault, but that of the Government in not keeping faith
with them. I will now make a few remarks in regard to
the religious sentiments of Joseph Brant; he was, I am
informed, a thorough-going Churchman, and entertained
high respect for the missionaries and the word of God.—
He assisted in the translation of the Gospel of St. Mark into
Mohawk, and other portions of the Holy Scriptures, as

well as the book of Common Prayer, which were printed
and distributed amongst the Christian portion of the Six
Nations, and I have every reason to believe were productive of much good. If I am rightly informed, Brant
was the principal means of the erection of this church, now
the oldest in Canada, and procured the bell which has so
often summoned the people of God together to worship in
his holy courts ; and has tolled for hundreds of those whose
bones now lie in that sacred yard. I am informed that it
tolled, when Brant died, twenty-four hours. I have been
informed, by one of his people, that after the Six Nations
had settled on this river, the Indians had a great feast, and
through the influence of the pagans, the Mohawks were
induced to assist in making and setting up a large idol at
the eastern entrance of the Mohawk Castle. Captain
Brant was absent when this took place, and on again
visiting the Grand River, and seeing this image (like
Moses, when he came down from the Mount and saw the
golden calf), his anger was kindled, and he immediately
ordered the idol to be cut down and destroyed. This
speaks loudly for the Christianity of Captain Brant, as it is
quite evident that he was jealous for the honour of Almighty
God, who, blessed be his name, is no respecter of persons,
but in every nation he that worketh righteousness is accepted of him. I am happy to learn that our white friends
have it in their hearts to erect a monument to the memory
of the Indian brave, that succeeding generations may see
and know the hero after whom the town of *Brantford* is
named. This is all I have to say."

The following correspondence is a demonstration of patriotic and sympathetic feeling which does credit to their enlightened Christianity :—

Indian Subscription to the Patriotic Fund, and the reply of Her Majesty's Government.

The Messissauga Indians of the New Credit Settlement in Tuscarora, in full council, made a grant of £25 currency, to the Patriotic Fund, and forwarded the following requisition and letter, through D. Thorburn, Esq., S.I.A., to his Excellency Sir Edmund Head :—

" NEW CREDIT, *July 7th*, 1855.

" £25.

" Required by our tribe, the sum of twenty-five pounds, currency, to be placed in the hands of our Great Father, Sir Edmund Head, as a subscription from our tribe to the Patriotic Fund in England, and the amount to be charged to our annuity of lands ceded to the Crown.

(Signed)   " JOSEPH SAWYER,⎫
                 " PETER JONES, ⎰ *Chiefs.*"

" *Witness :*—JAMES TOHECOE."

" BRANTFORD, *July 16th*, 1856.

" DEAR SIR,

" I have much pleasure in transmitting to you the enclosed requisition for £25 currency, from the Messissauga Indians of the New Credit Settlement, being the amount of their subscription towards the Patriotic Fund in England, and which is designed as an expression of their deep sympathy for the poor widows and orphans of the brave warriors of the allied armies who have fallen in the field of battle.

" I am sure it will rejoice your heart to know that your Red Indian children not only feel a great pleasure in offering their mite to the cause of humanity, but that, to my certain knowledge, they accompany their gift with their sincere and earnest prayers to Almighty God, that success may attend the armies of the allies, and speedily procure that honourable peace which may conduce to the prosperity and happiness of all nations, and thus cause the cries of the widow and orphan to be heard no more in the land. May God grant it.

" I have the honour to be,

" Dear Sir,

" Your obedient servant,

" PETER JONES, *Chief.*"

" To D. THORBURN, Esq.,

" *Supt. Indian Affairs, &c., Cayuga.*"

" INDIAN OFFICE, CAYUGA, *Sept. 22nd,* 1855.

" REV. AND DEAR SIR,

" I have this day received from the Superintendent-General a letter of the 18th instant, with a copy of a despatch from the Colonial Secretary, Sir W. Molesworth, of the 19th ultimo, acknowledging the receipt of a bill of exchange for the sum of twenty pounds three shillings and sevenpence sterling (£25 currency), as a contribution to the Patriotic Fund from your tribe, the Messissauga, which despatch you will please to make known to the tribe by command.

" I have the honour to be,

" Dear Sir,

" Yours faithfully,

" D. THORBURN, *Supt.*"

" To the Rev. PETER JONES,

" Chief, Messissauga, New Credit Indians."

(COPY:)

" Downing Street, *Aug.* 19*th*, 1855.

" Sir,

" I have to acknowledge your despatch (93) of the 26th ult., enclosing a bill of exchange for twenty pounds three shillings and sevenpence sterling, being the amount of subscription by the Messissauga Indians to the Patriotic Fund.

I request you will convey to the chief and Indians the thanks of Her Majesty's Government for this contribution, and the sense entertained by Her Majesty for the sympathy expressed on behalf of the widows and orphans of the allied armies engaged in the present contest.

      " I have, &c.,

    (Signed)   " W. Molesworth."

" *To* Gov. Sir Edmund Head, *Bart.*"

When the French first came to Canada, the Indians entered into an alliance with them; but no sooner was Canada conquered by the English, than all the Indians threw off their allegiance to the French, and gladly entered into a treaty with the British Government. This treaty, down to the present day, has not been violated. The old chiefs often mention these treaties in their councils, using at the same time a striking metaphor, in which is apparent their superior attachment to the English. They say that when the French came, they bound their hands together with an *iron chain;* but that when the English came, they broke asunder that chain, which had already become rusty, and then their great Father, the King of England, bound their hands together with a *silver chain,* which he promised should never rust and never be broken.

PRESENTED
in the Year 1832,
BY HIS MAJESTY
King William IV
TO
Ka-kiwe-quon-abi
(REVᴰ PETER JONES)
a Indian of that portion of
THE GREAT CHIPPEWAY
NATION located at the River Credit
IN UPPER CANADA

GEORGIVS III DEI GRATIA BRITANNIARVM REX. F. D.

The treaty then made with the Indians placed them as allies with the British nation, and not subjects; and they were so considered until the influx of emigration completely outnumbered the aborigines. From that time the Colonial Government assumed a parental authority over them, treating them in every respect as children. No one' will deny that the Indians have been more kindly treated by the British Government than by the American. The former have always protected them from the impositions of wicked white men; but the latter, in too many instances, have driven and chased the poor red man further and further to the west; and if they had not of late years shown more compassion towards him, he must soon have been driven into the Pacific Ocean.

It was kind in the Government to act as guardians of the poor defenceless Indians, and to protect them from the frauds of unprincipled white men; but, at the same time, I think that some acts of the Colonial Government cannot be considered as doing full justice to the natives. I now refer to the manner in which some of the tribes have been compelled to surrender their territories.

Indians at the present time enjoy no political rights or advantages. They cannot vote at elections for members of Parliament, nor sit as jurors, however qualified they may be, simply because they have no title-deeds for their lands. I feel confident that these things act as a powerful check to their advancement in the arts of civilized life. I have often heard them say that it is not much use for the Indians to aim at the exalted privileges of their white neighbours, as they will never be permitted to enjoy them. I know of no legal impediment to their possessing such rights; the difficulty lies in the tenure by which they hold their lands. It is my firm conviction that many of the

Indians are sufficiently instructed in the knowledge of civil affairs to be able to use the rights of British subjects as judiciously as many of their white neighbours. The names of numbers might be inserted were it of any avail. May the time soon come when my countrymen will be able to walk side by side with their white neighbours, and partake in all the blessings and privileges enjoyed by the white subjects of her most gracious Majesty the Queen!

THE INDIANS' OPINION OF THE AMERICANS.

The Canadian Indians, and those in the Western States, have a very poor opinion of the Americans. They call them *Keche Mookomon* (the Big Knives), from their having massacred, during the American war, many of the Indians with cutlasses and dirks. They imagine that all the Yankees hate the Indians, and would gladly exterminate them from the earth; they also consider them as rogues and traitors. Entertaining such views, it is no wonder that they look upon them with distrust. The following anecdote will illustrate the fact :—

An Indian Chief on the Grand River was applied to, separately, by two white men, for a certain piece of land. One was an old honest Canadian Dutch farmer, well known to the chief. The other was a Yankee stranger, who came with many extravagant promises of what he would do for the Indian if he would only let him have the land, far outbidding his competitor. The chief gravely listened to these offers, and then coolly replied to the Dutch farmer:—"My friend, I have known you these many years, and have never heard of your cheating an Indian, or sending him away from your house hungry." Then, pointing to the stranger, he said :—" This man wants my land ; his mouth is all sugar, and his words very sweet, but

I do not know what is in his heart. I therefore turn away from his sweet words, and let you have my land."

THEIR OPINION OF THE NEGRO RACE.

They consider the Negroes were made inferior to other races of the human family, and deeply commiserate their unhappy state in being bound with the iron band of slavery. They imagine that the Indian comes next to the Negro in the endurance of wrongs inflicted by the white man ; and with this idea they call them "our fellow-suffering brethren." With many of the tribes there is a great aversion to intermarriages with the Africans. The Indians boast of their freedom, and say they would sooner die than be treated as beasts of burden !"

The following extract from a letter to the Author, from an Indian visiting Paris, will show their opinion of the French people :—

"PARIS, *Oct.* 19*th*, 1854.

"MY DEAR BROTHER,

". . . . Last Saturday we saw the great chief of France, and his great chief woman ; the great chief of Belgium, and his great chief woman ; and some hundreds of their people . . . These things we did for them :— We played the Indian ball-play, shot at marks with our own bows and arrows, false scalping, war dance, paddled one of our birch-bark canoes in a beautifully made river, among swans, wild geese, and ducks. After the two great chiefs and their great chief women had much talk with us, they thanked us, got into their carriages covered with gold, drawn by six beautiful horses, and drove to the wigwam of the great chief of France. We followed them, and the great chief's servant, who wears a red coat, and much gold and silver, and a hat in the shape of half-night-sun, took us into one of the great rooms to dine. Everything on the table was gold and silver; we had twelve clean plates. Many came in while we were eating, and it was great amusement to them all. . . . .

"Paris is much handsomer than the city of London; very clean.

"The French people wear much hair about the mouth, which makes them look bold and noble; but our friend Sasagon, who has no taste for beauty, says that it would puzzle any one of our people to find where the Frenchman's mouth is; and that a person having much hair round his mouth makes him look like one of our Indian dogs in North America when running away with a black squirrel in his mouth.

"The French women carry big and heavy loads on their backs, on what we call tetoomaugun, same as our women do; they do it because they are industrious. Here, again, Sasagon says, 'that the French women would make good wives for the Ojebway hunters.'

"The French people are very gay in their dress, and yet I think they are not so selfish and proud as most of the English.

"There are no ragged people or beggars in Paris. We have not seen a single person intoxicated since we have been here.

	" KEEKAUNIS,
" *To* KAHKEWAQUONABY,	MAUNGWADAUS,
or REV. PETER JONES."	or GEORGE HENRY.

The following is the opinion the Author formed of England and its inhabitants on his first visit, in the year

1831 (extracted from a letter to his brother, Mr. John Jones, dated London, December 30th, 1831):—

. . . . " I have thought you would be pleased to hear my remarks, as an Indian traveller, on the customs and manners of the English people, and therefore send you the following, made from actual observation :—

" The English, in general, are a noble, generous-minded people—free to act and free to think; they very much pride themselves on their civil and religious privileges; in their learning, generosity, manufactures, and commerce; and they think that no other nation is equal to them.

" I have found them very open and friendly, always ready to relieve the wants of the poor and needy when properly brought before them. No nation, I think, can be more fond of novelties than the English; they will gaze upon a foreigner as if he had just dropped down from the moon; and I have often been amused in seeing what a large number of people a *monkey riding* upon a *dog* will collect, where such things may be seen almost every day. When my Indian name, *Kahkewaquonaby*, is announced to attend any public meeting, so great is the curiosity, the place is sure to be filled. They are truly industrious, and in general very honest and upright. Their close attention to business produces, I think, too much worldly-mindedness, and hence they forget to think enough about their souls and their God; their motto seems to be 'Money, money; get money, get rich, and be a gentleman.' With this sentiment they fly about in every direction, like a swarm of bees, in search of the treasure which lies so near their hearts. These remarks refer to the men of the world, and of such there are not a few.

" The English are very fond of good living, and many who live on roast beef, plum pudding, and turtle soup, get very fat, and round as a toad. They eat four times in a day. Breakfast at eight or nine, which consists of coffee or tea, bread and butter, and sometimes a little fried bacon, fish, or eggs. Dinner at about two, P.M., when everything that is good is spread before the eater; which winds up with fruit, nuts, and a few glasses of wine. Tea at six, with bread and butter, toast, and sometimes sweet cake. Supper about nine or ten, when the leavings of the dinner again make their appearance, upon which John Bull makes a hearty meal to go to bed upon at midnight.

"The fashion in dress varies so much, I am unable to describe it. I will only say, that the ladies of fashion wear very curious bonnets, which look something like a farmer's scoop-shovel; and when they walk in the tiptoe style they put me in mind of the little snipes that run along the shores of the lakes in Canada. They also wear sleeves as big as bushel bags, which make them appear as if they had three bodies with one head. Yet, with all their big bonnets and sleeves, the English ladies, I think, are the best of women. . . . .

"P. JONES."

CHAPTER XIX.

Illustrations of Faith.

THE late James Young, Indian, informed me that one Sunday morning, as he was on his way to the house of God, he overtook Widow Waubanosay. Before he came up to her he heard her talking, as if some one was with her. When she heard his footsteps behind her, seeing it was her class-leader, she said, " O my brother, I am only talking with Jesus as I walk along, and he makes me very happy in my heart." This, of a truth, is walking with God. W. W. is one of our most holy women. God is with her.

ANSWER TO THE PRAYER OF FAITH.

A teacher at Grape Island once requested the Indians to pray for his unconverted brothers and sisters living in the States. Upon his arrival home he found them all converted to God. His mother met him and told him the good news, saying that she could not account for their remarkable conversions, as no special means had been employed. The teacher then unfolded the mystery.

STRONG FAITH IN CHRISTIAN INDIANS.

The Rev. J. Messmore stated that when he was a missionary on the Grand River, a chief, with a party of his warriors, came to drive the Methodist Indians and their preachers away from the settlement. The Christians were assembled at their place of worship when the party arrived. They told their enemies that "Jesus Christ was stronger than the children of the devil, and that God would take care of them." They then joined in prayer; after which, one of the Indian speakers went out, and, mounting a log, preached to them with such power that the chief and his warriors were soon melted into tears. They then went into the church and united with the Christians in worshipping the true God. The next sabbath the chief was among the penitents at the altar, crying to God for mercy : he soon found peace, to the joy of his soul, and united himself with the people of God, whom he had so recently sought to persecute.

RESIGNATION UNDER AFFLICTION.

Thomas Magee, a pious Indian exhorter, was bereaved of his children one after another. When his seventh child was taken from him, after I had preached a funeral sermon, he rose up in the congregation and said :—" Brothers and Sisters,—I am now about to bury my seventh child ; I do not murmur at what the great Spirit has done in taking away my children ; I now feel that there are seven cords reaching down from heaven to my heart, and that these cords are pulling me up towards heaven, and not one shall be broken until I reach to the end of them, and then I shall meet my dear children again."

Polly Sunegoo is a pious, intelligent Indian woman. In the early part of her religious life she passed through deep afflictions, which she bore with Christian fortitude. Her children died one after the other; her husband was at this time given to intemperance, which was a great trial to her; her last promising son was drowned in the mill-race at the

River Credit, and her only daughter lying apparently at the point of death. In all these afflictions religion was her only consolation, and she was often heard to sing,—

> " My company before is gone,
> And I am left alone with Thee," &c.

PERSECUTION FOR CHRIST'S SAKE.

The Rev. J. Messmore informed me that when he was labouring on the Grand River Mission, an Indian woman being converted to God, her ungodly chief withheld from her her blanket, and two dollars in cash, telling her that she must either give up the Christian religion or lose her presents, &c. She replied—" By and bye the blanket will be burnt up and the silver melt away; but the good religion I have found will never leave me,—it will comfort my heart here, and carry me to heaven when I die."

John Caleb, an Indian youth at Muncey Town, when about twelve years of age, was converted to the Christian religion, and became very anxious to learn to read and write. He was much opposed by his parents, who were heathens, and threatened to take his gun and horse and sell them for the fire-waters, if he did not give up going to the meetings and school. John told his parents that he thought more about serving the Great Spirit than he did about his gun or his horse, and would therefore rather lose all he possessed than give up his school and religious meetings; and more than this, he modestly told them he would rather suffer death than disobey what the Great Spirit had commanded him to do. John then prayed earnestly for the conversion of his parents, and that good Being who hears and answers the prayers of faith gave

Q

him the desires of his heart in their sound conversion.
Let young persons never be discouraged; God will surely
answer their prayers, if offered up in sincerity and faith.

FAITHFUL CONVERTS, AND THEIR DESIRE FOR INSTRUCTION.

Faithfulness of an Indian Woman at Hudson's Bay.—The
late Rev. James Evans stated, at a missionary meeting, that he
met with an old Indian woman in the Hudson's Bay territory
who was converted at St. Marie seven years previous to his
meeting her. She informed him that for five years she had
been living among the pagans. The first three years of her
sojourn in that country she had year after year looked for
the arrival of a missionary, but no missionary came. She
then gave up all hopes of ever again hearing the words of
the Great Spirit, and resolved to serve him alone as well as
she could, and she kept her resolution in the midst of pagan
darkness and numerous temptations, until she had the joy
of seeing the face of a missionary. She expressed many
thanks for this great privilege, and stated she had been
brought to the knowledge of the Christian religion through
the labours of John Sunday, at the Sault St. Marie.

Saugeeng Indians ask for Spiritual Guns.—Some of the
Saugeeng Indians came to me at the Credit, and said—
"We have come to ask for guns to shoot our enemies, as
we are engaged in war." I asked them what they meant.
They replied, that they had come to ask for our translation
of the Holy Scriptures, which they called their *spiritual
guns.*

THE FLATHEAD INDIANS SEEKING FOR THE WHITE MAN'S RELIGION.

It was stated in the American paper that a deputation
of Flathead Indians had arrived at some western towns,

enquiring after the white man's religion, saying that "some of their Indian traders had informed them that the white man had his religion written in a book, which told him all he was commanded to do, and that they had come to ask for a missionary to tell their people the words of that good book." These poor Indians travelled between two and three thousand miles on foot, seeking for a messenger of peace to publish unto them the good tidings of salvation!

When the work of conversion first commenced at the Sault St. Marie by the preaching of John Sunday and others, so great was the desire to hear the word of God, that an Indian woman who was encamped on an island, finding the canoe gone, took her two children, and, slinging one on each shoulder, *forded* the river, which was about three feet deep, and thus reached the meeting, which was held on the mainland.

CHRISTIAN LIBERALITY.

George Killsnake's Missionary Ox.—When I was stationed at Muncey, George Killsnake drove a young ox to the Mission House, and said that he had subscribed four dollars to the Missionary Society and two dollars to the Bible Society, and that he had brought the ox from Moravian Town in order to sell it to get money to pay these debts, but that he had found no market on the road. I gave him his price for the beast; he was much delighted, and at once paid his subscriptions. This Indian had driven his ox upwards of thirty miles.

TRINKETS CONTRIBUTED BY NEW CONVERTS.

When the work of God commenced among our Indian tribes, many of them had silver brooches, ear-bobs, arm-

Q 2

bands, and nose-jewels, which they threw into the missionary collections with great apparent pleasure. These contributions were sold to jewellers, and the proceeds applied in helping on the blessed work. I have often known the poor Indian women make baskets and brooms previous to a missionary meeting, that by the sale of these things they might have a little money in time for the collection.

INDIANS PREPARED TO RECEIVE THE GOSPEL BEFORE IT WAS PREACHED TO THEM.

The Rev. A. Prindle informed me that the first Methodist missionaries sent to Canada were instructed to visit and preach to the Indians; but such was their want of faith, that he and his companions laughed at the idea as a fruitless effort. Their unbelief arose from the abject state in which the Indians were at that time.

Soon after this the same minister states that when Dr. Bangs was travelling in Canada, he conversed with some Indians at Duffin's Creek on the subject of religion. The chief burst into tears, and catching the preacher round the neck, said, " I will be a Christian and you shall be my minister."

P. WOMPEGOOSH AND HIS DEER-HUNTING.

P. Wompegoosh, an Indian residing in the township of Waterloo, on the Grand River, came on a visit to the Credit for the purpose of hearing the words of the Great Spirit. Being much interested, he tarried longer than he expected. On his return home, he found his family out of provisions and very hungry. P. Wompegoosh rose up very early in the morning in search of deer ; he travelled till the middle of the afternoon without seeing a sign of one. He now began to despair ; in this emergency he made known his wants to the Christian's God, and began to call aloud on him. To his first prayer he received no answer. He then travelled on some distance, again praying aloud as before that God would give him deer for his family. On rising from his knees, he looked and saw three deer standing not far from him; taking his rifle he shot one on the spot; when he discovered he had killed it, he again fell upon his knees and returned thanks to God. As he rose from his thanksgiving behold he saw another standing within gun-shot; as soon as he could load, he shot the second, and again gave thanks. After this he went in search of the third, and soon killed him. He was thus provided with an abundant supply for his family. Surely " God is a prayer-hearing, and a prayer-answering God, a very present help in time of trouble !"

OLD JEEKIB AND HIS OLD WIFE.

Among the Credit Indians there was a very tall, good-natured old man, named Jeekib. He and his wife used to get drunk together. On one occasion I saw the old woman beating her husband on his head and back. The old man, instead of resisting the blows, kept himself perfectly com-posed, saying, "Wawanee, wawanee;" that is, "Thank you, thank you." This enraged his wife the more, and when she saw she could not hurt him, she sat down and wept bitterly.

OBJECTIONS TO BECOMING CHRISTIANS.

Pashegezhegwashkum, a chief of the Beldom Indians and a noted pow-wow, after listening to the preaching of the white man, brought forward his objections to the Christian religion by saying, " The white man makes the fire-water, he drinks, and sells it to the Indians, he lies and cheats the poor Indian. I have seen him go to his praying-house in Malden, and as soon as he comes out I have seen him go straight to the tavern, get drunk, quarrel, and fight. Now the white man's religion is no better than mine. I will hold fast to the religion of my forefathers, and follow them to the far west."

Old widow Wahbuhnoosay accompanied a party of Indians to Toronto, to sell baskets and brooms. They returned by the cars as far as Hamilton. The old woman had never been in them before. She was observed to sit perfectly quiet. When she got out, she threw herself down flat on her face. The conductor told the Indians to find out what was the matter with her; when she replied, " I am waiting for my soul to come."

AN INDIAN'S REPLY TO A CHALLENGE.

The Indian has more sense than the white man. The duellist may possess some *physical* bravery, but he lacks the moral courage of the Indian, who, when he was challenged, replied, " I have two objections to this duel affair; the one is, lest I should hurt *you*, and the other is, lest you should hurt *me*. I do not see any good that it would do me to put a bullet through your body—I could not make any use of you when dead ; but I could of a rabbit or turkey. As to myself, I think it more wise to *avoid* than to put myself in the way of harm ; I am under apprehension that you might hit me. That being the case, I think it advisable to keep my distance. If you want to try your pistols, take some object—a tree, or anything about my size ; and if you hit that, send me word, and I shall acknowledge, that had I been there you might have hit me."

FIRST INTERVIEW BETWEEN A WHITE MAN AND INDIANS.

When the Dacatos first saw a white man they immediately took him prisoner. The white man shewed them a gun he had in his hand, and by signs told them that if he should point it to them it would kill them. The Indians appeared incredulous, and having placed one of their men a short distance from him, requested him to try the power of his gun. The white man declined. They then found a dog, which the white man shot dead on the spot. As soon as they heard the report of the gun, and saw its effects, they ran off in great alarm. They then called the white man *Uhnemekee*, that is, *the Thunder God.*

HONESTY OF AN INDIAN.

One day, an Indian solicited a little tobacco of a white man, to fill his pipe. Having some loose in his pocket, the white man gave him a handful. The next day the Indian returned in search of the man who gave him the tobacco. "I wish to see him," said the Indian. "Why so?" inquired some one. "Why, I find money with the tobacco." "Well! what of that? Keep it; it was given to you." "Ah!" said the Indian, shaking his head, "I got good man and bad man here," pointing to his breast. "Good man say, Money not yours; you must return it; bad man say, 'Tis yours; it was given to you. Good man say, That not right; tobacco yours, money not yours. Bad man say, Never mind, nobody know it; go buy rum. Good man say, O, no; no such thing. So poor Indian know not what to do. Me lie down to sleep, but no sleep; good man and bad man talk all night, and trouble me. So, now me bring money back; now me feel glad."

ANECDOTE OF AN INDIAN PREACHER.

While Mr. Kirkland was a missionary to the Oneidas, being unwell, he was unable to preach on the afternoon of a certain sabbath, and told good Peter, one of the head

men of the Oneidas, that he must address the congregation. Peter modestly and reluctantly consented. After a
few words of introduction, he began a discourse on the
character of the Saviour. " What, my brethren," said he,
" are the views which you form of the character of Jesus ?
You will answer, perhaps, that he was a man of singular
benevolence. You will tell me that he proved this to be
his character by the nature of the miracles which he
wrought. All these, you will say, were kind in the extreme. He created bread to feed thousands who were
ready to perish : He raised to life the son of a poor
woman who was a widow, and to whom his labours were
necessary for her support in old age. Are these, then,
your only views of the Saviour ? I tell you they are lame.
—When Jesus came into our world, he threw his blanket
around him, but the GOD *was within*."—*Dwight's Travels.*

INDIAN LOYALTY, AND LATE AMERICAN BRIGANDS.

The following letter is from a native Indian, who has
been educated in the Methodist Mission schools, and is now
an interpreter and teacher at the River St. Clair Mission.
He is one of those whom Sir F. Head has said Christianity had " decimated,"—one of those whom it was recommended to send to the Manitoulin Island to "feed " upon
"fish " and "berries that grow in the interstices of the
rocks." The vein of pleasant wit which pervades this letter
renders it very amusing. It also shows that the operations
of the Methodist Missionary Society are not less favourable
to loyalty than they are to piety, sobriety, and industry.
We are glad to perceive from this letter that even in
Michigan, the Americans are now assisting to prevent
lawless incursions of mobs, which have collected on their
frontier, upon the Canadian territories.

" ST. CLAIR MISSION, *July 20th*, 1838.

" DEAR SIR,—I send these few lines for to say to you that we have been troubled very much by the rebels ; so much so that we are in fear we get as savage as our fathers were in all the wars under the British flag. We have to be up every night in watching them, and go to sleep in day-time like bats and owls : we have to carry our guns and toma-hawks, war-clubs and scalping-knives, while our heads are decorated with feathers, and faces painted. I am thinking that if they will yet continue a little longer, we shall have to dress ourselves in such a way that it will make them fall like dead men on the ground just by seeing us, without the war-whoops and yells. Though the Yankees are now assist-ing us in trying to keep them away from robbing some of the stores on these frontiers, yet we are in fear that they will yet continue to trouble us ; for they are just like the artichokes on the American side, that the hogs cannot root them all up, they will come up and grow in spite of all the laws can do to prevent them.

" I am, Sir,

" Your very dear Indian friend,

" GEORGE HENRY.

" To Rev. E. RYERSON, Toronto.

" P.S.—The rebels did come over on our side a few weeks ago, and robbed one store ; but a few of the savages drove the unfortunate fellows over again, and chased them on the other side too.   " G. H."

Bishop Hedding relates the following incidents :—

" When at Grape Island Mission I had a meeting to allow them to ask any question they might desire. It was astonishing and sometimes amusing to hear the questions they proposed. A squaw said ' She heard her boy read in the Testament that a man and his wife were one; now, supposing that the squaw is converted and her husband is a drunkard—when they die will the Indian go to Heaven with the squaw, or must she go to hell with her husband, seeing they are one?' Her husband was a drunkard.

"When addressing them I had for my interpreter a large, stout, fine-looking Indian, who had been an old warrior. They called him Captain Beaver. He appeared to be solemnly engaged in religion, and deeply affected with its great truths. Before his conversion he had been a great sinner, he had killed one wife, and in a drunken frolic threw a child out of doors into the mud, and stamped it to death. When preaching to them on the intercession of Christ, the whole congregation were greatly affected and cried aloud, so that I was obliged to stop for some time before they could hear me. Captain Beaver bowed himself nearly double, and cried aloud, 'Oh, oh!' I was told by the missionary that this doctrine of the intercession of Christ had probably not been taught them before, and it was the discovery of it for the first time that so greatly affected them.

"When visiting the Indians residing at the River Credit one Monday morning, a converted Indian came to me and said, 'Yesterday I crossed the River Credit in a canoe, and the salmon were thick all around me; and he no run away, for he know Christian Indian would not catch salmon on Sunday.'"

CHAPTER XX.

THE concluding chapter of this volume was to have embraced the following subjects:—"The present state and future prospects of the North American Indians." As the author ceased from his labours before the commencement of this chapter, it is deemed sufficient to insert his suggestions on the subject, expressing as they do his unaltered opinions up to the day of his death. The queries, as will be seen, are numerous, and embrace a wide field. The answers of the author, having all the authority of a life of labour and observation, cannot fail to interest.

Answers to the Queries proposed by the Commissioners appointed to enquire into Indian Affairs in this province.

Query No. 1.—How long have you had an acquaintance with any body of Indians?

Answer No. 1.—Being an Indian on my mother's side, I am well acquainted with the habits, customs, and manners of the Chippeway nation of Indians to whom I belong. The tribe or clan with whom I have been brought up is called *Messissauga*, which signifies the eagle tribe, their *ensign* or *toodaim* being that of the eagle. I also lived for several years among the Mohawk Indians on the Grand River, by whom I was adopted. Since my entering upon the work of a missionary, I have travelled very extensively among all the Indian tribes in this country, and am therefore well acquainted with their former and present state; but, as I belong to the River Credit Indians, I intend to confine my remarks principally to them.

Query No. 2.—What has been their improvement during that time in their moral and religious character, and in habits of industry?

Answer No. 2.—Previous to the year 1823, at which time I was converted to Christianity, the Chippeway and indeed all the tribes were in a most degraded state; they were pagans, idolaters, superstitious, drunken, filthy, and indolent; they wandered about from place, living in wigwams, and subsisted by hunting and fishing. Since their conversion, paganism, idolatry, and superstition, have been removed, and the true God acknowledged and worshipped. The Christians are sober, and comparatively clean and industrious; they have formed themselves into settlements, where they have places of worship and schools, and cultivate the earth.

Query No. 3.—Do you find them improved in their mode of agriculture to any extent, since you first became acquainted with them?

Answer No. 3.—Many of them have made considerable progress in farming, but not to the extent they would have done if they had been settled on their own farm lots. The Credit Indians live in a village, and some of them have necessarily to go a mile or two to their farms, which has been a great hindrance to their improvement. Before their conversion very few of them raised even Indian corn, but now many of them grow wheat, oats, peas, Indian corn, potatoes, and other vegetables, several cut hay and have small orchards. I find the Indians at Muncey Town far behind their brethren at the Credit in agricultural industry.

Query No. 4.—What progress have they made in Christianity?

Answer No. 4.—Considerable; many of them can repeat the Lord's prayer, the ten commandments, and the Apostle's creed. They also understand the leading articles of our holy religion. I have translated the Book of Genesis, the gospels of Matthew and John, with other portions of Scripture, which they have now in their possession. They have made some proficiency in singing, are tolerably well acquainted with the rules of sacred harmony, and have a hymn-book translated into their own language, which is in constant use.

Query No. 5.—Since their conversion to Christianity are their moral habits improved? What effect has it had upon their social habits?

Answer No. 5.—Christianity has done much to improve their moral, social, and domestic habits. Previous to their conversion the women were considered as mere slaves; the drudgery and hard work was done by them; now the men treat their wives as equals, bearing the heavy burdens themselves, while the women attend to the children and household concerns.

Query No. 6.—Do they appear sensible of any improvement in their condition, and desirous of advancing?

Answer No. 6.—Very much so, and feel grateful to those who instruct them. They are still desirous of advancing in knowledge, seeing their white neighbours enjoy many comforts and privileges which they do not possess.

Query No. 7.—Are any of the Indians still heathens? What efforts have been made to convert them? And what obstacles have prevented their conversion?

Answer No. 7.—There are no heathens at the Credit, Alnwick, Rice Lake, Mud Lake, Snake Island, Balsom

Lake, narrows of Lake Simcoe, Cold Water, St. Clair, and
Moravian Town; but there are a number at Muncey Town,
some at Sahgeeng, Big Bay, and the Grand River.   I
believe all the Indians at Walpool Island are pagans.*
There are a few among the Oneidas settled on the Thames
at Muncey, and a number of Pattawatimees wandering
about in these western parts who are in a most deplorable
state of poverty and degradation.   Efforts have been made
to introduce Christianity to most of the pagans by missionaries of various denominations, but principally by native
teachers.   The obstacles to their conversion arise from
their strong partiality to the ways of their forefathers, and
their prejudices to the white man's religion.   I am happy
to state that the Wesleyan Missionaries, aided by native
teachers, have never yet failed to introduce Christianity
among a body of Indians.

Query No. 8.—What, in your opinion, is the best mode
of promoting their religious improvement?

Answer No. 8.—To combine manual labour with religious
instruction; to educate some of the Indian youths with a
view to their becoming missionaries and school teachers, as
it is a well known fact that the good already effected has
been principally through the labours of native missionaries.

Query No. 9.—Do the children in the Indian schools
shew any aptitude in acquiring knowledge?

Answer No. 9.—Considering they are taught in a strange
language, they show as much aptitude as white children.

Query No. 10.—What, in your opinion, is the best mode
of promoting the moral, intellectual, and social improvement of the Indians?

Answer No. 10.—The establishment of well-regulated
schools of industry, and the congregating of the several

* This island is now under Christian instruction.

scattered tribes into three or four settlements, which would be a great saving of expense to the Government and to missionary societies, at the same time it would afford greater facilities for their instruction in everything calculated to advance their general improvement.

Query No. 11.—Can you offer any suggestions on the expediency and best means of establishing schools of industry for the Indian youth, and the best system of instruction to be adopted in them?

Answer No. 11.—I would respectfully refer the commissioners to my letter on this subject, addressed to them, dated November 21st, 1842.* In addition to what is there stated, I am happy to add that most of the Indian youths who have been educated at the academies have become respectable, and are now usefully employed in instructing their countrymen.

Query No. 12.—Do the Indians show any aptness for mechanical arts? And if so, to what arts?

Answer No. 12.—I know several Indians who have become pretty good mechanics with little or no instruction. At the Credit Mission there are two or three carpenters and a shoemaker. At Muncey we have one blacksmith, and some carpenters and tailors. By a little more instruction they would soon become good workmen in any mechanical art. The only drawback which I have observed is a want of steady application to their respective trades.

Query No. 13.—Is the health of the Indians generally good, or otherwise, as contrasted with the white population in their neighbourhood?

Answer No. 13.—From observation I am led to conclude that in general they are not as healthy as the white population. I apprehend this arises from their former mode of

* See Appendix O.

living, when they were frequently exposed to excessive fatigue and fasting, to carrying heavy burdens, drunkenness, and injuries inflicted on each other when in this state. These things have laid the foundation of many pulmonary complaints from which the present generation are suffering.

Query No. 14.—Do you find the Indians on the increase or decrease in numbers, irrespectively of migration? If the latter, what, in your opinion, is the cause?

Answer No. 14.—Previously to their conversion to Christianity they were rapidly decreasing. Before the white man came to this country the old Indians say that their forefathers lived long and reared large families, and that their diseases were few in number. In my opinion the principal causes of their decrease have been the introduction of contagious diseases, which hurried thousands off the stage of action; their excessive fondness for the *fire-waters,* and want of proper care and food for the children and mothers. I am happy however to state that this mortality has been greatly checked since they have abandoned their former mode of life.

I have kept a register of the number of births and deaths of the Credit Indians for several years past. After their conversion they remained stationary for some years; but, latterly, there has been a small increase from actual births. I have also observed, in other tribes, that the longer they hav eenjoyed the blessings of civilisation, the more healthy they have become, and the larger families they have reared.

Query No. 15.—Is there in your opinion any means of checking the excessive mortality among the Indians, if such prevails?

Answer No. 15.—In my opinion the best means is to promote industry and regular habits amongst them, and to have a good medical man stationed at or near each Indian settlement. I have known many of them suffer much, and die for the want of medical aid. It is also my opinion that intermarriagés with other tribes of people would tend greatly to improve their health. Many of the small tribes are degenerating on account of their having continued for ages to marry into the same body of Indians. Hence the necessity of concentrating the scattered tribes.

Query No. 16.—Do the Indian men or women frequently intermarry with the whites ?

Answer No. 16.—When this country was first visited by the whites it was a common practice for white men to take Indian wives, but at present it seldom occurs. As far as my knowledge extends, there are only three or four white men married to Indian women, and about the same number of Indian men married to white women.

Query No. 17.—Is there any marked difference in the habits and general conduct between the half-breeds and the native Indians ? If so, state it.

Answer No. 17.—I think there is. The half-breeds are in general more inclined to social and domestic habits. I have always found them more ready to embrace Christianity and civilization than the pure Indian, who, in his untutored state, looks upon manual labour as far too degrading to engage his attention.

Query No. 18.—In cases where intermarriages with the whites have taken place, do you find the condition of the children of the marriage improved ?

Answer No. 18.—I think they are, especially as regards their health and constitution.

Query No. 19.—Do the Indian women frequently live with white men, without being married ?

R

Answer No. 19.—I know of no instances in all the tribes with which I am acquainted.

Query No. 20.—Does the birth of illegitimate children among the unmarried women occur frequently? And in what light is the circumstance viewed by the Indians?

Answer No. 20.—Such occurrences are not so frequent as when the Indians were in their drunken state; and when they do occur it is regarded as a great sin, and the mother loses her reputation as a virtuous woman.

Query No. 21.—Do any of the Indians enjoy all, or any, of the civil and political rights possessed by other subjects of Her Majesty?

Answer No. 21.—Not any to my knowledge; except the protection of law which I believe every alien enjoys who may visit or reside in any part of her Majesty's dominions. I am fully persuaded that, in order to improve the condition of the Indians, all the civil and political rights of British subjects ought to be extended to them so soon as they are capable of understanding and exercising such rights.

Query No. 22.—Are there any instances of Indians possessing such rights, besides those of the children of educated white men married to Indian women?

Answer No. 22.—I know of none.

Query No. 23.—In your opinion have the Indians the knowledge and ability to exercise any of those rights?

Answer No. 23.—In my opinion, some of the Credit Indians, and a few at other settlements, are so far advanced in knowledge as to be able to exercise some of those rights, such as voting for Members of Parliament, township officers, &c., and to sit as jurors.

Query No. 24.—Can you offer any suggestions for the improvement of the condition of the Indians?—For the application of their presents, the expenditure of their annuities, and the proceeds of the sales of their lands?

Answer No. 24.—I would most respectfully suggest—

1st.—The importance of establishing schools of industry as soon as possible, that there may be no further delay in bringing forward the present rising generation.

2nd.—In order to promote industry among the Indians, agricultural societies ought to be formed at each settlement, and rewards offered to such as might excel in any branch of farming. This would excite a spirit of emulation, and be productive of good results.

3rd.—In forming an Indian settlement, I consider that each family ought to be located on his own farm lot, containing 50 or 100 acres of land, with the boundaries of each lot marked out and established.

4th.—I am of opinion that it would have a beneficial tendency were titles given to the Indians by the Government, securing their reserved lands to them and their posterity for ever. In offering these suggestions I do not mean to say that it would be prudent to confer titles individually on the Indians, but on the whole tribe. At present they hold no written documents from Government, and they frequently express fears that they will, at some future period, lose their lands. This fear acts as a check upon their industry and enterprise. In suggesting the impropriety of giving individual titles, I consider at the same time it would be well to hold out the promise to the sober and industrious, that when they shall have attained to a good knowledge of the value of property, and have established a good character, they shall have titles given them.

5th.—The power of the chiefs is very different from what it was in former times, when their advice was listened to, and their commands implicitly obeyed. Immoral acts were

R 2

then punished, and the offenders submitted without a murmur. But I am sorry to say, at present, many of the young people ridicule the attempts of the chiefs to suppress vice. I would humbly suggest that the Legislature, in its wisdom, take this subject into consideration, and pass an Act incorporating the chiefs to act as councillors, and the Superintendents of the Indian department as wardens. Bye-laws could be passed for the regulation and improvement of the several communities of Indians, such as the enactment of a moral code of laws, performance of statute labour, the regulation of fences, &c., &c.

6th.—I think it very desirable that something should be done for the Pottawatimees who wander about in these parts. They are in a state of great poverty and degradation, and an annoyance to the white inhabitants wherever they go. They have no lands in this province, having recently come over from the United States. I would, therefore, suggest the propriety of locating them, and thus bring them under the influence of civilization and Christianity.

7th.—Feeling a deep interest for the welfare of the Muncey Indians residing at Muncey Town, I beg to call the attention of the Commissioners to their state. They are an interesting people, strongly attached to the British Government; and during the last American war rendered essential service in the defence of this province. If the Government could do something in the way of assisting them in their farming, it would afford great satisfaction, and be the means of facilitating their civilization. They receive no annuity from Government, and consequently have no means at their command to help forward their improvements.

8th.—With regard to their presents, I would respectfully

suggest the propriety of issuing them at their respective settlements. This would prevent some of the tribes being obliged to leave home, very often to the great damage of their crops, in order to travel to a distant post to receive the Queen's bounty.

9th.—It is my opinion that the annuities payable to the Indians for lands ceded to the Crown ought to be applied in promoting agriculture and education among them.

10th.—The proceeds of the sales of their lands ought to be invested in good securities, and the interest paid annually, and applied to such purposes as may improve their condition.

11th.—I would suggest the propriety of rendering annually detailed accounts of the receipts and expenditures of the annuities, and the proceeds of the sales of their lands, and that the same be laid before the Indians in council for their satisfaction and information.

All which is respectfully submitted.

(Signed)   PETER JONES,
                     Missionary and Indian Chief.
Muncey Mission House,
   Feb. 6th, 1843.

APPENDIX.

(A.)

ARRIVAL OF THE BLOOD-HOUNDS IN FLORIDA.

(From the *New York New World*, 1840.)

WE learn from the *Madisonian*, that an officer of the army, just arrived in Washington from St. Augustine, reports that a vessel with thirty-three blood-hounds, from Cuba, had entered one of the ports of the peninsula before he left. The purposes for which they are imported have not been disguised. They are to be employed in hunting down the miserable remnant of the Seminoles in Florida.

We have never read anything more strikingly illustrative of the inhumanity and injustice of this war than these remarks of Mr. Poinsett. It is then, for a country benign to the Indians, but deadly to the whites, that we are contending ! Of what advantage can it be when we obtain it ?

" In what an inhuman attitude," says the *Madisonian*, " does this development show this government before the civilized world ! A great, powerful, and magnanimous nation of fifteen millions of freemen, hunting down with blood-hounds a wretched squad of Indians, dwelling in a country which no white man can inhabit after it is conquered ! A war which will complete the solitude of a desert, by destroying the remnant of life that remains in it !"

When Spain armed herself with blood-hounds to extirpate the wretched aborigines of Cuba, a general cry of execration and horror rose from civilized Europe at the unparalleled spectacle ! When Great Britain turned the hostility of the savages within our borders against our forefathers, the measure was denounced by Lord Chatham as a stain upon her national honour. With what degree of condemnation will the good and wise of every country and age regard the attempt of our Government to extirpate, by means so terrible, from a region to which their habits and constitutions are

peculiarly and exclusively adapted, the poor remains of a once great
and powerful tribe, who, in the unintentionally pathetic language of
the Secretary of War, are "hemmed in by the sea, and must defend
themselves to the uttermost."

(From the *Albany Argus*.)

We have been unable to persuade ourselves that the Government
had become so utterly insane and degraded as to think of prose-
cuting its wanton and inglorious war in Florida with BLOOD-
HOUNDS ! But we are startled by a report that a "detachment"
of these brute "allies" have actually arrived ! Still we doubt. For
the honour of the Republic—for the honour of civilization—for the
honour of human nature, we hope that our cup of national infamy
may not be filled to overflowing. Enough of dishonour already
attaches to this sanguinary war. The integrity of a flag of truce
has been for the first time violated. We commenced the war without
cause, other than the desire to rob the Indians of their lands. Defeat
and disgrace, under the just auspices of the God of battles, has so
far attended our efforts. One commanding General informed the
Government that the swamps for which we were fighting are not
worth the medicine used to save a remnant of the army from
untimely graves. And yet the same besotted councils which set
the war on foot, persist in proceeding, with no purpose, it would
seem, but to allow an army of speculators to "pick and steal," and
to sink the nation deeper in its ignominy.

Is Mr. Van Buren, after bringing ruin, bankruptcy, and distress
upon the people, about to sign and seal a covenant of eternal infamy
by a mode of warfare which is forbidden by the laws of civilization,
and which is abhorrent to every sentiment and feeling of justice and
humanity ?

(From the *New York Commercial Advertiser*.)

We are not quite old enough to remember the time when the
biped blood-hounds of France sent their blood-hounds into the
human hunting-grounds of St. Domingo. But we do remember
the shuddering which conversation upon the subject created when
we were young. Little did we then expect to see the day that we
should be called upon to chronicle like transactions of barbarity
against an administration of the government founded by the spotless
Washington.

(B. AND C.)

AN interesting inquiry has for a considerable time past engaged the attention of the curious, both in Europe and of America, concerning the present existence and local situation of the remains of the lost ten tribes of Israel. A German publication assigns to a large portion of them the great plains of Bucharia, in Central Asia; others have contended that the American Indians are the true descendants of that stock. In favour of the latterargument a work* has recently been published, from which we extract the following analogy between those tribes and the ancient Israelites. The parallel is striking, and well worthy attention. "They [the Indians] are living in tribes, with heads of tribes; they have all a family likeness, though covering thousands of leagues of land, and have a tradition prevailing universally that they connect that country at the North-west corner. They are a very religious people, and yet have entirely escaped the idolatry of the old world. They acknowledge one God, the Great Spirit, who created all things, seen and unseen. The name by which this being is known to them is *Ale*, the old Hebrew name of God; he is also called *Yehowah*, sometimes *Yah*, and also *Abba;* for this great being they possess a high reverence, calling him the head of their community, and themselves his favourite people. They believe that he was more favourable to them in old times than he is now; that their fathers were in covenant with him, that he talked with them, and favoured them. They are distinctly heard to sing, with their religious dances, Hallelujah, and praise to Yah; other remarkable sounds go out of their mouths, as *shilu yo, shilu he, ale-yo, he-wah, yohewah,* but they profess not to know the meaning of these words, only that they learned to use them upon sacred occasions. They acknowledge the government of a Providence overruling all things, and express a willing submission to whatever takes place. They keep annual feasts, which resemble those of the Mosaic ritual; a feast of first-fruits, which they do not permit themselves to taste until they have made an offering of them to God; also an evening festival, in which

* "A View of the American Indians," by Samuel Worsley.

no bone of the animal that is eaten may be broken ; and if one family be not large enough to consume the whole of it, a neighbouring family is called in to assist : the whole of it is consumed, and the relics of it are burned before the rising of the next day's sun. There is one part of the animal which they never eat, the hollow of the thigh. They eat bitter vegetables, and observe severe fasts, for the purpose of cleansing themselves from sin ; they also have a feast of harvest, when their fruits are gathering in ; a daily sacrifice, and a feast of love. Their forefathers practised the rites of circumcision ;* but not knowing why so strange a practice was continued, and not approving it, they gave it up. There is a sort of jubilee kept by some of them. They have cities of refuge, to which a guilty man, and even a murderer, may fly and be safe."

(D.)

In reading over a paper read before the Ethnological Society, London, by James Kennedy, Esq., LL.B., I find his opinions on this subject accord with my own. He says—" With regard to North America, there seem to have been two great divisions of people among the Indians inhabiting the eastern and western countries of that continent. They both bore the general colour and appearance of the Mongol or Asiatic race ; but those on the west alone had the obliquity of eye peculiar to the Mongolians ; that peculiarity extending down to Mexico, Central America, and still further south, evidencing their origin from the Mongols of the north-west of Asia. In the eastern countries of North America, this strongly-marked peculiarity was not found, as Dr. Morton has also stated in his great work, ' Crania Americana ;' while the Indians there were distinguishable by manners equally indicative of their distinct origin ;" . . . "while we find the nations of the east and west sides of North America equally savage and bloodthirsty, yet those on the east had some particular customs or practices unknown to those of the west ; or, if not unknown, yet

* Years after the foregoing was written, the author was informed that it is a well-attested fact that in their drunken brawls the Munceys frequently reproach the Iroquois in an epithet of derision identical with that of circumcision, for having practised it in olden times.

not in general use among them ; such as the wampum, the calumet, and pipe of peace, the shaving of the head, the practice of scalping, the rite of circumcision, and the building of mounds. All these customs or practices are clearly traceable throughout what we may call Scythia or Tartary, especially that of building mounds, which, common as they are in the eastern half of North America, are still more common throughout Siberia and all Tartary ; from which quarter, therefore, we may conclude that the progenitors of that family of American Indians originally came." . . . "Such analogies and considerations, *primâ facie,* give us considerable reason to expect that we ought to look for the origin of the various American nations in the countries to which they refer ; and thus, according to the theory I maintain, the ethnologist ought to look to Tartary ; to compare the languages of the people on the eastern shores of North America ; while to trace the origin of the various tribes on the western coasts, down to Central America, he ought to compare their languages with those of the nations who inhabit the eastern parts of Asia. Were this course to be sedulously followed, I feel persuaded that very extraordinary analogies might be discovered, and the question of origin and unity of race even might be settled."

(E.)

HOW AN INDIAN CAN DIE.

(*From the St. Paul Democrat.*)

A TOUCHING instance of this characteristic trait, occurred at the late engagement between a small war party of the Chippewas and a greatly superior party of Sioux, near Cedar Island Lake. The Chippewas, who were *en route* for a scalping foray upon the Sioux villages on the Minnesota, here fell into an ambuscade, and the first notice of danger which saluted their ears was a discharge of fire-arms from a thicket. Four of their number fell dead in their tracks. Another named the War Cloud, a leading brave, had a leg broken by a bullet. His comrades were loth to leave him, and, whilst their assailants were re-loading their guns, attempted to carry him along with them to where they could gain the shelter of a thicket a short distance to the rear. But he commanded them to leave him, telling them that he would show his enemies how a Chippewa could die.

At his request they seated him on a log, with his back leaning against a tree. He then commenced painting his face and singing his death-song. As his enemies approached he only sang a louder and a livelier strain ; and when several had gathered around him, flourishing their scalping-knives, and screeching forth their demoniac yells of exultation, not a look or gesture manifested that he was even aware of their presence. At length they seized him and tore his scalp from his head. Still seated with his back against a large tree, they commenced shooting their arrows into the trunk around his head, grazing his ears, neck, &c., until they litterly pinned him fast, without having once touched a vital part. Yet our hero remained the same imperturbable Stoic, continuing to chant his defiant strain, and although one of the number flourished his reeking scalp before his eyes, still not a single expression of his countenance could be observed to change. At last one of the number approached him with a tomahawk, which, after a few unheeded flourishes, he buried in the captive's skull, who sank in death, with the song still upon his lips. He had, indeed, succeeded well in teaching his enemies "how a Chippewa could die." A few days afterwards they were taught how a Chippewa could be *avenged*.

(F.)

ALEXANDER HENRY relates the death and burial of a child who had been scalded. He says :—" I did not fail to attend the funeral. The grave was made of a large size, and the whole of the inside lined with birch bark. On the bank was laid the body of the child, accompanied with an axe, a pair of snow-shoes, a small kettle, several pairs of mocassins, its own strings of beads; and because it was a girl, a carrying belt and a paddle. The kettle was filled with meal. The last act of the mother (crying over the child) was that of taking from it a lock of hair for a memorial, that by this she should discover her daughter in the land of spirits, as she should take it with her. In this she alluded to the day when some pious hand would place in her own grave, along with the carrying

belt and paddle, this little relic, hallowed by maternal tears."—
(Page 150.)

J. CARVER'S TESTIMONY:—" Whilst I remained among the Indians, a couple whose tent was adjacent to mine lost a son of about four years of age. The parents were so much affected at the death of their favourite child, and they pursued the usual testimonies of grief with such uncommon rigour, as through the weight of sorrow and loss of blood to occasion the death of the father. The woman, who had hitherto been inconsolable, no sooner saw her husband expire, than she dried up her tears, and appeared cheerful and resigned. As I knew not how to account for so extraordinary a transition. I took an opportunity to ask her the reason, telling her that I should have imagined that the loss of her husband would rather have occasioned an increase of grief than such a sudden diminution. She informed me that, as the child was so young when it died, and unable to support itself in the country of spirits, both she and her husband had been apprehensive that its situation would be far from happy ; but no sooner did she behold its father depart for the same place, who not only loved the child with the tenderest affection, but was a good hunter, and would be able to provide plentifully for its support, than she ceased to mourn. She added, that she now saw no reason to continue her tears, as the child, on whom she doted, was happy under the care of a fond father, and she had only one wish which remained ungratified, which was, to be herself with them. Expressions so replete with unaffected tenderness, and sentiments that would have done honour to a Roman matron, made an impression on my mind greatly in favour of the people to whom she belonged, and tended not a little to counteract the prejudices I had entertained, in common with other travellers, of Indian insensibility, and want of parental affection. Her subsequent conduct confirmed the opinion I had just imbibed, and convinced me that, notwithstanding this apparent suspension of her grief, some particles of that reluctance to be separated from a beloved relation, which is implanted either by nature or custom in every human heart, still lurked in hers. I observed that she went almost every evening to the foot of the tree, on a branch of which the bodies of her husband and child were laid ; and, after cutting off a lock of her hair, and throwing it on the ground, in a plaintive song bemoaned its fate."

(G.)

" OLD JACK'S PINE-TREE GOD."

ON the west side of the Grand River, in the township of Waterloo, formerly stood a lofty pine-tree, with a large spreading closely matted top, which had a most imposing appearance from the distant hills, as this tree was taller than any others within view. On the top of this tree the eagles for many generations were wont to build their nests and rear their young, so that other lofty trees, towering rocks, and declivities, might become inhabited by the representatives of the "thunder-god." Old Jack, the Indian, whose hunting-grounds lay within the shadow of this remarkable tree, thought that he must have a god to worship, and therefore dreamed or fancied that this tree was to be his munedoo, or god, who would grant him and his family long life and success in hunting. He and they made periodical visits to it, bringing with them the best of the game they had taken, and offering the same at the foot of the tree. The offering was made in the usual manner, namely, by boiling the game, and burning part of it as a burnt offering, and the remainder being eaten by the invited guests, or by portions of the family. But old Jack would not taste a mouthful of it himself, as he intended that it should be a whole sacrifice. If the heathen are led to see the necessity of a whole consecration of the animal or thing offered, in order that it may be an acceptable sacrifice, how much more important is it, under the Christian dispensation, that we present ourselves living sacrifices to God in the name of the Lord Jesus, who having given himself a sacrifice for the sins of the world, has opened the way to the mercy-seat, that all mankind may come to God and obtain salvation. When passing through that part of the country, I have repeatedly gazed upon and admired old Jack's tree. I have recently heard that the white man has been so daring and profane, as to fell to the ground the poor Indian's god, which no doubt was drawn to the saw-mill, and then made into lumber to build the white man's wigwam. How would the descendants of Jack, with the eagles that nestled on the branches of this tree, wail and lament to see that their father's god has fallen to rise no more! This is but too emblematical of the fate of the red man of the forest. The white man comes, and as he advances the trees vanish before him ; thus the poor Indian disappears, as if crushed by the falling of the immense forests.

During the summer of 1837, whilst on a missionary tour to the Manitoulin Islands, we passed on the north-east shore of Lake Huron, an island on which was a large and curious rock, presenting the appearance of a turtle with its head pointing towards the west, as if overlooking the waters in that direction. We landed, in order to examine the *stone turtle*, as we had been informed that the heathen Indians frequently offered their devotions and sacrifices to it. On approaching, we found several pieces of tobacco lying beneath the head, which had been left by the poor superstitious Indians, in order that they might meet with no disasters whilst journeying in the direction they supposed this blind inanimate god to overlook.

The caverns, or hollow rocks, in the mountains which surround Burlington Bay, were once noted as being the abodes of gods, and especially when explosions were said to take place. Before the country was settled in the vicinity of the mountain which extends round the head waters of Lake Ontario, explosions were frequently heard, which the superstitious Indians attributed to the breathing or blow-ing of the munedoo, but which no doubt were caused by the bursting of sulphurous gas from the rocks. The poor Indians now say that the munedoos have such an abhorrence to the white people coming near their abodes, that, like the red men of the forest, they leave their once consecrated retreats unprofaned by the presence of the pale faces, and retire back into the interior. Near the Credit village, at the foot of a pointed hill, is a deep hole in the water, which is said to be the abode of one of the water-gods, where he was frequently heard to sing and beat his drum. When the white people began to frequent this place for the purpose of taking the salmon, this munedoo took his departure during a tremendous flood caused by his power, and went down the river into Lake Ontario.

(H.)

INDIAN TRAGEDY.

A MICHIGAN correspondent of the *Rochester Democrat* details the following tragedy in savage life. If an Indian could write the story he would head it—"The Scathe of Fire-Water :"—

"In the spring of 1837, Nogisqua, an Indian of the Pottawatimees tribe, residing in this vicinity, having pawned his gun and part of his clothing from time to time to a man named John N——, for intoxicating drink, the trader proposed to the Indian that if he would sell him a certain cream-coloured pony belonging to his squaw, and a present from her father, Bawbish, a chief of their tribe, he would give up his gun and clothing, and let him have more strong drink from time to time until the price agreed upon was paid. To this Nogisqua agreed, and privately gave up the pony, which was sent off farther west.

"It appeared that his squaw, having some suspicion of what was going on, employed her younger brother to watch the result and inform her; which it appears he did. Upon the return of the Indian to his camp, partly intoxicated, his squaw, highly enraged, accused him of selling her pony. She became more and more enraged at his indifference about the affair, and at length declared she would kill him. He handed her his scalping-knife, and drawing aside his hunting shirt and making his bosom bare, coolly exclaimed, ' *Kina poo !* '—(kill away.) She instantly plunged it to its handle in the Indian's breast, which caused his death in a few minutes.

"Her father, the Indian chief, being then absent some twenty or thirty miles east, a runner was despatched to inform him. Soon after, Mr. Fowle says he saw him pass by his house with a sad countenance for the place of the murder.

"A heart-rending duty now devolved upon the old chief. His word was to acquit or condemn his agonized daughter, according to Indian usage from time immemorial. Horror reigned in the breast of her father. His daughter was the handsomest squaw of her tribe, and a darling child; and the wails of his relatives, together with his own sympathies, rolled upon the mind of the chief like the rushings of the mighty deep upon the lonely rock in the sweeping storm. The crisis in the chief's mind was at hand. He must judge. No other tribunal was in the Indian code of criminal justice. The performance of this duty required more than Roman firmness. He had nothing to do with the goddess of Mercy. The Great Spirit, and the blood of his murdered son-in-law, seemed to say, ' Bawbish, according to the customs of your forefathers for ages past, now decide justly !'

"The chief, like agonized Joseph, when he made himself known to his brethren, could contain himself no longer. His integrity as Indian chief prevailed. He rolled his troubled eye for the last time upon his darling daughter, then upon his kindred, and upon a portion of his tribe that stood before him, and then to the Great Spirit for firmness. The storm of agony in the mind of the chief had passed away, and, in deep sorrow, he decided that his daughter ought to die by the hand of the nearest of kin to the murdered Indian, according to their custom for ages past. The person of the father, chief and judge, then withdrew, with nothing but his integrity to console him, which the whole world beside could neither purchase nor bribe.

" Upon enquiry, it was decided that Jonese, a brother of Nogisqua, then south, near Fort Wayne, should execute the sentence. Accordingly, a runner was sent for him, and he came without delay. After hearing what was deemed his duty, the cry of a brother's blood from the ground on which he stood strung every nerve, and gave tone to every muscle for revenge.

"There were white persons present at the execution, who relate it as follows :—The brother proceeded to the fatal Indian camp, and after sharpening his scalping-knife to his liking, and performing several ceremonies customary with their tribe since their acquaintance with the Catholic missionaries, he took the victim by her long flowing hair, and led her to the front of the camp. Then, with his scalping-knife, he made an incision in her forehead in the form of a cross, bared her bosom, and plunged the knife to the handle in her body. A shriek, a rush of blood, and a few dying groans and convulsions followed, and the fair form of the handsome squaw lay stiff in death.

" From the time of the murder until the execution, the female relatives of the murderess never left her, the time being spent in lamentations over the young squaw. After the execution, both bodies were buried together in a sand-bank, where they now lie side by side. The Indian squaws became reconciled, and all seemed satisfied that no other atonement could have been satisfactory.

"Since the events related, the remnant of the tribe has been removed to the great west, together with their chief, whom the strongest inducements the world could present could not jostle out of the path of justice.

"Thus perished," says my informant, "the best Indian and handsomest squaw of their tribe—the victims of the whisky-cellar—who is far more guilty than either of the others of a moral wrong." My informant also says, "that from first to last, there was manifested no desire to escape or evade the fate of the unfortunate young squaw."

(I.)

1. Brothers,—
2. A great deal of land
3. And a great deal of water
4. Is between us.
5. You have never seen us,
6. And we do not know your faces;
7. But you and we pray to the same Great Spirit
8. Who made the red men and the white men.
9. We are brothers.
10. Brothers,—
11. You have given up a great deal of land
12. To the chiefs of the white men.
13. We are sorry to hear it.
14. The chiefs of the white men try to persuade you to go further back in the woods.
15. We are sorry to hear it.
16. For times to come we will tell you what you must do.
17. You must never drink fire-water.
18. The white men gives fire-water,
19. To make your brains like dung ;
20. He then laughs at you,
21. And you go further back in the wood.
22. Brothers,—
23. You must learn to get dollars.

24. To get dollars, rear sheep
25. And pigs, cows and horses,
26. Turkeys and geese.
27. Brothers,—
28. At the end of every six moons
29. Take some of the animals
30. To the towns of the white men,
31. To sell them for dollars.
32. Brothers,—
33. Lay up corn and dried grass for yourselves
34. And for your animals during winter ;
35. If you have more than you want,
36. Sell some of your corn
37. To the white men, your neighbours.
38. Brothers,—
39. Cultivate your good land,
40. Sow potatoes and corn,
41. Beet and rye,
42. Oats and onions.
43. Oats are very good when ground into meal.
44. Onions are very good when cooked with meat and with deer's meat.
    Brothers,—
45. Cut down good trees,
46. And saw them into planks ;
47. Send the planks to the town
48. And sell them for dollars.
49. Brothers,—
50. Buy with the dollars
51. Blankets and kettles of iron,
52. Cotton shirts and cotton for the squaws—
53. Buy spades and round knives to cut the corn—
54. Buy axes and hand-saws—
55. Buy light ploughs made of iron.
    Brothers,—
56. Do not sell any more land.
57. Tell your children not to sell any more land.
58. If the Governor says
59. "Give me some of your land,"

60. Say to him " No, we have cleared off trees,
61. We work at it, we sow seed,
62. We will not leave it,
63. We will not go farther back in the woods."
    Brothers,—
64. Do not speak words which cut to the Governor ;
65. Speak to him word of " sugar," make him your friend.
    Brothers,—
66. Try to get title-deeds from the Governor—
67. Title-deeds for the land where you live now.
68. Go to the Governor
69. And say to him,
70. " We have cleared the land from trees,
71. We have sowed, and we have cut corn,
72. We have built houses and barns :
73. Give us a title-deed for our land."
74. If the Governor does not give the title-deed the first time,
75. Go to him a second time—
76. If he will not give it the second time,
77. Go to him again, and again, and again,
78. Until you get the title-deed.
79. The writing must be registered in the council-house for writing.
80. Keep the title-deed in your church :
81. Show it to your sons and to your daughters.
82. May the Great Spirit keep fire away from his house.
    Brothers,—
83. We are glad to hear that many red men can read the great word,
84. And that they love the Great Spirit who sends it.
85. It is sent to the red man and the white man.
86. We are glad to know that you have missionaries and schools in some of your towns.
    Brothers,—
87. Settle in little towns.
88. Attend to the great word which the missionaries read to you.
    Brothers,—
89. Send your little ones to school.
90. Come out of the wigwam and out of darkness,
91. And dwell in the light.

Brothers,—

.92. May the Great Spirit teach you to kno w and to love the great word.

93. May you receive it into your hearts.

London, August 22nd, 1837.

Sent by us through Shawundais, or John Sunday, to the Chippewas and the other Indians, their neighbours, we wishing that they may all improve in religious knowledge, and in all those useful arts and acquirements which have, till now, made the white men superior to their red brothers.

(Signed)   AUGUSTUS D'ESTE,
THOMAS HODGKIN, M.D.,
ROBERT ALDER.

(J.)

Copy of a Despatch to his Excellency SIR GEORGE ARTHUR, *Lieut.-Governor of the Province of Upper Canada, &c., &c., &c.*

DOWNING STREET, *28th March,* 1838.

Sir,—The Indian missionary, Mr. Peter Jones, and the secretary to the Wesleyan Missionary Society, Mr. Alder, have lately been in communication with me relative to the application preferred by the former on behalf of certain of the Indian tribes in Upper Canada, for title-deeds of the lands which they now hold under the Crown. I enclose herewith for your information copies of the letters which they have addressed to me.

I need scarcely state that, in considering these letters, I have not failed to advert to the opinions expressed in Sir Francis Head's despatches of the 18th October and 8th November last. I am, of course, sensible how much weight is due to Sir F. Head's opinion on such a subject, and with my present information I should much doubt the expediency of adopting to the letter the propositions contained in the accompanying letters.

Yet, I must think that some measure may be taken for removing the uneasiness which is said to exist among the Indians in regard to their land. With this view, I should propose that at the first general meeting of the Indians an assurance should be conveyed to them, in the most formal and solemn manner, that her Majesty's Government will protect their interests, and respect their rights, in regard to the land on which they are settled.

It might be explained to them, that for the sake of themselves and their posterity, it would not be advisable to deliver into their hands the title-deeds of their property ; but that those title-deeds should be drawn up in writing, and recorded in the office of the Commissioner of Crown Lands, of the fact of which record, any person or persons deputed on their behalf may convince themselves by inspection ; that these title-deeds so recorded should be considered by the Government as equally binding with any other similar documents ; and that if the Indians, or any other individual among them, should at any time desire to sell or exchange their land, the Government would be ready to listen to their applications, and to take such measures as should be most consistent with their welfare and feelings.

It appears to me, that if a measure of this nature were adopted, any reasonable apprehensions in the minds of the Indians would be allayed, while the danger of their becoming the victims of deception would be avoided.

It would also tend to draw closer the connection which unites them with the Executive Government, and to cherish those feelings of affection with which they regard the Sovereign of the British dominions.

I am aware, however, that there may be impediments to such a course which have not occurred to me ; and I do not, therefore, desire you to consider the foregoing instructions as imperative. But I should be anxious, that, if not the precise measure which I have suggested, some other of a similar description should be forthwith adopted.

In furnishing me with a report of the steps which you may take in this matter, I request that you will advert to the statement in Mr. Jones's letter, respecting the annuity granted to the River Credit Indians, in return for their lands ; and that you will supply me with an explanation of the alleged reduction of the sum which had been agreed upon as a permanent payment.

I have the honour, &c.,

(Signed)   GLENELG.

To Mr. JOSEPH SAWYER, *and the River Credit Indians.*

LEEDS, 22nd May, 1838.

MY DEAR BROTHERS,—For your information I here send you a copy of Lord Glenelg's despatch to his Excellency Sir George Arthur, our new Governor. You will perceive from the despatch that her most gracious Majesty's Government have been pleased to listen to our words, which you sent over to England by me, and that there is a fair prospect of having all our wishes and desires attended to by the government of our Great Mother the Queen.

My Brothers,—I rejoice to tell you that I never saw the sun rise so bright and clear upon my fellow-Indians as at the present time. O, may no evil-minded person rise to obscure the clear sky by throwing dust in the air!

My Brothers,—Be united in all your important matters. Union is strength. Let the glory and honour of the Great Spirit, and the welfare and happiness of your children for ever, be your rule and chief object, and then I am sure there will be but one opinion amongst us all.

My Brothers,—God has heard our cries when we called upon him, about our sorrows and fears. Let us, then, ever trust in Him who has the control and the disposal of the hearts of kings, queens, and rulers. When I first heard that Lord Glenelg had sent such a favourable despatch to our governor, I shed tears of joy; I could not help weeping. Let us then thank God and take courage.

My Brothers,—I would now advise you, before you speak to Sir George Arthur, to consult with the Rev. J. Stinson and the Rev. Egerton Ryerson, as to the best mode of obtaining the title-deeds, which Lord Glenelg has been pleased to recommend to be given to us. Brother Evans, I think, would also be glad to assist in this matter, as I know him to be a warm friend to the poor Indians.

My Brothers,—It appears to me that his lordship's plan of having the title-deeds recorded in the office of the Commissioners of Crown Lands is an excellent one, as it will prevent any of our people from selling or making away with their lands. When I return to Canada I shall talk to you more on this subject.

My Brothers,—I am glad that his lordship has been pleased to request an explanation to be given about the reduction of our land payments. I advise you to get a copy of the agreement or bond from the office of the Indian department in Toronto. The agreement will show for itself what was understood by both parties when our fathers surrendered their territories to the crown of Great Britain.

My Brothers,—I rejoice to tell you that our Great Mother the Queen, and all the officers of the Government, love the poor Indians, and desire to do them good. I am glad also to say that all the Christians in England love and pity our people; and I am persuaded when you hear this, and read the accompanying despatch, you will love the queen and the British nation more than ever. God save our great and noble queen!

My Brothers,—I am glad to learn that in the midst of the late disturbances in Canada you have been kept and preserved in peace, and that you have not suffered in your religious enjoyments and zeal for God on account of them. O be thankful, my brothers, that the Great Spirit has been pleased to preserve and deliver our country from the wicked designs of those who would gladly imbue the province in carnage and bloodshed, with a view to separate us from the fostering care of the mother country.

Dear Brothers,—I am happy to inform you that myself and my dear Newish enjoy good health and peace. The English Christians take much pains to raise money in order to send missionaries among the poor heathen in different parts of the world; we ought, therefore, to be very thankful for what they have done for us. I am now trying to get the Wesleyan Missionary Committee in London to establish a central manual labour school. They have given me encouragement to hope that they will take up the subject and put one in operation. I feel very anxious to see an institution of this kind established amongst us, for I am fully persuaded that our children will never be what they ought to be until they are taught to work and learn useful trades, as well as to learn to read and write.

We hope to be able to leave England for home about the 1st September next, but this will depend on the success I may have on those matters I have still to attend to. I am glad I came to England, for if I had not come just at the time I did, I doubt whether we should ever have obtained the deeds or the arrears of our payments. Now my beloved brothers, neighbours, and relatives, I must close my paper talk, and I shake hands with all the brothers, sisters, and children in my heart.

Write to me as soon as you receive this, and tell me all that is in your hearts. You will be pleased to read all these words in a full council. Pray for me.

I remain, my dear brethren,
Your brother and servant in the work of the Lord,
PETER JONES,
or KAHKEWAQUONABY.

After the reading of the above despatch and letter in Council at Credit, the Chief Sawyer delivered a lengthened speech on the beneficial influence of Christianity on the religious and social state of the Indians. The following is the part of the chief's speech which relates to Lord Glenelg's despatch:—

"My Brothers and Young Men,—We have often petitioned our Great Father, and made our wants known to him; but he did not hear us, he did not attend to our wants. But at last we have sent our words to our Great Mother the Queen; and now you see how soon she has sent out this despatch to her lieutenant-governor to attend to our wants. What is he reason of this? I don't know any other reason, but because the Mother loves the children better than the Father. Now we have a queen instead of a king; and a mother is more ready to hear the cries and to relieve the wants of the children."

The above was heartily responded to by all the Indians in council. Their acclamations were almost deafening.

COPY OF A PETITION TO THE QUEEN, FROM THE CREDIT INDIANS, PRAYING TO HAVE THEIR LANDS SECURED TO THEM.
4TH OCTOBER, 1837.

To Her most gracious Majesty Victoria of the United Kingdom of Great Britain and Ireland, Queen, Defender of the Faith, &c., &c.

The humble petition of the undersigned sachems, principal chiefs, and warriors of the Messissauga tribe of the Chippewa Nation of

Indians of the River Credit, in the Home District, in the province of Upper Canada, on behalf of themselves and the people of the said tribe.

May it please your Majesty,—We are the descendants of the original inhabitants of the soil, who formerly possessed this, their native country, in peace and harmony long before the French, the ancient enemies of your people, came over the great waters and settled upon our territories : then your people came too, and with great valour drove away the French and took Quebec, and the British colours have ever since waved over the land of our forefathers.

We have been happy and contented to live under the protection of such a great and powerful empire ; and we acknowledge, with gratitude to the great Father of all, the good we have enjoyed under British Government. Our people have been civilized and educated, and the Gospel of Jesus Christ has been preached to us. We have also learned the ways of the white people ; they have taught the children of the forest to plough and to sow.

Our people are now very few in number ; the white people have settled all around us, but our Great Father, King George the Third, allowed us to reserve a tract of land at the River Credit ; and the parliament of this nation has acknowledged this tract of land to be ours, and has forbid the white people from disturbing our fisheries. Our good queen will be pleased to hear that many of our children have been taught to read and to write. Some time ago, our people in council said it was proper now to divide the land, so we gave some of them small farms of about fifty acres, to be held by them and their posterity for ever. Our people have begun to improve their farms ; they wish to sell the produce at market and buy goods from the white people, but they are afraid to clear much ground, because they are told by evil-minded persons that their farms can be taken away from them at any time. These people say the land is not our own, but belongs to your Majesty. Did your Majesty buy it from us, or from our forefathers ? We know that our people in times past have sold lands to our late father the king, but we never sold our lands at the Credit.

Will your Majesty be pleased to assure us that our lands shall not be taken away from us, or our people, who have begun to cultivate their farms ; and will your Majesty be pleased to permit us to go on dividing our lands among our people as our people in council think best. Our people and our children then will continue to cultivate the wild lands of our forefathers, and will be contented and appy, and will pray that your Majesty may long live, and reign over our people as their most gracious queen and sovereign.

And your petitioners, as in duty bound, will ever pray.

NAWAHJEGEZHEGWABY,
   JOSEPH SAWYER, Chief.

MANOONOODING,
   JAMES CHEEHOK,

PIPOONNAHBA,
   JAMES YOUNG.

KEZHEGOWININE,
   DAVID SAWYER.

TYENTENNEGEN,
   JOHN JONES.

NAWAHJEGEZHIGWABY,
   JOHN CAMPBELL.

PAMEGAHWAYAHSING,
   ISAAC HENRY.

MASQUAHZEGWUNA,
   MOSES PAHDEQUONG.

NEGAHNUB,
   LAWRENCE HERCHMER.

SASWAYAHSEGA,
   THOMAS MAYER.

MAHYAHWEGEZHIGWABY,
   JOHN KEGHEGOO.

OOMINEWAHJEWEEN,
   WILLIAM HERCHMER.

KANAHWAHBAHNIND,
   WILLIAM JOHN.

PAMEGEWAHNWABY,
   JOHN PETER.

CHEWIMOOKA,
   JOHN M'COLLUM.

PAHOOMBWAWINNDUNG,
   THOMAS SMITH.

AHGHAWAHNAHQUAHDWABY,
   PETER OLDS.

NAHWAHQUAYAHSEGA,
   SAMUEL FINGER.

TAWAHSING,
   JAMES TAHWAH.

ANEWAHKOOGE,
   JOHN WESLEY.

MOOKEJEWUNOOKA,
   GEORGE KING,

NANINGAHSEYA,
   WILLIAM JACKSON.

*In Council at the River Credit,
the 4th day of October, 1837.*

(K.)

The following account of a noted conjuror was furnished by the late Rev. James Evans, August, 1835 :

Oozhuskah, a native Indian of the Ojebway tribe, now resides at Mackinaw. He was once one of the lowest and most abandoned

of that profligate class of Indians who have measurably forsaken
their native wilds, and linger about the settlements of the whites.
His stature is small ; his frame, worn down with age, and debilitated
by former dissipation, presents a strange ghastliness of appearance,
which would almost excite the belief that Oozhuskah is a deserter
from the land of departed spirits. But, however fearful and suspicious his character may have *once* been, those acquainted with
him *now* do not fear him ; his spirit, formerly wild, untameable,
and intriguing, is at present gentle, honest, guileless. His name
once stood unrivalled as a prophet, and he was considered invincible as a warrior.

"The missionaries stationed at Mackinaw had often faithfully tried
to instruct him in the knowledge of God ; but he always responded
to their instructions with the most supercilious contempt, and their
lessons were apparently "pearls cast before swine." But they were
not lost. They were lodged in the memory of Oozhuskah. He
narrated them to his wife, who was as drunken as himself, but
when sober these lessons formed a fruitful theme of conversation.

" In the winter, as usual, Oozhuskah chose his hunting-ground,
some fifty miles from Mackinaw : here, with no companion but his
aged squaw, he pitched his lonely tent, in the recesses of the forest.
Here, the inebriating draught was beyond his reach ; they had time
for reflection and for converse. They had not long occupied their
quarters, when Mekagase was taken ill ; Oozhuskah's conjuring
songs and Indian medicines could not cure her. During this severe
illness she retained her senses. The truth of heaven dwelt upon
her mind ; her understanding told her she was a wretch, a sinner,
that she had all her life persisted in doing knowingly and wilfully
wrong. Death stared her in the face, and she was afraid to die ;
her conscience convinced her she was unprepared, and that as
a consequence of her wickedness she must expect misery hereafter.
Trembling on the threshold of eternity, she humbled herself, prayed
to the Great Spirit in compassion to forgive her, to blot out her
sins, and receive her departing spirit.

" Suddenly, the fears of Mekagase were taken away ; joy filled
her heart, and she felt indescribably more happy than when in
youth she had joined the Indian dance around the evening fires of
her tribe. In short, she experienced what the Apostle designates
' joy unspeakable and full of glory !' From that hour her disease

abated. She felt she was a new creature, and, unlike too many enlightened Christians, she did not reason herself out of the faith; but, taking the simple testimony of the Spirit bearing witness with her own, spoke of her hopes and her joys to Oozhuskah, with ecstacy and confidence; she warned him of his folly and wickedness with such convincing testimony that his heart was touched. He prayed to the Great Spirit; the radiance of Divine truth beamed on his benighted understanding, melting his hardened heart; and in ten days from his wife's remarkable conversion, Oozhuskah could heartily join with her in offering their morning and evening orisons to the Great Spirit in praise of redeeming grace.

When the hunting-season was over they returned to Mackinaw, where they lost no time in making known the change wrought in their feelings; and from that day to this they have tested the verity of their conversion by well-ordered lives and godly conversation.

"Oozhuskah narrated to me the following account of his former life :—' From the earliest period of my recollection, inspired by the traditions of my tribe, I had an insatiable thirst to become a prophet. . . . . To accomplish this object, I commenced a fast. I partook of no kind of nourishment for twenty days, excepting the broth of a little boiled corn, after the going down of the sun. On the twentieth day I caused my tent to be erected alone in the forest : I entered it, and on that evening ate nothing. I was almost famished with hunger; my skin clave to my bones; and I had barely strength to stand on my feet. Nearly fainting, I laid down in my tent, determined to die or obtain the object of my desire. I lay until nearly midnight, when suddenly a man entered my tent. ' What are you doing? Why are you here? and what do you want?' said he. I replied, 'I am fasting, almost dead, and must soon perish with hunger.' Before I had time to say more, he rejoined, ' Follow me ;' and it seemed as if my spirit left my body. I rose and went out of my tent; he then took me by the arm, and we both ascended into the air, and moved on with the utmost ease and rapidity.' Oozhuskah then related the adventures of his journey; how his long fasting had gained the approbation of the gods, and how they made him a mighty prophet. . . . . After this he found himself in his tent extremely hungry; he partook of some food, and slept sweetly. When he awoke the next morning he felt proud, considering himself superior to all the Indians around him. From this time all the promises of the gods were fulfilled, till the illness of Mekagase, 'when,' he adds, ' I was led by her conversion to examine myself, and saw that I was a wretch, and a child of the devil. Then I prayed to the Great Spirit, and he heard and forgave me.'

"At that time I had a large collection of medicines, some to kill and some to cure : I threw them all away, and my hawk* has not since visited me, and God grant he never may. I was the most wicked of men ; my converse with the strange man of the cave made me proud, but it did not make me happy. But I bless God that now a Spirit unseen communes with my heart; and though it does not teach me how to destroy my enemies, it teaches me to forgive and love them."

(L.)

CONVERSION OF A MEDICINE MAN.

(From J. Sunday's Journal, October 17th, 1833.)

To-day a medicine man, who used to oppose us, came and said he would give up his enchantments and listen to our teaching. The cause of the change is this :—He had a daughter whom he tenderly loved, and being taken sick, he tried his utmost skill to cure her, but could not. His munedoo would not be entreated for her, and his medical enchantments would have no effect ; but his beloved daughter died. When the child was past recovery, and was given up to die, a pious son affectionately sat by her for three days and nights, and scarcely slept the whole time, but continued to watch and pray for her, that she might be prepared for death. After the sister died, the young man dreamed he saw a ladder that reached to heaven, and that his sister ascended on it. He told the dream to his father. This greatly comforted him, and when he reflected that

---

* The bird he chose for his messenger to communicate with his familiar spirits.

his pagan skill had failed him when he most needed help, and that the new religion taught such affection and faithfulness as that of his son to his sister, and that the Great Spirit had heard his prayer, and shown that his daughter was safe and happy, he resolved to change his worthless religion for that which gave him comfort in affliction.

(M.)

JOHN CHIEF, AND MERCHANT'S SOUL IN CLAY BANK.

Extract of a Letter to P. JONES, *from* JOHN SUNDAY, *Muncey Town, November 12th,* 1850.

" THERE are many magicians here. I will name one John Chief. This man pretends he can do a great thing. One Indian has been sick for some time. He has been Christian some years, and now he has turned into pagan; he believed that the magicians could cure him, so he got John Chief to come to him and at the same time sent an Indian to get whisky for the magician. When John Chief came he told some men to make *Jeesuhkon* (conjuring wigwam), and when finished he went into it. The conjuror then said to the sick man :—' Your soul is gone away from you, and is now in the bank of the river, it is with the munedoos, who reside on the high clay bank, where it has been all the time. If you wish your soul to come back to you again I can send one of the sky-men, or *Medawwhmagwug,* and bring it back again.'

' The sick man said :—' I shall be very glad if my soul comes back to me again.'

" So John Chief send one of his sky-men to go and bring the sick man's soul, and in a short time he returned, and then the magician said to the sick man :—' Your soul is now in you. The sick man asked his soul what was the cause of his leaving him? The soul replied :—' I will tell you the reason, it is because you became a MERCHANT last spring, this is the reason why I left you.'

" John Chief then said, ' he would so blow upon his mouth as to blow his soul up and down in his body and make it stay in.'

John Chief did so, and the sick man was very glad that his soul got back to him again."

John Sunday, in his peculiar satirical manner, adds :—

" Tell our Indian brethren, never, never to desire to become merchants, lest their souls should leave them, as did this sick man's."

Notwithstanding all the power and vanity of John Chief's munedoos, the poor backsliding sick man died, and his soul in earnest left his body.

———— ——

(N.)

At a Conference held at Colborne-on-Thames, the 27th January 1841 : — *Present :* The Superintendent of Indian Affairs ; Rev Richard Flood, Rev. Solomon Waldron (*Missionaries*) ; and the Chiefs of the Delawares, Oneidas and Chippewas.

The Chief, CANOTING, arose and said, that he was appointed to speak for the three tribes, and addressed the Superintendent as follows :—

" *Father,*—We have met in council, to take into consideration a subject which has engaged the attention of our white brethren throughout the country. We mean the destruction of the monument erected on Queenstown Heights to the memory of a great warrior, who, like Tecumseth, fell in defence of his sovereign. We have a few chiefs and warriors still living who fought under the command of the great and good General Brock ; and we remember when he travelled on that road (the Long Woods) he said to us, ' I bring my sword to fight against your enemy and mine ; and now I tell you plainly, they must not throw us down ; rise, follow me, that your children may partake of all the privileges which you have ever enjoyed under the protection of your great Father.' These words struck deep into our hearts, and with one shout we flew to aid him. Our hearts are yet afflicted by the loss of many a brave chief and warrior who fell in that war ; and when we heard that the ashes of that warrior had been disturbed, and the monument shattered by the hand of the cowardly white man, our indignation was aroused, and we all declared our abhorrence of such wickedness against the will of the Great Spirit, who was pleased to place him there.

" *Father*,—The three nations here assembled have agreed to subscribe each the sum of ten pounds, towards the re-construction of his monument ; and we request you to communicate to our great father, Sir George Arthur, our sentiments on this subject ; and to assure him that it is our firm determination to retain the same zeal, loyalty, and devotion, that glowed in the bosoms of our forefathers, who bravely defended the Royal Standard, under which we have the happiness to live, and to claim the proud distinction of British subjects.

"*Father*,—We salute you and our friends the missionaries, with a hearty shake of the hand.

(Certified)   J. B. CLENCH, S. I. A."

To our Brother SIR GEORGE ARTHUR, *Lieutenant-Governor of the Province of Upper Canada.*

" *Brother* —The chiefs, warriors, and people of the Six Nations Indians, heard with feelings of the greatest horror, that white men from the American Nation had desecrated the grave of the brave and lamented warrior, Sir Isaac Brock.

"The to ab of the brave warrior has always been esteemed sacred among us, from the earliest period to which the tradition handed down to us from our fathers extend.

" *Brother*,—It has given to the chiefs, warriors, and people of the Six Nations, great pleasure to hear that you, our brother, called a meeting of your white people, at the spot where the brave warrior fell, fighting in defence of his and our country ; and that it was resolved to erect anew a monument sacred to his memory, to record his valour to future generations.

" *Brother*,—We and our fathers endured the fatigues and privations of war, fighting by the side of the illustrious dead, and wish to contribute from our funds the sum of seventy-five pounds, to forward the speedy completion of the work ; to commemorate our veneration for the name of our illustrious and valiant brother, deceased ; and to record our horror at the perpetration of so base a deed as the destruction of the tomb where his hallowed remains have been interred.

T

"*Brother*,—We have transmitted to our Chief Superintendent an order for that amount, which we request may be paid for the above purpose, out of our funds in the hands of Government.

"In the name and on behalf of the Six Nations.

"Moses Walker.
"John S. Johnson.
"Peter Green.
"Aaron Frazer.
"Noah Powlis.
"Peter Powlis (X his mark).

"*Witness*—J. Martin,
"*Sup. Ind. Dep.*"

To our Great Father, Sir George Arthur, K.C.H., *Lieutenant Governor of the Province of Upper Canada, and Major-General Commanding Her Majesty's Forces therein, &c.*

"*Father*,—Our ears have been shocked in hearing that some person or persons have had the wickedness to destroy the sacred grave of our late Great Father,Major-General Sir Isaac Brock, the brave hero of Upper Canada.

"*Father*,—We cannot find language sufficient to express our utter detestation of such an outrageous conduct.

"*Father*,—Some of our people fought and bled by the side of that brave chief. He was so brave that he feared no death. He was beloved by all the red coats, and by all the inhabitants, and by all your red children.

"*Father*,—We shall ever remember the debt of gratitude we and our children owe to that great chieftain. Whilst your red children were sitting together, like a family of helpless children, in danger of being tomahawked, the brave hero flew with only a few brave warriors to our rescue. His wisdom, skill, and bravery, saved us from the destroying enemy.

"*Father*,—Our hearts were made very glad, when we heard that your Excellency, and your great officers and inhabitants of Upper Canada, were about to re-construct the grave of our late Great

Father ; and, as a tribute of respect to his memory, we wish to give ten pounds, out of our annual land payments, towards re-building the same.

"*Father*,—We feel truly grateful to the British Government, for the kind care they have ever manifested towards us.

"*Father*,—We love our Great Mother the Queen, and all her children over the great waters.

"*Father*,—We are happy and contented to live under the protection of such a wise, good, and powerful Government ; and we hope nothing shall ever separate us from the protecting hand of our Great Mother the Queen ; and may the blessing of our Great Spirit rest upon Her Majesty — upon her great chiefs — and upon her people. This is all we have to say.

"Signed in behalf of the River Credit Indians.

> "JOSEPH SAWYER.
> "PETER JONES.
> "JOHN JONES.
> "THOMAS SMITH.
> "JAMES YOUNG.
> "DAVID SAWYER.

"*River Credit*,
  "*January, 2nd*, 1841."

The QUEEN's *Thanks to the Indians who subscribed for the Rebuilding of Brock's Monument.*

(*Copy*)
"CHIEF SECRETARY'S OFFICE,
  "*Kingston, June 22nd*, 1841.

"SIR,—I am commanded by the Governor-General to inform you that Her Majesty's Government having had before them a pamphlet containing the addresses connected with the subscription of the Indian tribes in Upper Canada, in aid of the re-construction of the monument of Sir Isaac Brock, His Excellency has been directed to convey to these tribes the thanks of the British Government and nation for their zealous co-operation in this patriotic undertaking, and to renew to them the assurance of the Queen's regard for their welfare.

T 2

" You will have the goodness to communicate to the Indians who took part in the subscription the sentiments which Her Majesty has been pleased to express on the subject.

> "I have the honour to be, Sir,
> "Your most obedient humble Servant,
> "(Signed) T. W. C. MURDOCK,
> "*Chief Secretary.*

"S. P. JARVIS, Esq.,
"*Superintendent of Indian Affairs, &c. &c.*
"Upper Canada."

(O.)

Copy of a Letter to the Hon. Commissioners appointed to enquire into Indian Affairs.

MUNCEY MISSION HOUSE, *Nov. 21st,* 1842.

" GENTLEMEN,—I beg to inclose, for your consideration, a copy of my letter to Dr. Luckey, and his reply, on the subject of the School of Industry at Missouri.

"From the knowledge I have of the Indian character, and from personal observation, I have come to the conclusion that the system of education hitherto adopted in our common schools has been too inefficient. The children attend these schools from the houses of their parents, a number of whom are good pious Christians, but who, nevertheless, retain many of their old habits ; consequently, the good instructions they receive at school are in a great measure neutralized at home. It is a notorious fact that the parents in general exercise little or no control over their children. Being thus left to follow their own wills, they too frequently wander about in the woods with their bows and arrows, or accompany their parents in their hunting excursions. Another evil arises from their not being trained to habits of industry, so that by the time they leave the schools they are greatly averse to work, and naturally adopt the same mode of life as their parents.

"Under these considerations, I am very anxious to see manual labour schools established among our people, that the children may be properly trained and educated to habits of industry. I see nothing to hinder the entire success of such a plan, and as the school in the Missouri country is answering the most sanguine expectations of its promoters, we may safely conclude that the same success would attend the like operations among our Indians. I am happy to inform you that all the Indians with whom I have conversed highly approve of the project. They are ready and willing to give up their children to the entire control and management of the teachers.

"I beg also to state that, in my opinion, unless something be done in this way, the Indians will for ever remain in their half-civilized state, and continue to be a burden to the British Government and the missionary societies. But, on the contrary, by the blessing of the Almighty on our proposed efforts, I see no reason why they may not be raised in their condition, so as to become useful subjects of our Great Mother the Queen, and an ornament to society. I do not mean to insinuate that our past efforts to Christianize and civilize the red man of the forest have altogether proved abortive; far from it, we have many examples at our various mission stations of industrious Indians who cultivate their farms to the best of their knowledge; such have been induced from religious principles to abandon the chase, and turn their attention to husbandry; but we have observed that in general, where this motive is wanting, the Indian still adheres to his old habits.

"With regard to the means, I would suggest that part of the expenses be borne out of the Indian's land payments, and the other out of the Parliamentary grant to the Indian department. I cannot help expressing my opinion that a large amount of that grant might be saved by curtailing the expenses of the department. The Wesleyan Missionary Society of the Canada Conference, who are very anxious to see such schools in operation, would, in all probability, aid in their establishment and support.

"I am not able to make any positive estimate as to the amount necessary for the erection of the buildings, &c., &c., as that will depend on the magnitude of the establishment. I should suppose that a school that would accommodate 100 scholars might be put in operation for about £1,500, or £2,000 currency.

"I beg to inform you that when I was in England, in the year

1838, I brought this subject before the Colonial Secretary, Lord Glenelg, who was pleased to forward a despatch to his Excellency Sir George Arthur, recommending the Colonial Government to take the matter into consideration, and, if practicable, to do something in the way of promoting the general welfare of the Indian tribes."

" I have the honour to be,

" Gentlemen,

" Your most obedient and humble Servant,

(Signed)   " PETER JONES,

" Indian Missionary and Chief.

" *To the Hon. Commissioners on Indian Affairs, &c., &c., Kingston.*"

RICHARD BARRETT, Printer, 13, Mark Lane, London.

Books Lately Publifhed.

5, Bifhopfgate Without, London.

Crown 8vo, Illustrated, price 6s.

Settlers and Soldiers; or, the War in Taranaki.
Being a Chapter in the Life of a Settler. By Rev. THOMAS GILBERT, formerly Paftor of the General Baptift Church, Ditchling, Suffex.

Crown 8vo, Illustrated.

Malta under the Phenicians, Knights, and
Englifh. By WILLIAM TALLACK, author of "Friendly Sketches in America."

Crown 8vo, price 6s.

The Stockman, and other Tales. Illustrative
of Life in Australia. By HORACE EARLE, Esq.

Cloth extra, 1os. 6d., Illustrated.

Will Adams. The Firft Englifhman in Japan.
A Romantic Biography. By WILLIAM DALTON.

Crown 8vo., cloth, price 3s. 6d., poft free.

Narrative of Ten Years' Imprifonment in the
Dungeons of Naples. By ANTONIO NICOLÒ, a Political Exile.

Just published, crown 8vo., 5s.

Friendly Sketches in America. By WILLIAM TALLACK. Contains Notices of Viſits to Friends in Indiana, Ohio, Philadelphia, New York, and New England, with deſcriptions of Scenery, Colleges, Schools and Cities; and Anecdotes of Waſhington, Whittier, Macaulay, &c. Particulars of the diviſions of the American Friends into " Orthodox," " Hickſite," " Evangelical," and " Wilburite." Notices of Unitarianiſm, Slavery and Politics, &c.

Poſt 8vo., cloth, price 6s. 6d.

A Memoir of William Allen, F.R.S. By the Rev. J. SHERMAN, of Surrey Chapel.

Poſt 8vo., cloth, price 4s. 6d.

Curioſities of London Life; or Phaſes, Phyſiological and Social, of the Great Metropolis. By C. M. SMITH.

Poſt 8vo., cloth, price 10s. 6d.

The Three Archbiſhops. Lanfranc—Anſelm— A'Becket. By WASHINGTON and MARK WILKS.

Crown 8vo., cloth, price 4s. 6d.

The Campaner Thal; or, Diſcourſes on the Immortality of the Soul. By JEAN PAUL FR. RICHTER. Tranſlated from the German by JULIETTE GOWA. Second Edition.

Crown 8vo., cloth, price 4s.

The Half-Century; its Hiſtory, Political and Social (1800 to 1850). By WASHINGTON WILKS. With a chronological table of contents, and a tabular arrangement of the Principal Officers of State from 1800 to 1850. Second Edition, reviſed, and containing a Supplementary Chapter.

London : A. W. BENNETT, 5, Biſhopſgate Without, E.C.

www.ingramcontent.com/pod-product-compliance
Lightning Source LLC
Chambersburg PA
CBHW021217270326
41929CB00010B/1169